PENGUIN BOOKS
MISSING IN ACTION

Pranay Kotasthane is deputy director at the Takshashila Institution, where he teaches public policy, geopolitics, and public finance. His current area of research is semiconductor geopolitics. Pranay co-hosts *Puliyabaazi*, a popular Hindi podcast on public policy and politics.

Raghu S. Jaitley is a public policy and political economy enthusiast. He co-writes *Anticipating the Unintended*, a popular newsletter on Indian public policy.

T0166936

ADVANCE PRAISE

'There have been many books about Indian society but none so far about the Indian state. *Missing in Action* fills that gap, and how! Kotasthane and Jaitley are two of our finest thinkers, and their writing combines a surgeon's precision with a poet's art of revealing the unseen. They paint both the big picture and the small details. This book is a masterpiece that will be essential reading 50 years from now. If you want to understand India, you should read *Missing in Action*.'

—Amit Varma, Creator of *The Seen and the Unseen* Podcast and *The India Uncut* Blog

'*Missing in Action* is a thoroughly engaging, entertaining, and educational book. The book helps readers understand why the Indian State is the way it is—powerful yet ineffective, well-intentioned yet weak, and ambitious yet underperforming. A must-read for everyone!'

—Rohini Nilekani, Philanthropist, Author of *Samaaj Sarkaar Bazaar: A Citizen-First Approach*

'The policy outcomes are the result of the three important forces: society, market and the Government. This wonderful book by Pranay Kotasthane and Raghu S. Jaitley beautifully tells you why and how this happens. Their pedagogical strategy is deceptively simple but very effective. The book has many real-life examples of both policy triumphs and disasters in our country and the authors lucidly explain the how and why. I would urge you to read this remarkably perceptive book that is analytically rich while making the learning ride very enjoyable.'

—Vijay Kelkar, Chairman, Thirteenth Finance Commission and former Finance Secretary, Government of India

MISSING IN ACTION

Why You Should Care About Public Policy

ACTION

PRANAY KOTASTHANE
RAGHU S. JAITLEY

PENGUIN BOOKS

An imprint of Penguin Random House

PENGUIN BOOKS

USA | Canada | UK | Ireland | Australia
New Zealand | India | South Africa | China

Penguin Books is part of the Penguin Random House group of companies
whose addresses can be found at global.penguinrandomhouse.com

Published by Penguin Random House India Pvt. Ltd
4th Floor, Capital Tower 1, MG Road,
Gurugram 122 002, Haryana, India

First published in Penguin Books by Penguin Random House India 2023

ISBN 9780143459378

Typeset in Bembo Std by Manipal Technologies Limited, Manipal

www.penguin.co.in

We Salute Those Who Strive to Strengthen the Indian Republic in Ways Small and Big

Contents

III *SAMAAJ*

Making Public Policy Interesting Again

Yeh jo public hai yeh sab jaanti hai [The public knows everything]

—A song from the film *Roti* (1974)

Why This Book?

You, dear reader, have no shortage of reading choices. A pile of unread physical books, a long list of e-books, and many web browser tabs are probably staring at you expectantly. So, our first task is to explain why you should consider devoting that scarcest of resources—attention, not time—to this little book of ours.

Public policies are all around us. They influence our choices, behaviours, and incomes. More so in the Indian context, given the State's wide-ranging ambitions. Despite this pervasiveness, public policy can be inaccessible, boring, or both. Because of this, quite contrary to what Rajesh Khanna (the star of *Roti*) would have us believe, *yeh public sab nahin jaanti hai* (the public doesn't know it all). As Trump would have said, this book is an attempt to *Make Public Policy Interesting Again*.

Ironically, the public doesn't question the one institution that can make rules, bend them, and punish others for breaking the laws it creates. Those who can afford it prefer not to think about the Indian State because they have already given up on it. Those who can't afford it have resigned themselves to a State that can give occasional handouts and provide short-term benefits. That much benevolence is enough for them to be grateful. Either way, we seldom pause to reflect on why the Indian State works the way it does.

This book aims to change such perceptions through sketches from everyday experiences to illustrate India's tryst with public policymaking. By the end of this book, you will have gone through some fundamental concepts of the public policy discipline. You will be able to look at the endless stream of political news differently. At least, that's our hope.

Before moving ahead, a moment to explain what this book is and, more importantly, what it is not. For this book, we have picked real Indian public policy stories. We are neither policy experts nor government 'babus' nor seasoned politicians. While we have formally studied public policy and economic reasoning, we consider ourselves students who keenly observe, analyse, and write about the Indian public policy realm.

This purpose brought us together to start a public policy newsletter—*Anticipating the Unintended*—in 2019. What began as a fun way for us to keep our writing muscles active turned out to be beneficial to our many readers who engaged with us every week. To take these lessons to a broader audience, we took on the challenge of writing this book.

This book is not the work of a government official. So, if you are looking for insights into public administration, it is sure to disappoint. Neither is it academic work; there are no experiments, equations, regression models, or pilot studies. Instead, we refer to key ideas from existing academic research. Nor is this book a work of journalism. There are no formal interviews or ground-zero reports. What you will find instead is a collection of stories, some attempts at humour, and many counterintuitive ideas. Each story will offer a public policy concept, idea, or framework as the key takeaway. These ideas, we believe, are the building blocks for understanding Indian public policy issues.

You might wonder, why should you, a common Indian citizen, bother about learning public policy concepts; shouldn't we take these ideas to those who make policy—our politicians and bureaucrats—instead? We believe that in a democracy, the government *mirrors* the society more often than it *directs* our choices. And so, with this book, we want to address the demand side of the public policy pipeline.

It is our strong belief that if Indian citizens are better equipped with public policy fundamentals, three things are likely to happen.

One, our governments will be more accountable, and they won't be able to take us for a ride as often. We will be able to anticipate the faults and benefits of policies before they are put in place instead of being left to 'kindly adjust' to the consequences.

Two, we will be able to sharpen our demands from our governments. We will be in a better position to understand the limits of government actions. We might then be able to articulate our demands from our governments and discourage actions that could make us worse off.

Finally, better public policy understanding will raise the level of public discourse. Much of our current public discourse is a partisan sniping contest. A policy is judged not by its consequences, sometimes not even by the intentions behind it, but by the party—and sometimes just one person—that backs it. When this happens, policy discussions are bound to descend into identarian one-upmanship contests.

Armed with the knowledge of public policy fundamentals, we can steer such debates towards solutions, trade-offs, and, hopefully, a better future.

On Your Mark

In the previous section, we used the phrase 'counterintuitive ideas' with a lot of thought. Since public policy is all around us, understanding it is as much a process of unlearning as it is about learning. Unlike perhaps a history graduate learning about quantum mechanics, there's no clean slate, to begin with.

In fact, it's quite the opposite. People come to every public policy issue with strong biases and emotional points of view. Equipping oneself with key ideas and principles from the public policy domain is hardly considered necessary for commenting on government policies. In that sense, public policy is like discussing Sachin Tendulkar versus Rahul Dravid instead of learning a subject such as physics. You might not have strong opinions about what's better—the electron or the proton—but you will have a tough time convincing die-hard fans of one policy about its weaknesses.

Therefore, a good place to begin is to think of the beliefs we need to let go of before learning public policy. We have put together a non-exhaustive list of eight such beliefs below.

Belief 1: What I Know Is Golden, So I Can't Let Go of It

The first step is being open to the process of unlearning. Our prescriptions for policymaking are shaped by our experiences, perceptions, and memory. Neither of the three sources is a true representation of reality. Hence, an unrelenting defense of what we have already learned is like falling into the trap of watching a sequel of a boring movie because you have already spent money on the first part.

Belief 2: Good Intentions Translate to Good Policies

This is a tough one to unlearn. This principle calls for dissociating the intentions behind a policy from its outcomes. Most government policies have noble intentions. Yet, many of them do not have the desired consequences. How should we, as citizens, judge government actions then?

The default response in India seems to be to evaluate a policy based on the stated intentions alone. Once things start going wrong, the blame is placed on poor delivery, corrupt politicians, and inefficient bureaucrats.

There are two problems with this approach of evaluating policies.

First, intentions are difficult to gauge. Few government policies are made with a stated malintent in any case. Thus, judging intentions is an unhelpful guide for evaluating policies.

Next, imagine we had an insight into the minds of our policymakers, and we could decipher their intentions perfectly. It would still be unhelpful to evaluate policies based on intent simply because even the best motives can lead to terrible consequences. Take the case of alcohol prohibition in Mumbai which began in 1949 with the noble intention of preventing alcoholism. As a policy, it turned out to be one of the reasons why the 'underworld' flourished in that city. First, it made bootlegging a viable business and encouraged smugglers to get into it. These operators then used this money to diversify into other illegal activities. Eventually, a strong police–underworld–politician nexus developed. There are a number of accounts tracing the rise of underworld figures such as Varadarajan Mudaliar and Haji Mastan to this well-intentioned policy called prohibition.[1]

As citizens, we must evaluate policies based on their intended and unintended consequences, and not fall into the trap of judging intentions.

---

[1] For a timeline of alcohol prohibition in Mumbai, read Riddhi Joshi, 'In Bombay, Prohibition Didn't Just Fail. It Spawned the Underworld', *Hindustan Times*, 17 April 2016. https://www.hindustantimes.com/india/in-bombay-prohibition-didn-t-just-fail-it-spawned-the-underworld/story-PSLIEhNprWpbBYHk3ZeMZK.html.

Belief 3: India's Bane Is That While the Policies Are Good, Their Implementation Is Bad

A common refrain in our public discourse follows this narrative—a 'fantastic' policy failed because its implementation was botched up. There was nothing wrong with the policy per se, it's just that the inept bureaucracy or worse—the evil citizens—that came in its way. This is a fallacy because a policy formulated bereft of implementation details cannot be termed a good policy.

By blaming implementation alone, we are letting governments off the hook easily. The government has resources and expertise at its command to anticipate at least some of the implementation challenges, stakeholder attitudes, and unintended consequences. Hence, we need to hold the government to higher standards when evaluating policies.

Belief 4: Certainty and Consistency of Views Over a Long Period Is a Hallmark of Good Policy Analysis

An evidence-based policymaking attitude demands that we don't let our ideology interfere with our judgement. Too often, we fall into the trap of defending an ideology we hold dear. When you feel yourself succumbing to this temptation, recall these words by Ambedkar:

> To a critic who is a hostile and malicious person and who wants to make capital out of my inconsistencies, my reply is straight. Emerson has said that consistency is the virtue of an ass and I don't wish to make an ass of myself. No thinking human being can be tied down

to a view once expressed in the name of consistency. More important than consistency is responsibility. A responsible person must learn to unlearn what he has learned. A responsible person must have the courage to rethink and change his thoughts. Of course, there must be good and sufficient reasons for unlearning what he has learned and for recasting his thoughts. There can be no finality in thinking.[2]

Belief 5: Economics Is About Picking Your Poison— Capitalism or Socialism

Economics is the bedrock of good policy. Given its focus on incentives, it provides a lens through which we can anticipate policy outcomes. For example, economic reasoning allows us to anticipate that a price cap on cinema tickets will raise the price of the popcorn sold at the stall outside it.

Economics is certainly not about eulogizing the patron saints of economic theories, whether it be Karl Marx or Adam Smith. As long as our efforts are aimed at substantiating why and how human beings behave, we can aim to have policies that can build the right incentives, nudges, or restrictions. Being wedded to an economic theory in the face of contradictory evidence is repeating the folly described in belief 3.

In reality, public policy is an applied discipline that requires understanding human motivations from different

---

[2] B.R. Ambedkar, *Dr Babasaheb Ambedkar Writings and Speeches*, Vol. 1 of 17 vols (Dr Ambedkar Foundation, 1956), 139.

lenses. Sociology, psychology, philosophy, ethics, are all immensely helpful. Even so, economics is the core discipline to understand policymaking.

Belief 6: Politics Is Disgusting

Discarding one's disgust for politics is a good starting point for learning public policy. In the satire *Yes Minister,* that unparalleled fount of knowledge, bureaucrat Sir Humphrey Appleby remarks, 'If the right people don't have power, do you know what happens? The wrong people get it: politicians, councilors, *ordinary voters* [italics ours]!' Sir Humphrey is only half-right. The worst enemy of governance is not opposition but apathy. The more people abdicate politics, the more it becomes disgusting. There is no other way out than to engage. There is no policy without politics.

Belief 7: There's No Good or Bad Policy; Only Better or Worse Outcomes

Thus far, we have been using the binary 'good policy' versus 'bad policy'. Reality doesn't come in these neat binaries. The best of policies also has negative consequences while policies with flawed designs may also have some positive fallouts. This is because of the nature of the State as an all-pervasive institution. Given that its actions impact millions of people, each with a different relation to the State, they feel the impact of the policy in different ways.

A ban might be terrible for a consumer, but it might supercharge the business of a smuggler. A price cap might seem beneficial to a consumer in the short term but it disincentivizes producers and harms the consumer in the longer term due to restricted choice.

Thus, it becomes important to analyse the costs and benefits of every policy and confront the trade-offs to decide whether a policy makes us better-off or worse-off. Grey is the only shade in policy evaluation.

Belief 8: A Well-Designed Government Policy Can Meet Several Objectives At Once

One institution or policy instrument optimizing for several goals is the bane of policymaking and institutional design. As if it wasn't enough that every government policy needs to balance equity, efficiency, and effectiveness, we also fall into the trap of trying to solve several problems with one policy. A classic example of a government policy trying to achieve way too many things at once is India's tax policy.

A common reason some government policies and institutions perform suboptimally is that they try to do hyper multi-objective optimization, ultimately creating a system that meets none of the objectives. Practising parsimony while thinking of desired policy outcomes is underrated.

Consider these eight ideas as landmines hidden in your pathway.

What's in the Book?

Think of this work as a 'pop' public policy book. Like all books of this genre, we let stories of Indian experiences take centre stage. That's because context is king in public policy. There are very few immutable, universal rules that apply across all countries. We believe that our discourse on government is anchored way too much on the stories and experiences of other countries.

The result is that public policy books end up discussing distant and unrelatable stories. For instance, you too would have come across a popular quote on WhatsApp. Attributed to Gustavo Petro, a former mayor of Bogota, the quote reads: 'A developed country is not a place where the poor have cars. It's where the rich use public transportation.' Reading about Bogota's transformation can give a misleading assessment that spending more on Bus Rapid Transit systems alone can bring about a similar change in India as well. However, what gets missed in transplanting such ideas unthinkingly is that context matters.

Bogota's public transport success is also about changing social attitudes, individual incentives, and guiding market behaviour. Many not-so-apparent, context-specific things need to fall in place to replicate successes from other policy environments. For this reason, this book is about Indian public policy centred on India's experiences.

Any individual is a part of three meta-institutions, each with its unique characteristics, follies, and strengths. These are the market, State, and society. Following this worldview, the book is organized into three independent sections. Section 1 (*Sarkaar*) tries to identify some key features of the Indian State, why it fails, and also why it succeeds. Section 2 (*Bazaar*) gives an account of how the Indian State interacts with markets and businesses. Section 3 (*Samaaj*) maps the relationship between the Indian State and society.[3] The chapters in each section are independent and can be read in any order. Each chapter discusses a prevalent idea, story, or myth in the popular discourse on Indian governance.

We hope, dear reader, you will find something useful in this book, something that will contribute to your understanding of Indians governing themselves. And we also hope you have fun while reading it.

As Crime Master Gogo famously said in *Andaz Apna Apna* (1994), '*Aaya hun to kuchh le kar hi jaayoonga*' [since I'm here already, I'll settle for the key takeaways].

---

[3] We've borrowed the terminology of Samaaj, Sarkaar, Bazaar from philanthropist Rohini Nilekani's articles on this theme. See https://www.samaajsarkaarbazaar.in/

I

Sarkaar

1

Reflecting on the Indian State's Origins

Who is that one ancient Indian you will find on city billboards, newspaper advertisements, and self-help books sold by the street side?

Kautilya or Chanakya, of course.

While his insights are now commonly invoked to sell real estate or to derive a listicle for corporate management, we forget that the *Arthashastra* at its core is about one abstract political institution that affects us in profound ways: the State.

The Beginning

Kautilya writes that in the absence of an effective king, *matsyanyaaya*—the law of the fishes—prevails. By this, what he means is that when the law is kept at abeyance, 'the strong do what they can and the weak suffer as they must'.[1]

---

[1] Thucydides (460–400 BCE), an ancient Greek theorist, reflected on the State in these words.

In that scenario, power becomes the only determinant of survival and success. Big fish eat small fish, and that's just the way the cookie crumbles.

Kautilya argues that it is only in the presence of a king who upholds the law that the weak can resist the strong. The king's dharma then is to ensure that the powerful do not trample over the disadvantaged. The king is duty-bound to punish the powerful who run amok. This primary function of the king is referred to as *dandaniti* (literally, the policy or practice of punishment) in the Indian philosophical tradition.

In this conception, the freedoms—'rights' in contemporary parlance—of individuals are not naturally ordained. They are a consequence of a political institution called the State that will use its power effectively and judiciously to protect these freedoms. Kautilya wrote:

> People suffering from anarchy as illustrated by the proverbial tendency of a large fish swallowing a small one (*matsyanyayabhibhutah prajah*), first elected Manu, the Vaivasvata, to be their king; and allotted one-sixth of the grains grown and one-tenth of merchandise as sovereign dues. Fed by this payment, kings took upon themselves the responsibility of maintaining the safety and security of their subjects (*yogakshemavah*), and of being answerable for the sins of their subjects when the principle of levying just punishments and taxes has been violated.[2]

---

[2] *Kautilya's Arthashastra*, translated by R. Shamasastry (1915), accessed 20 January 2022, http://www.columbia.edu/itc/mealac/pritchett/00litlinks/kautilya/index.html.

In this imagination, individuals metaphorically enter into a contract with a political institution. The terms of the contract are such that they submit some of their freedoms in return for the promise of security and well-being offered by the State.

In Western philosophy, this trade-off forms the basis of social contract theories. In *Leviathan* (1651), Thomas Hobbes argues that individuals cede all their rights in return for protection to a sovereign who is himself above the law. John Locke, writing after Hobbes, is more moderate. In his view, individuals surrender only some of their rights (liberty) to a government that rules by the consent of the governed. The primary role of the State then is to prevent the strong from harming the weak and ensure that every person is given an equal opportunity to succeed.

Even though we no longer have kings who 'rule' over people, what hasn't changed is the purpose of the Indian State. It exists to prevent *matsyanyaaya*. A lofty goal, isn't it? For this reason, the State as an institution is unparalleled in human society. Understanding it is key to understanding ourselves. That's where this book begins.

The Modern State

Although the fundamental motivation underlying the need for the State hasn't changed, the nature of this institution has evolved over time. The labels that we commonly apply to States today, such as 'liberal democracies' can be traced back to the Age of Enlightenment.[3] It was an age of reason where philosophers questioned the orthodoxies of religion and morality that were drawn from it. It marked the secession of the social and the political from the realm of the spiritual. The separation of the State from the church, as it was called. This opened up the thinking of how people should organize themselves to conduct their affairs in the community without the overbearing weight of religion. The eventual outcome was the evolution of the State with its arms of legislature, executive and judiciary as we now know it.

Hence, before understanding the specifics of the Indian State, it is useful to understand the current status of the three assumptions that underlie all modern democracies: the omnicompetent citizen, a limited role for the State, and political parties as just one of the several important institutions.

Assumption 1: The Omnicompetent Citizen

The first foundational assumption was that of an 'omnicompetent' citizen—a citizen who knew almost everything that was happening around her and could be

---

[3] The Age of Enlightenment (also known as the Age of Reason or simply the Enlightenment) was an intellectual and philosophical movement that dominated the world of ideas in Europe in the 17th and 18th centuries. The Enlightenment included a range of ideas centred on the value of human happiness, the pursuit of knowledge obtained by means of reason and the evidence of the senses, and ideals such as liberty, progress, toleration, fraternity, constitutional government, and separation of church and State.

trusted to make decisions in a democracy. This was the basis for the touching faith in the abilities of any individual citizen to have an equal voice in what's good for society. This wasn't a terrible assumption to make at the time. The world was a simple place. Most of the economy was dependent on hunting and farming. Families had lived on their land for generations and could be trusted to know what was good for them. That the citizens could make full sense of their world wasn't therefore considered a stretched assumption.

What do we make of this assumption today? Democracy is founded on the belief that public opinion matters. But as society has become more advanced, knowledge more specialized with a wider range of issues impacting our lives, citizens find it difficult to inform themselves about all the issues impacting their lives. The world is getting infinitely more complex with advances in technology and specialization in knowledge. A large proportion of people live in cities and frequently move between them. They see and make sense of only a narrow sliver of the world that's around them every day. In fact, almost a century back, Walter Lippman already had misgivings about the idea of an 'omnicompetent' citizen. He probed this in his two seminal books—*Public Opinion* (1922) and *The Phantom Public* (1925). As Lippman wrote, 'The real environment is altogether too big, too complex, and too fleeting for direct acquaintance.'[4]

The ordinary citizen 'lives in a world he cannot see, does not understand, and is unable to direct'.[5] This leads

---

[4] Walter Lippman, *Public Opinion* (Transaction, 1998), 16.

[5] Walter Lippman, *The Phantom Public* (Transaction, 1925).

to an inevitable discrepancy between 'the world outside and the picture in our heads'.[6] This 'pseudo environment' in our heads is what we use to form political and public opinions. This is what political parties and media work on to create narratives. For Lippman, this was the flaw with the democratic ideal of public participation in decision making. They are coming at it with the 'most inadequate picture'.

Democracy needs competent citizens. If majority of the voters aren't able to make sense of the real world around them to make clear-headed judgements, what's the point of it all?

Lippman's response to this problem was in the role of experts. Representative politics 'cannot be worked successfully . . . unless there is an independent, expert organization for making the unseen facts intelligible'.[7] An enlightened oligarchy of experts is the answer. In Lippman's prescription, the expert is a disinterested participant with deep mastery of an area who advises those in power within the government or administration. As Lippman writes, 'The power of the expert depends upon separating himself from those who make the decisions, upon not caring, in his expert self, what decision is made.'[8]

For Lippman, this separation of responsibilities is critical for the functioning of the democracy. The role of the ordinary public is restricted in mobilizing themselves to elect their representatives on the basis of their performance (real or promised), which in turn depends on how they have

---

[6] Lippman, *Public Opinion*, 3.

[7] Ibid., Introduction, xvi.

[8] Ibid., 382.

used the experts to frame laws and policies. Lippman has no illusions about the capabilities of popular governments that sway to the moods of the public. They need guidance from experts. Citizens neither possess the knowledge nor the competence on the wide range of issues that concern their world nor can this be taught to them. The best hope for democracy, therefore, is to have detached experts who have the ears of those at the helm.

It is fair to say that the role of experts has become larger from the time Lippman wrote those words almost a century ago. They became central to the democratic systems worldwide. For a few decades in the post-war era this equilibrium between the public, the representatives, and the experts worked just as Lippman had imagined. Experts weighed in on everything—defence, environment, economics, social issues—and soon there emerged a market for experts. This is usually a good thing so long as there's a way to calibrate expertise. Else, you will soon find biased charlatans and wannabes peddling their expertise to inch their way up to those in power. By the 1980s, lobbying (as it came to be called) became a career option. In a marketplace of ideas, lobbying is natural. But vested interests willing to outspend others soon vitiated this marketplace. The stories of the 'Big Pharma' or the 'Big Tobacco' lobbies twisting scientific expertise to their advantage are legion.

There was another problem too. Something more genuine than insidious lobbying. A familiar issue in social sciences that underpins public policy discussions is what's called the replicability problem. Unlike natural sciences, social experiments done in a closed group or a sample quite often don't replicate the same results when using a different or larger sample. There have been numerous instances of this where famous social science theories have failed the test. Only in the last few years, this problem has been acknowledged and there are now attempts to address this problem.

By the turn of the twenty-first century, experts were no longer seen in the same light as before because of these reasons. For the public looking on from the outside, policymaking had become the preserve of think tanks, regulatory bodies, advisory committees of public intellectuals, economists, academics, and other such cabals of elites. A combination of complacency, lack of intellectual integrity in questioning market fundamentalism, the global financial crisis of 2009, and the rise of radically networked societies[9] on social media platforms meant the backlash against this elite was inevitable. The backlash arrived in the last decade, and it has been bad for elites. The experts have become discredited and internet echo chambers have taken their place. The citizen of today isn't omnicompetent like it was expected once; nor does she trust experts, the group Lippman thought would mediate between her and the government. This is new territory for citizens in a democracy.

---

[9] A Radically Networked Society is defined as a web of hyper connected individuals possessing an identity (imagined or real), and motivated by a common immediate cause. From Nitin Pai & Pranay Kotasthane (2016). 'Liberty & Security in Radically Networked Societies: A Challenge for Every Generation' in *Liberalism in India, Past, Present and Future, Essays in Honour of SV Raju* (pp.123-145), ed. Parth Shah.

Assumption 2: A Limited State

The second foundational assumption was the nature of the role of the State (therefore, the government) in the affairs of its citizens. It was expected that the State would concern itself with political matters, law and order, and the management of its treasury. Over the past two centuries, this has changed. The rise of nation-states, increasing globalization of trade, the need to manage the macroeconomy, and the desire to apply the progressive values of enlightenment more thoroughly within society have meant that the State is significantly more pervasive than ever. Despite the rhetoric of 'big bad government' of the Reagan–Thatcher era, the State in the US and the UK has continued to become bigger. The threat of global terror and cyber warfare has given the State further license to intrude on the privacy of its citizens. There is no retreat for the State or the government. This power in the hands of the government has skewed the balance in its favour over other arms of the State. We have to rethink the relationship between citizens and the government and the system of checks and balances. The Enlightenment might have been the age of reason that gave us this system. We need an age of reimagination today to address this change.

Assumption 3: The Political Party as Just Another Institution

The third foundational assumption was the featherlight concept of the political parties in electing a government to helm the State. We call this featherlight because political science philosophers like Edmund Burke or Thomas Paine viewed political divisions as emerging from differences on fundamental issues such as the role of the individual, State, and church than from tribal loyalty to a community, kinship, or other emotional reasons. The idea that party boundaries could be sharp and distinctive wasn't anticipated by them. Since the primary axis of confrontation during the Enlightenment was between reason and religion and their roles in the social and political spheres, the notion of political parties was somewhat limited. There's nothing in the literature of those times to suggest that political parties and their divisions exercised the minds of intellectuals. The idea that domestic politics could be adversarial like it is today would have been a shock to them.

To be fair to them, the partisanship that's on display today in most democracies would surprise even those who were familiar with the politics about half a century ago. Parties worked on issues together; there were many who could work across the aisles on key policies that had a long-term impact on society, and this notion of being in a 'permanent campaign' mode was absent. As the State continued to grow bigger with an outsized influence on the economy, there was more at stake for political parties to be in power. The other side wasn't just another party with a difference of opinion. It was the enemy. Capital and media played into this sharpening of division. The centrality of the party system and the division of the society, media, and capital along party lines is a reality in most democracies today. The tribal loyalties have only gotten sharper, and almost every issue is viewed through a partisan lens. This has meant a retreat of citizens into media echo chambers full of voices that reinforce their biases. There can never be any agreement or even engagement with the other side, and life is full of performative gestures to demonstrate your purity to your in-group. These will have their own consequences.

The changes in these three foundational assumptions mean we must rethink the democratic process in today's times. This is true for all democracies in the world. For India, there are a few more factors that have changed since it turned into a republic in 1950.

The Indian Case

First and foremost, the term State (*rajya*) itself is a confusing term in the Indian context. Political entities such as Karnataka or Goa are listed as states under the Indian Constitution. In common parlance, the term refers to these non-sovereign, political entities. But when we use the term 'State' in this book, we are referring to the 'Republic of India'—a political institution that came into being on 26 January 1950.

As the preamble to the Indian Constitution tells us, on that day, in an abstract sense, 'we, the people of India' solemnly resolved to constitute India into a new political entity. The Indian Constitution essentially describes, in excruciating detail, the relationship between this newly formed political entity and the Indian citizens. Think of it as a user's manual that describes the Indian State to Indian citizens, to government functionaries in India, and to the world at large. It is a physical manifestation of the social contract that Kautilya and Locke wrote about.

The Indian State that came into existence in 1950 was a fundamentally different institution from its predecessor. Prior to Independence, the colonial government was answerable to the British Parliament. The pre-Independence legislative structures in India had limited scope and its members were chosen by a very limited electorate. The governmental structure was designed for consultation and efficiency, rather than representation and accountability.[10] Thus, in independent India, the aim of the Indian leaders was to establish a State whose government represented a broad section of the society, was accountable to the electorate, and able to hold together a nascent nation.

As a result, a bicameral parliamentary democracy with a federal character, an independent judiciary, and a professional army controlled strictly by a political leadership came into being. This meant that the Indian Parliament became the supreme legislative body of India representing the majority will of the people. The Indian Parliament was made up of the President and the two Houses—Rajya Sabha (Council of States) and Lok Sabha (House of the People). The people who constitute the government were made replaceable through specific procedures laid down in the Constitution. The members of the Lok Sabha were to be elected through an election based on universal adult suffrage every five years.

Horizontally, the government was divided into three arms—the Executive, the Legislature, and the Judiciary, each of them having different functions within the government. Vertically, the Indian government was structured on the concept of federalism. Governments

---

[10] Vernon Hewitt, 'A Cautionary Tale: Colonial and Post-Colonial Conceptions of Good Government and Democratisation in Africa', *Commonwealth & Comparative Politics* 44, no. 1 (March 2006): 41–61, https://doi.org/10.1080/14662040600624437.

were to be formed at provincial and union levels. Each level was to have an independent sphere of administrative and legislative competence along with independent tax bases. The federal system of government was preferred for the Indian State as it aligned with the many identities— pan-Indian and sub-regional—that have characterized Indian society for centuries.

Seventy-five years after its creation, governments have come and gone, and leaders have moved on to other worlds, but the *Republic of India* still remains. This might seem anodyne at first, but look at India's neighbourhood and you will understand why this is a significant achievement. Take the case of Afghanistan over the last hundred years. The Kingdom of Afghanistan, a State that was formed in 1926, was replaced in 1973 by the Republic of Afghanistan. This republic was replaced by the Soviet-allied Democratic Republic of Afghanistan six years later. In 1996, the Taliban created another new State—the Emirate of Afghanistan, which was again replaced by the Islamic Republic (after the Taliban regime was toppled post 9/11) in 2001. By 2021, the Taliban's Islamic Emirate of Afghanistan had been reinstated. With each of these transitions, the relationship between the governed and the government changed significantly. Though Afghanistan is an outlier, many other States in India's neighbourhood have witnessed either an outright overthrow of the State or multiple significant revisions of their constitutions.

Coming back to India, if there's one thing to learn from our neighbouring States, it is that there can be no finality in State-building. The Republic of India has also evolved since its founding moment in three significant ways.

One, the modern conception of the Indian State with its emphasis on individual liberty, the primacy of law, and universal adult franchise was not rooted in the local context and tradition. The social ethos that has governed Indians place the primacy of family, caste, and community over the individual. Religion had a role in this. The lack of industrialization and organic modernization like that seen in western Europe was possibly another reason. The idea of an individual sacrificing herself for the greater good of the group always had a powerful draw in India. The notion of enlightened individual self-interest was foreign to this society. Gandhi, who understood this, believed a decentralized structure of democracy, with village panchayat-like bodies at the heart of it, could be more suited to the Indian ethos. But these views weren't taken seriously because they either seemed too idealistic to be implemented or were viewed with suspicion by those who felt the need to overhaul the Indian social structure premised on caste.

Over time, ideas like secularism and socialism were added to the Constitution, and there were more direct interventions in social and religious issues by the government. Through the long years that various Indian principalities were ruled by the royalty of different stripes and hues, there was one thing that was constant. The State rarely interfered in the social and religious customs of its people. A reformist king or a minister was always playing with fire. The ossification of the Indian society on caste lines with its inhumane rituals was a result of this policy of non-interference. The modern Indian Constitution in its intent was a stark departure from this tradition. It was fashioned to be a tool for not just an economic and political revolution, but a social revolution.[11] Later in the book we will discuss the Hindu Code Bill and how even the most ardent champions of the Constitution found the State's desire to reform social practices that drew their legitimacy from the religious realm as difficult to swallow. There was resentment in sections of society who considered these moves motivated by political gains and bided their time to undo them. The vilification of this Nehruvian consensus and the pushback against liberalism that has gained traction in recent times are perhaps manifestations of this repressed angst. In a way, this is the society catching up with politics. We haven't seen the end of it yet.

Two, we might have got ourselves a brand-new constitution in 1950, but that didn't mean we were fully able to break from the colonial past. What we inherited was a system that cared to enrich itself more than its citizens and extractive institutions that were designed to treat Indians as subjects. Despite the republic's promise to overturn this ruler–subject dynamic, the dissonance remains. Being colonial overlords of a huge population can be a heady feeling. The evidence of this is all around us. The civil servants and ministers live in the colonial bungalows left behind by the Raj with a retinue that would have made a Raj-era sahib proud. Traffic is cleared for cars with a red light (*lal-batti*) on top because their time is more important than the thousands who wait and watch. All kinds of State representatives are exempt from things that ordinary

---

[11] Granville Austin, one of the foremost scholars of the Indian Constitution, claimed that the document's primary purpose was to reform the Indian society through constitutional means.

citizens face in their everyday lives—paying toll, standing in queues at airports, the list is endless. The laws, the police procedures, the guidelines on how the State procures things (more on this later), the way we assess the performance of the State are all relics of an extractive State of the past. The modern Indian State might have taken on a benevolent garb and is perhaps more responsive than the colonial State but the tools it has are all of the past. The citizens have gladly accepted this for whatever little kindness they get in return. The idea that the State is to serve the people is not in their bones. The 'sarkaar' as the mai-baap of people is deeply embedded in our psyche.

Three, we called India a union of states, but we centralized power in the union government as part of our design. There were reasons for this, including the point made above about inheriting a colonial system. The coming together of over 600 princely states into the union meant no one was quite sure what shape and form local governing bodies or state governments would take. There was a lack of trust in their allegiance to the union, and any weakness by the union might have been exploited by them. The union had to be stronger at the centre. Also, the task of nation-building in the wake of the great tragedy of Partition meant there was a desire to centralize power to directly manage the affairs of the provinces. Communal strife was an ever-present danger and there was no guarantee that, left to themselves, the provinces would be able to control it. Also, the early success of Soviet-style central planning in the USSR was a great influence among policymakers of that era. Nation-building was seen as a grand project managed through elaborate five-year plans by a central planning commission. This consolidation of power by the union has only strengthened over the years.

The chapters in this section ruminate on these key characteristics of the Indian State. Chapter 2 begins by asking if being 'anti-national' is seditious in order to understand the profound difference between the Indian State, the Indian nation, and Indian governments. In Chapter 3, we locate the Indian State through its interactions with society and markets. Chapter 4 tries to address that favourite contemplative Indian question—'why are our governments like this only?' Chapter 5 analyses the 'ambition versus capacity' paradox that characterizes the Indian State. Chapter 6 addresses another popular lament about the Indian State— do we have 'too much' democracy? The dominance of the political party as an institution of governance is the focus of Chapter 7. Finally, the section ends with a chapter that discusses the State's role as an enforcer of law and order in society.

2

A Political Science Toolkit

If you are of a certain age, you probably remember the Vikram–Betaal stories. They appeared in *Chandamama*, a popular children's weekly magazine, and later there was even a popular Doordarshan serial featuring them. To stick to the bare details of the tale without getting into its finer points, the wise king Vikramaditya had to carry Betaal on his shoulders while maintaining a vow of silence. En route, Betaal would tell him a story that would end with an intriguing conundrum. He would then ask Vikram for the solution, warning him that if he were to deliberately remain silent, his head would be blown to bits. Vikram would, of course, have the solution and proceed to answer, thus breaking his vow of silence. Betaal would then fly back to the top of the tree from where Vikram had picked him up in the first place. This cycle would repeat itself (about twenty-five times).

In today's India, if there's a conundrum one could pose to Vikram, it would be this: who is an anti-national? Because these days you can never be sure. Sedition charges are generously distributed. Is there a way to make sense of this?

A recent round of this conundrum played out in 2021. In February that year, the Delhi Police arrested a young woman, Disha Ravi, and charged her with sedition and criminal conspiracy. The reason: she was an editor of a shared online document (called the 'Toolkit'), which was used to 'peddle support for the secessionist Khalistan narrative in the guise of farmer protests'. She was then jailed, but a Delhi Court later granted her bail.

This case brought back several old questions into the limelight. What exactly is 'sedition'? Can someone who doesn't identify themselves as Indian be termed seditious, or can merely criticizing a government's policies become seditious under some circumstances? Are sedition, anti-nationalism, and dissent any different from each other?

In our view, these questions cannot be answered unless we understand what the terms 'the Indian State', 'Indian nation', and 'Indian government' mean. So, let's take a detour to the high school political science curriculum before returning to the question of sedition.

The State, as we have discussed, is an abstract political institution. In the introduction to this section, we discussed how states came into being to prevent *matsyanyaaya.* Another connected definition of the State comes from Max Weber who defines it as 'a human community that (successfully) claims the monopoly of the legitimate use of physical force within a given territory'.[1] To ensure that all its individuals'

---

[1] Drawn from 'Politics as a Vocation' (1919) by Max Weber, a seminal essay of political science and sociology.

liberties are protected, a State is invested with the power
to use violence and prevent other belligerent groups from
terrorizing individuals. It is for this reason that a State
maintains armed institutions like the police and the army.

By this definition, an anti-State act would be the one
that challenges the State's monopoly over the legitimate
use of physical force. In other words, an act of violence or
the use of force by anyone other than the State becomes
anti-State. In a few Indian languages, such an anti-State act
would translate to *raajdroha*.

The government is a temporary governing body of the State.
If the State is imagined as a corporation, the government
is like its management. A State is semi-permanent. It will
live on until it is overthrown or replaced and a new social
contract is established. Unlike the State, the government is
composed of a set of specific *people*. When the electorate
votes, they choose their government and not the State.

By this definition, an anti-government act would be the
one that criticizes the policies, strategies, and directives of
the governing body in power.

Finally, *a nation* is a mental construct, an act of personal
imagination. Social anthropologist Ernest Gellner defines
this concept precisely yet comprehensively thus:

> Two men are of the same nation if and only if they
> recognize each other as belonging to the same nation.
> In other words, nations maketh man; nations are
> the artefacts of men's convictions and loyalties and
> solidarities. A mere category of persons (say, occupants
> of a given territory, or speakers of a given language, for
> example) becomes a nation if and when the members of

the category firmly recognize certain mutual rights and duties to each other in virtue of their shared membership of it. It is their recognition of each other as fellows of this kind which turns them into a nation, and not the other shared attributes, whatever they might be, which separate that category from non-members.[2]

In other words, nations are imagined.[3] People belong to the same nation only if *they* consider themselves to be so.

An anti-national act could thus be of two types. One that denies the existence of such an imagined community. For example, libertarians could argue that only individuals matter and not the groups that these individuals are a part of. And the other view imagining a nation along lines different from the dominant belief. For example, communism sees workers across the world as one 'nation'.

What Is Sedition Then?

With these concepts understood, we are now in a position to understand sedition.

Sedition laws can lie on a continuum. In dictatorships and party-States, sedition laws are applied wantonly to criticisms of the government. That is, being anti-government is regarded as seditious. In most modern democracies, however, sedition laws punish only those anti-State actions that have the capability to directly challenge the State's

---

[2] Ernest Gellner, *Nations and Nationalism* (Basil Blackwell, 1983), 7.

[3] Benedict Anderson, in his book *Imagined Communities: Reflections on the Origin and Spread of Nationalism* (1983), defines the nation as an 'imagined political community'.

authority. Thus, criticism of the Republic of India would not count as sedition, but inciting violence against the police would count as sedition.

Similarly, being anti-national is not the same as being seditious. An anti-national person doesn't imagine herself as Indian. Though we personally believe that nationalism is a net positive, it is perfectly reasonable for someone else to not think along the same lines. The act of denying one's association with the Indian nation, criticizing it, or spreading the word about it, is anti-national but not criminal or seditious. In fact, the Republic of India protects the rights of people to express anti-national, anti-government, and even anti-State views in a peaceful manner.

The Indian Sedition Law

Now we are in a position to understand a law that often gets discussed in India: sedition. India's sedition law i.e., Section 124A of the Indian Penal Code has colonial origins. In British times, being anti-government was reason enough to be labelled seditious. On this basis, Tilak, Gandhi, and scores of other leaders were tried for sedition by the colonial government.

After Independence, there was a case for the sedition laws to be taken off the books. That never happened. Sedition law continued in its colonial avatar. But its application changed. First, only anti-State acts were penalized—as against anti-government ones—as a result of a right to freedom of speech and expression. In subsequent court rulings, the applicability of sedition was further truncated. Only those anti-State acts that had the tendency to incite violence or disturb law and order were deemed to be seditious.

This dissonance between the original definition and application continues to this day. See for yourself. Section 124A of the Indian Penal Code, colloquially called the sedition law, reads:

Whoever, by words, either spoken or written, or by signs, or by visible representation, or otherwise, brings or attempts to bring into hatred or contempt, or excites or attempts to excite disaffection towards, the Government established by law in India, shall be punished with imprisonment for life, to which fine may be added, or with imprisonment which may extend to three years, to which fine may be added, or with fine.

Explanation 1.—The expression 'disaffection' includes disloyalty and all feelings of enmity.

Explanation 2.—Comments expressing disapprobation of the measures of the Government with a view to obtain their alteration by lawful means, without exciting or attempting to excite hatred, contempt or disaffection, do not constitute an offence under this section.

Explanation 3.—Comments expressing disapprobation of the administrative or other action of the Government without exciting or attempting to excite hatred, contempt or disaffection, do not constitute an offence under this section.

Note how wide-ranging this provision is. Even disloyalty and all feelings of enmity towards the government count as sedition. Now, read the qualifier that the Supreme Court added in *Kedar Nath vs State of Bihar* in 1962.

... the sections aim at rendering penal only such activities as would be intended, or have a tendency, to create disorder or disturbance of public peace by resort to violence. As already pointed out, the explanations appended to the main body of the section make it clear that criticism of public measures or comment on Government action, however strongly worded, would be within reasonable limits and would be consistent with the fundamental right of freedom of speech and expression. It is only when the words, written or spoken, etc. which have the pernicious tendency or intention of creating public disorder or disturbance of law and order that the law steps in to prevent such activities in the interest of public order.[4]

In non-legalese, for an action to count as seditious, its connection with violence is necessary according to the Supreme Court, but that's not what the original framing in the Indian Penal Code says.

This dissonance is a problem to such an extent that the same judge presiding in two similar cases (Disha Ravi's and Safoora Zargar's), referred to the same 1962 judgment, and yet reached two opposite conclusions. In Safoora Zargar's[5] case, bail was denied on the grounds that the connection of an act with violence is not necessary. In the Disha Ravi case, bail was granted on the grounds that the connection of an act with violence is necessary.

---

[4] 'Kedar Nath Singh vs State of Bihar on 20 January, 1962', accessed 28 January 2022, https://indiankanoon.org/doc/111867/.

[5] Safoora Zargar is a student activist who was jailed for her alleged role in the riots that broke out during protests against the Citizenship (Amendment) Act, 2019.

The other problem is the political economy of India's sedition law. Because it is construed as a grave anti-State offence, it is cognizable, i.e., investigation and arrest can happen based on just a First Information Report (FIR). It is also non-bailable i.e., bail is subject to the decision of a session's judge. Such strict provisions mean that the police authorities have an incentive to slap sedition charges indiscriminately. By the time charges are cleared, many years pass by. The process becomes the punishment.

The Way Forward

Broadly, there are three ways out. The first method would be to revise the sedition law to end the dissonance between the text and its subsequent interpretation. Make the link with violence a necessary condition for the application of sedition.

A second way is to scrap the law altogether. If the tendency to cause violence is what triggers sedition, there are enough laws in place to address such actions. Even if this law were to be struck down, provisions to punish acts inciting violence against State, government, or other people will still be applicable.

A third way out is to address the political economy question by making sedition a bailable and non-cognizable offence. With nothing to gain by slapping the additional charge of sedition, its usage is likely to decline. A solution with a similar effect is to make police personnel comply with additional requirements before arresting a person for sedition. The Bombay High Court tried to do this in the

Aseem Trivedi case[6] by issuing guidelines to police personnel listing specific preconditions. A failure to adhere to these guidelines made the police officer liable to dereliction of duty. To what extent these guidelines have been adopted since then is not clearly known.

Perhaps, the second solution is the ideal one. But it's also the most unlikely one in the current situation. We, in fact, run a real risk of going the other way—sedition laws might well go back to punishing anti-government utterances. Given this reality, focusing on changing the incentives of the police might be more practical.

For now, these lines from Disha Ravi's bail order that explain the difference between anti-national, anti-State, and anti-government clearly, need to be paid attention to:

> Citizens are conscience keepers of government in any democratic Nation. They cannot be put behind the bars simply because they choose to disagree with the State policies. The offence of sedition cannot be invoked to minister to the wounded vanity of the governments. Difference of opinion, disagreement, divergence, dissent, or for that matter, even disapprobation, are recognized legitimate tools to infuse objectivity in state policies. An aware and assertive citizenry, in contradistinction with an

---

[6] Aseem Trivedi, a cartoonist, was charged with sedition in 2012 on allegations that his cartoons had not only defamed Parliament, the Constitution, and the emblem, but also tried to spread hatred and disrespect against the government.

indifferent or docile citizenry, is indisputably a sign of a healthy and vibrant democracy.[7]

What happened in the toolkit case was neither new nor surprising. In 2016, the same story of dissent leading to slapping of sedition laws unfolded in the Jawaharlal Nehru University (JNU) campus. Why then is it so easy for our governments to label dissent as seditious, while the social contract with the State permits us to oppose government policies?

The cycle of dissent–protest–arrest that we witness so often points to a fundamental paradox: we have compromised the Indian Republic for the sake of democracy. Let us see how.

There is no universally accepted definition of democracy, but it literally means the 'rule of the people' as against rule by a monarch. In reality, it can be defined as the rule of the majority. What constitutes a majority can vary but at the bare minimum, a democracy means that whatever the majority of the populace agrees to will be carried out by the State.

In a pure democracy, therefore, the majority rules in all cases, regardless of the consequences for individuals or for those not in majority. For example, the city-states in ancient Greece were democratic, and so, it was within the laws of the State for Socrates to be killed through a majority sanction. Centuries later, in the JNU case, if a majority of

---

[7] Livelaw News Network, 'Citizens Can't Be Put Behind Bars Simply Because They Disagree with State Policies : Delhi Court In Disha Ravi Bail Order', 23 February 2021, https://www.livelaw.in/top-stories/citizens-behind-bars-disagree-state-dissent-sedition-disha-ravi-toolkit-170279.

people support the arrest of a student because what he said is 'seditious', it would not violate the principles of democracy per se. But it's the Indian Republic that prevents a majority from using its coercive power against individuals or groups with lesser power. This might come as a surprise to many of us who have been taught in civics that 'a republic is merely a State where the leader of the government is not a hereditary position'.

Conceptually, a republic is governed by the *rule of law* and not the *rule of men or women*. This means that law is the supreme power in a republic and not a monarch. Rule of law also implies that laws apply to everyone in the State. This does not mean that the head of the State has the same powers as ordinary citizens, but it means that even the head of the State can only act in accordance with the laws that specify his/her duties and actions. In a republic, the highest aspiration of anyone in political life ought to be to obey the rule of law as well as to enforce it.

A corollary of the rule of law is that a republic recognizes certain inalienable and individual rights for its citizens, which are formalized in a bill or a charter. Every citizen, by default, possesses these rights and a document such as the constitution specifies how these rights will be protected.

And so, it's this Indian Republic that prohibits the majority from running roughshod on the basis of its numerical strength. In a republic like India, the Constitution limits the power of governments and groups, in order to protect the individual's rights.

The conflict between democracy and the republic is a long one. There have been many times when individual freedoms have been abrogated in the name of upholding the greater good, of securing India and its citizens. The first strain between the two aims came up with the first amendment of the Indian Constitution, which introduced the concept of 'reasonable' restrictions.[8] The amendment made it easier for the State to regulate speech if they violated 'sovereignty and integrity of India, the security of the State, friendly relations with foreign States, public order, decency or morality or in relation to contempt of court, defamation or incitement to an offence'. The introduction of the word 'reasonable', along with vaguely defined reasons for the restrictions, added ambiguity—it locked the media, the executive, the legislature, and the judiciary in a four-cornered contest that continues to this date.

At its core, the toolkit case was a reflection of this conflict between democracy and the republic.

Wrapping Up

A charitable way to reason out the recent attempts at labelling anti-government protests as anti-national or worse anti-State is ignorance.

---

[8] The First Amendment to the Indian Constitution was made by the Interim Government dominated by Congress Party members and led by the Interim Prime Minister Jawaharlal Nehru. Since these amendments took place less than a year before the first Parliamentary elections, there were no formal Opposition parties involved in the debate. Of the changes that were made, the most controversial were those pertaining to the limitations on the freedom of speech and expression guaranteed under the Indian Constitution.

Can you protest against the government and yet be a nationalist? The answer is yes, of course. That's what a democratic republic like India allows us. Anti-government expressions are important means to ensure that 'we, the people' are masters, not subjects.

And is being anti-national being anti-State? This is an even more important difference. Because the nation is an imagined idea, a democratic republic must allow a citizen to have alternate imaginations of the nation. Of course, some nationalists may not like these ideas and would prefer a common imagination. Peaceful means to persuade and make the case for the Indian nation is a valid recourse for them. But the usage of violence and threat of violence against anti-nationals would be against the rights that the Indian State gives to individuals—whether they are anti-nationals or not.

Violence in the name of nationalism is anti-national and anti-State, both.

3

Maai-Baap Sarkaar

Jitne bhi tu karle sitam,
hans hans ke sahenge hum

[We will happily take all your tyranny in our stride—the
song that kind of sums up the relationship between the
Indian citizen and the State.]

Neeraj Chopra won India's first athletics gold ever at the
Tokyo Olympics 2020. Immediately after his victory, two
kinds of narratives played out in the Indian media. The first
narrative was about government apathy. It went something
like this: Chopra won not because of the government
but *despite* it. The government failed to provide adequate
support and facilities, and yet the athlete went on to win the
gold medal. Immediately, a counter-narrative sprung up.
The Sports Authority of India (SAI) put out several numbers
in the media to the effect that between 2016 and 2021,
Chopra received government support worth Rs 7 crore,

and that he was inducted into the Indian government's flagship program, the Target Olympics Podium Scheme (TOPS) in 2018, which paved the way for his success.

Notice how both these stories place the government as the side-hero. Both story arcs assume that it is the government's responsibility that Indian teams must win Olympic medals. We hardly question whether the government is the best institution to achieve this goal. And if not, whose job should it be to win Olympic medals? This question is a good starting point to locate the institution called the Indian State in our society.

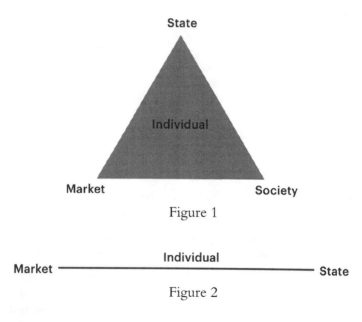

Figure 1

Figure 2

The conventional view of politics considers just two agents of change—the State and the market (Figure 2). This dichotomy implies that the solution to all our problems rests with either the State (represented by its agent—the government) or the market. In this view, society is like a patient that gets operated on by the State or the market.

But such a view misses out on another important part of an individual's human experience—her human network or the society that she lives in. If we were to place the individual at the centre, there are not two, but three institutions she is a part of—the market, the State, and the society (Figure 1).[1] The underappreciated point is that the nature of the three institutions is such that each of the three is better at certain things and worse at some others. They are complementary.

For example, the State is very adept at employing force. For an individual, through an instrument like the Constitution, the State ensures that *matsyanyaaya* doesn't prevail, i.e., it ensures that the only determinant for her survival is not the power she can exercise over others. The State essentially provides the individual with a sense of security.

Concurrently, this institution is worse at many things. Efficient usage of resources is not its strength, as any company run by the government amply demonstrates. The State also cannot account for the variety and preferences of all individuals. Changing social behaviours through the State requires immense capacity, oversight, and enforcement. Like Alexis De Tocqueville said succinctly, 'A government knows only how to dictate precise rules; it imposes the

---

[1] Raghuram Rajan's *The Third Pillar: How Markets and the State Leave the Community Behind* (Penguin Press, 2019) explores the interplay of these three forces in an American context.

sentiments and the ideas that it favours, and it is always hard to distinguish its counsels from its orders.'[2]

A market, on the other hand, is arguably more efficient than the government. For individuals, the market provides them the opportunity to be productive, differentiate themselves, innovate, and excel. The primary medium through which the market operates is trade. Voluntary exchanges in markets enable people to specialize in different goods and services. Trade becomes a positive-sum game benefiting all parties. At the same time, the market is oblivious to equity concerns. If an exchange is forced, as it was in the case of slavery, it can increase inequity. Moreover, the market does not concern itself with the individual's need for belonging. You might order an organic product from the hills of Himachal Pradesh on Amazon but you are unlikely to identify yourself with the producer. The market enables transactions, not relationships.

That's where a third institution comes into play— society or more appropriately, civil society. From an individual's perspective, it fulfils her need for belonging. It provides a framework for norms and values. Society, being closest to the individual, can also potentially respond the quickest to her needs. Sometimes, societies can even plug the failures of governments and markets. But just as markets and governments can fail, societies fail too. A society is susceptible to majoritarianism, tends to be conservative, and can suppress individual expression.

So, in a sense, there are not two but three actors of change. From an individual's point of view, we need a world

---

[2] Alexis de Tocqueville, *Democracy in America*, Vol. 3 *(Liberty Fund), Of the Use That Americans Make of Association in Civil Life*, 901.

where she is able to extract benefits from each of the three while each covers the others' weaknesses. For example, we want the State to prevent majoritarian excesses of society and the market to prevent the sucking away of initiative and innovation that States tend to do.

While we broadly understand the strengths and weaknesses of the State and markets, society is what we know the least about. So, let's zoom in on this institution.

A civil society is 'an aggregate of non–governmental organizations and institutions that manifest the interests and will of citizens'.[3] Apartment WhatsApp groups, philanthropies, and local governments where citizens have the power to determine its agenda are all part of this construct called civil society. Broadly, there are three ways in which civil society groups can be a part of the solution.

One, philanthropy. Andrew Carnegie's public library legacy, the Bill and Melinda Gates Foundation's work on healthcare, JSW's (Jindal Steel Works) role in India's Tokyo Olympics performance, and the Tata's contribution to research establishments (Tata Institute of Fundamental Research, Tata Institute of Social Sciences, to name two) fall under this category of civil society initiatives.

Philanthropy is particularly important because when we have an overstretched and under-resourced State, there are too many competing demands on its limited resources. For example, it is difficult to see how the Indian State can prioritize art, sports, or environment over Indians' material well-being especially with over 20 per cent of its

---

[3] Shahajadi Khanom, 'Civil Society and Democratization Process in Developing Country: A Review', *International Journal of Research and Innovation in Social Science* 2, no. 8, August 2018, 5.

population below the poverty line. In fact, it might even be unconscionable for the State to do so. Such gaps can be filled by civil society initiatives like philanthropy. By working in these areas, civil society can complement the State instead of substituting it.

Two, social movements. Social movements are initiatives aimed at self-correcting the underlying organizational fundamentals of society. Such movements are often led by reformers, of which we had quite a few in India. Ram Mohan Roy's contribution to the abolition of Sati, D. K. Karve's work in women's education, Jyotirao Phule and Periyar's efforts to eradicate caste discrimination, and Baba Amte's rehabilitation of leprosy patients are all successful examples of civil society-led reform.

The third category of civil society initiatives is aimed at correcting market failures: situations in which allocations of goods and services are suboptimal. Non-governmental groups that mobilize people to plant more trees in the city, or clean lakes, or raise awareness about noise pollution are a few examples of this category. Economist Elinor Ostrom's work documents many self-governance initiatives for managing the common pool resources. One of the failures that people often talk about is the tragedy of the commons—a situation where a shared resource declines in quality due to individuals prioritizing their self-interest over community needs. For instance, people would often say that our forest cover was reducing because a few individuals were overexploiting the shared resource through excessive logging or slash and burn cultivation. The common wisdom when Ostrom wrote said that the only way to preserve a forest in such cases was to take it away from the community and either nationalize it or privatize it. Her work found that tragedy of the commons is, in fact, not inevitable. In *Governing the Commons* (Cambridge University Press, 1990), Ostrom documented several cases of common resources across the world where the community—and not the State or market—had institutionalized self-governance mechanisms successfully.

The Indian Context

What we have so far spoken about the three institutions is something that applies globally. But in India, the imagined role of the State dominates both the markets and the society. Created in the backdrop of a deeply fractured, poor, and unequal society, the Indian Constitution came hardcoded with a social revolution algorithm.

Until then, the idea of social revolution by constitutional methods was not common. A conservative document like the Constitution served primarily to establish rights and institutions in a society, and protect its citizens from an overreaching State. To use a document like that to bring about a social revolution was a bold and imaginative experiment. Our personal bias is in favour of this laudable experiment. Maybe it was this that held India together in its infancy. Nevertheless, as the *introduction* chapter says, even the best of policies can have unintended consequences. So too was the case with this idea of a 'revolutionary' Indian welfare State.

Over time, we kept adding new things to the already long list of things that the State should do. The State became the *maai-baap sarkaar*—a nanny State that interferes excessively in matters of personal choice, economy, and society. Even today, many of us instinctively want it to do more regardless of its capabilities. The mismatch between the State's ambition and competence only kept growing. Because the State was overly concerned with reforming the society, it miserably failed at the task it was supposed to be doing: upholding law and order, policing, or providing basic public services. The Indian State's expenditure on risk-coping social protection measures such as fuel and food subsidy and employment guarantee far exceeds the expenditure on basic public services.[4] Even after seventy years of Independence, over 20 per cent of our population continues to live in extreme poverty, many dense habitations have poor access to schools, water, and electricity, and law, order, and public safety show little improvement.

Next, the citizen at the margin refused to take up acts of compassion, empathy, or philanthropy. This is because she considers that the execution of these functions is, in fact, the raison d'être of the State. Citizens are more likely to claim that their tax contributions are by themselves their generous contributions towards social and behavioural change. Governments further exploited the State's primacy, imposing cesses, or even taking away forcibly from unsuspecting citizens to clean cities, to fund toilets—goals that actually need massive societal and behavioural changes, and hence require citizens as active stakeholders rather than passive taxpayers.

---

[4] Devesh Kapur and Prakirti Nangia, 'Social Protection in India: A Welfare State Sans Public Goods?', *India Review* 14, no. 1 (3 March 2015): 73–90, https://doi.org/10.1080/14736489.2015.1001275.

Because it is seen as a philanthropic actor out to do many good things, a variant of Stockholm Syndrome took root. The State's follies got ignored. Acts of wrongdoings by governments then became fait accompli, pushed aside as a collective cost that the society necessarily needs to incur in order to ensure that the State performs its welfare role. For example, the policy for reserving certain items for manufacturing by the small sector was a mainstay of the government's policy for small enterprises, for nearly 50 years. Under this policy, firms that used machinery above an arbitrarily defined threshold were prohibited from manufacturing certain items. While intended to generate more employment in the small sector, it had the opposite effect. Efficient firms with optimal mix of machinery and labour were booted out, and the total number of people employed across the sector in the production of these items fell. This policy was also one of the reasons why India lost out to China in manufacturing.[5] Despite being a resounding failure, the policy continued to be in place for nearly half a century, because the State was seen as doing 'good' things.

Once the State failed in providing basic public services, even well-meaning civil society initiatives were then directed towards plugging the government's leaky bucket. Instead of complementing the State, civil society initiatives began substituting the State. So, we do have philanthropy, but a lot of it is in areas that fall squarely in the domain of the State. For example, nearly 70 per cent of funds under the Corporate Social Responsibility (CSR) commitments

---

[5] We discuss this policy 'Items reserved for manufacture exclusively by the small-scale sector' in some detail in Chapter 17.

go to just two basic public services that should have been a high priority area of the State—health and education. Philanthropy for the big, bold tasks that governments can't do, like Carnegie's public library network, is yet to come of age.

Looking Ahead

Given the weak capacity of our omniabsent State, introducing new positive rights such as the right to education (RTE) or right to house ownership—without fixing chronic government failures—is counterproductive. Instead, we need to hold the State accountable for providing basic public services, judicial recourse, safety, and security to every Indian.

Back to Sports

There's no doubt that Indian athletes are capable of winning many more Olympic medals. But is it really the responsibility of the State?

With the three-point State–society–market framework, we can throw new light on this question. A low-income, democratic setting imposes certain constraints on governments, and for good reasons. A low-income setting implies that the government would have low enforcement, monetary, and intellectual capacities. Hence, it would be in our collective interest to have governments do fewer things and do them well. Moreover, unlike authoritarian regimes that can sponsor projects of national pride at the cost of other expenditure items, democratic governments are elected to prioritize areas that benefit a majority of the electorate. Taken together, governments—regardless of their intentions—will not (and probably should not) prioritize winning medals.

And that's perfectly okay. Since governments cannot be at the forefront in this area, we need to unleash the power of the two agents of change—markets and society. For sporting excellence, the complementary strengths of markets and societies are far more vital than government attention.

Consider the role of markets first. Not too long ago, cricket would be criticized by players of other sports for hogging all the popularity, attention, and resources. And then a commercial, entertainment-focused enterprise such as the IPL turned this argument on its head. The city-based league format pioneered in India though IPL proved to be a positive-sum game for other sports. It spawned similar leagues in several sports, even managing to bring kabbadi back to primetime TV screens. This commercial model energized many sports in ways that no government medals could have done.

At the amateur level, reforms in India's FDI policy finally brought world-class sporting retailers such as Decathlon to India. Earlier, the sports retailing scene was stagnant, with few old-style shops only catering to the demands of select, mass-market sports. By getting out of the way, the government helped change the sports equipment landscape for millions of budding sportspersons in the country. In short, markets are critical to creating lasting sporting success.

Now consider the role of the third agent: the society. Sports is definitely one such big, bold task that is ideally suited for philanthropy. Take the role that the MRF Pace

Foundation has played in producing fast bowlers in India. Or the contribution of the Tata Group in improving hockey facilities in Odisha. We need many more philanthropic initiatives of this nature.

Besides the well-established corporates, there are smaller non-profit organizations such as the GoSports Foundation and Olympic Gold Quest. These organizations sponsor and support talented Indian sportspersons so that they can become world-class. Perhaps, we need hundreds of such societal initiatives outside the government to achieve sporting excellence.

Just as creating one champion sportsperson needs sacrifices from many friends and family members, it takes contributions from the government, markets, and societies to create a sporting culture. We too can play a small role. Instead of ruing the lack of governmental support for our athletes, we need to contribute to societal initiatives dedicated to sports. This could mean local communities in urban areas pooling together resources to build infrastructure aimed at specific sports, sponsoring coaches, nutritionists, physiotherapists, and psychologists for local athletes, conducting small-scale tournaments and recognizing sporting achievements at par with academics. Even a modicum of success at national or international levels will start a virtuous cycle of sorts as we have seen with badminton, where private efforts of a few individuals have spawned multiple badminton coaching centres and a good assembly line of young players emerging from Hyderabad and Bengaluru. That, more than anything else, would be a perfect tribute to the spirit shown by the Indian contingent of the Tokyo Olympics 2020.

Finally, there's also a behavioural aspect to our relative lack of success in sports. It is about how we view sports and sportspersons. We think of sports as a career of last resort meant for the poor, the underprivileged, or those with no other redeeming ability. And this isn't just us alone. Cricket is often cited as a sport that is now a viable career option. This is partly true. Surely, the commercial success of IPL has meant there's a pool of about five hundred players in the last decade who have earned well for themselves. The cascading impact of IPL has raised the incomes at various levels of domestic cricket. But in a cricket-obsessed country where millions play or aspire to play cricket at competitive level, the count of those who can make a career out of it still remains small. Other sports fare worse. Our neighbours who were part of our society not so long back are the same. It is no wonder that Pakistan, Bangladesh, or Nepal also don't produce any world-class sportspersons. This view permeates the administration, investments, and support in sports right to the grassroots. Barring a few exceptions, there's never any real respect for talent in sports among those who run or those who follow sports.

It is not just about money. Our attitude towards athletes is marked by the same biases we bring to the table elsewhere—their background, their caste, their communication skills, or some other marker of their social rank. And once we have pegged them, we aren't shocked by the conditions in which they live, travel, or train. Their athletic prowess is of limited interest to us till they show up on screen during an Olympics or Asian Games. A few weeks later, we forget all about them. This is a societal failure we have to fix. The government throwing more money at the problem will not resolve social failures.

4

Why Is the Indian State Omniabsent?

Sadak, tum ab aayi ho gaon,
Jab saara gaon shahar ja chuka hai
[O road, you have reached our village now? When the
entire village has already migrated to the city. . .]

The perennial deficit between the intent of the government
and its actions on the ground are beautifully summed up in
these lines of the poet Mahesh Ch. Punetha.

To put it another way, if the Indian State were a
cricketer, it would be like Vinod Kambli's batting—
brilliant, enigmatic, but mostly disappointing. No wonder
that just like Indian society, the Indian State too continues to
confound observers. Development economist Lant Pritchett
called it a flailing State—not successful, nor a failed one
either, but one that swings widely. Sometimes, it's capable
of accomplishing amazing feats such as conducting elections
for crores of voters without breaking a sweat. Or it can
administer more than 25 million COVID-19 vaccines on a
single day. But these flashes of brilliance aside, it is mostly

mediocre and uninspiring. The public service delivery is poor, the implementation deficit is a subject for stand-up comedy acts, and corruption is the expected norm and established practice.

So, how do we make sense of this paradoxical entity?

In this chapter, we try to make sense of the Indian State by recalling how it responded in the first few months of the COVID-19 pandemic. An unsophisticated way to analyse the State is to think of it as a person. It has biases and fears, it likes to project a certain image of itself to the external world, it has a code of conduct (however warped), some formative influences that shape its thinking, and, maybe, a kind of character, or even, maybe, a consciousness. There isn't any academic rigour behind this anthropomorphic model. But humour us and just walk alongside us for some time.

When things are normal, the State, like any other person, plays multiple roles with various masks on—an enforcer of rules at home, a caring presence for those needing help, an ambitious go-getter outside, or a woolly-headed idealist. There's a way a person reconciles these identities—either by keeping tight boundaries or through some personal mythology she builds about herself. However, this slips during a crisis. That old cliché—adversity doesn't test character but reveals it—holds. In a way, then, a crisis and the response of the State to it is the best way to analyse it.

Republic of No

The Indian State, like all States, is coercive. Although, its power of coercion works best when it denies something; when it says no. The executive capacity isn't geared to enable the rights of citizens. But it is very effective at curtailing them. A State derives its legitimacy when it recognizes the 'reasons of belief' of its citizens and then exercises its monopoly of force over the citizens in a way that doesn't repudiate those beliefs. In India, this is easy. The one strong belief among its citizens is that of the State as a ruler with unlimited powers. The 'Republic of No' follows from here.

India responded to the spectre of COVID-19 contagion by suspending entry of international flights and enforcing a twenty-one-day national lockdown when the case count was about 500. The lockdown was announced in the evening primetime hour by the Indian prime minister, and citizens were given a grand total of four hours to fall in line. This massive social experiment provided a plot for many Netflix movies but that's beside the point.

This was the earliest any country had placed such restrictions, and it was seen by many as an overreaction. There's a generally held view, backed by the evidence of a huge number of 'avoidable' deaths, that the value of life is cheap in India. However, this isn't entirely true. There is also a counter narrative of multiple success stories—large-scale vaccination programmes, reduction in infant mortality, and control over communicable diseases—that suggest the State is effective in reducing avoidable deaths. Also, there's a collective memory that's still fresh among people and the administration of outbreaks going out of control. All of these meant the State had the will and the people were willing to live with a complete lockdown.

This was quite unlike other democracies. Citizens complied and the administration came down heavily on those who didn't. The local administrative machinery of the district magistrate, gram sarpanch, superintendent of police, and medical officer came together to contain the spread and manually contact trace anyone who might be in danger of spreading the virus. Communities developed their own protocol in restricting movements of their residents, and there weren't any dissenters who protested the imposed lockdown. In fact, those most affected by it, the millions of daily-wage migrant earners, walked back to their villages in a sad acceptance of their fates rather than protest the sudden shutdown. The Indian State and its citizens are perhaps at their most effective when they prevent things from happening.

An Instinctive State

The significant centralization of power that's part of the design of the Indian State often precludes a consensus-driven or a planned approach that considers likely scenarios and trade-offs. The upside is that the State can act extremely fast when it deems fit. The downsides are apparent. Decisions are often taken on instinct and repercussions are borne at leisure. Boldness is the measure of a decision, not its impact.

While the lockdown decision was quick and its implementation complete, it was evident within the first forty-eight hours that the consequences of the decision weren't thought through. With the economy grinding to a halt and an immediate relief package out of sight, the impact on small and medium businesses was severe. The inability to provide for migrant workers or contract workforce and the complete shutdown of the inter-state transport system led to a humanitarian crisis and possibly, the spread of the virus in rural areas. There was a delay in trying out other options to flatten the curve like digital contact tracing and rapid testing, widespread distribution of masks, and establishing social distancing guidelines at public places, which could have provided insights on how to lift the lockdown partially later. Also, the lack of communication on what scenarios could emerge at the end of the lockdown and thinking through an exit strategy was left for too late. 'Lockdown is the only option' was strongly communicated.

Reflexively Socialist

The Indian State doesn't yet see entrepreneurs and industrialists as employment generators and wealth creators. Sure, the State indulges in the rhetoric around this and occasionally rewards them, but it is wary of being viewed as industry-friendly. The State and the citizens reflexively think of the private sector as exploitative of the labour they use. The line between profiting and profiteering is very thin in their minds.

India provided for the lowest fiscal stimulus among large economies when its economy came to a standstill during the COVID-19 pandemic. The first fiscal package announced on 26 March 2020 had very little for the industry. The monetary package was primarily a deferral of the pain than providing a balm for it.[1] What was worse was

---

[1] Press Information Bureau, Government of India, 'Finance Minister Announces Rs 1.70 Lakh Crore Relief Package under Pradhan Mantri Garib Kalyan Yojana for the Poor to Help Them Fight the Battle against Corona Virus', accessed 28 January 2022, https://www.pib.gov.in/www.pib.gov.in/Pressreleaseshare.aspx?PRID=1608345.

that the State had used moral suasion since the beginning of the lockdown urging all establishments to not reduce salaries or lay off people. Businesses were therefore boxed in. They didn't have revenues, couldn't reduce their costs, and didn't get a fiscal relief package from the State. So, in effect, they were funding a relief package themselves. What's more, with the message to the private sector to not take any employee action, there was no groundswell of support among the vocal salaried class for lifting restrictions. The lockdown seemed like a State-sponsored trip to purgatory for the private sector.

Symbolism over Substance

States, the world over, revel in the symbolism of flags, emblems, seals, etc. to create an emotional attachment for their citizens. On these symbols, meanings drawn from the history of the nation, a cherished ideal or a common value, are bestowed. While the symbols remain mostly static, the relationship of the people to them is re-imagined by every generation. The Indian State loves symbolism. The fight for freedom from colonial rule was replete with it because people in India are uniquely moved by it. The Indian State has learnt that lesson well. It isn't merely keen on static symbols. It actively looks to create new ones.

The lockdown in India was unique in the way the government orchestrated events and symbols to rally people together at quick intervals. In other countries, in contrast, these gestures evolved organically from society. The Italians were singing in their balconies because they collectively felt better doing it. Nobody asked them to. The collective clanging of the plates or lighting of *diyas* or torches/lamps to honour those on the frontlines are the unique contribution of the Indian government to the global pandemic response. The overwhelming participation of the citizens across sections suggest an intuitive grasp the government has about the psyche of its people. It is a powerful tool to effect a change.

The Lone Political Axis

A Republic of No, instinctive, reflexively socialist, and privileging symbolism over substance—that's what this crisis reveals about the character of the Indian State.

This is also useful to understand why the lines that divide political thought in western democracies don't have much relevance in India. Left versus right, liberal versus conservative, or libertarian versus statist; these divisions don't animate Indian political discourse as much. Our core beliefs, that which the State continues to nurture to retain its monopoly over violence, are to be statist, socialist, and conservative. Those in opposition to these will remain a minority. It will always be an unequal battle. The real dividing line on political thought in India has always been identarian. This pits one imagination of the Indian nation with another, complete with their own imagined past, a lament of the present and a vision for an ideal nation.

That old cliché—the idea of India—is where the true political divide in India lies.

We Are Like This Only

The COVID-19 response of the Indian State also reveals a lot about our society. A key feature of Indian society is its hyper-diversity. Less charitably, it refers to the multiple issues the society is divided on. This diversity makes collaboration through purely societal means quite difficult. With societal collaboration having its peculiar problems in the Indian context, a more widely accepted cooperation pathway is the one where the State is at the forefront. That's because the Indian elites (taken to mean anyone with a graduate degree) still harbour an overwhelmingly benevolent view of the State. There are sharp divisions about who should be in power, not so much about what they should be doing.

To draw this out further, we go back to an old and well-regarded book *Public Finance and Public Choice: Two Contrasting Visions of the State* (MIT Press, 1999) in which two legendary economists argue about the role of the State. James Buchanan, one of the leading lights of the public choice theory, is suspicious of the government. Richard Musgrave, one of the founding fathers of public finance school, views the beneficial functions of the government sector quite favourably.[2] If we think of this as a continuum with Buchanan's and Musgrave's views on the opposite ends, Indian society has consistently been on Musgrave's side.

Why is it so? One explanation comes from path dependence. The colonial experience made people inherently suspicious of both businesses and markets.

---

[2] James M. Buchanan and Richard A. Musgrave, *Public Finance and Public Choice: Two Contrasting Visions of the State* (The MIT Press, 1999), https://doi.org/10.7551/mitpress/5688.001.0001.

Therefore, the other mechanisms through which societies express and fulfil their needs and wants—as against the State—were perpetually handicapped.

The second explanation comes from the social revolution experiment that the Indian State took onto itself after Independence, which we discussed in Chapter 3 (*Mai-Baap Sarkaar*). One unintended consequence of this experiment has been that the State is now seen as the only vehicle for driving any change. In the current political context, this image of the State as a benevolent actor gets amplified when it is represented by an individual who enjoys charismatic authority—perhaps a consequence of measuring decisions by their boldness rather than by their outcomes. This is why the State remains our society's go-to troubleshooter. It explains why India largely complied with a State-sanctioned lockdown.

Omnipresent and Omniabsent

While the first COVID-19 wave in April 2020 gave a good glimpse into the *nature* of the Indian State, the second wave, a year later, told us a lot about the *size* of the Indian State. We witnessed how the State was ill-equipped to provide basic healthcare facilities, and many thousands died due to the unavailability of oxygen cylinders. And yet, a common gripe you would have heard is how the Indian State is just too big. The most common portrayal of our government institutions is an old, musty-smelling office with a lot of busybodies or more precisely, busy-looking bodies. Inefficiency, wastage, and corruption are the features that come to mind. So, how do we make sense of the size of the

Indian State—is it too big or too small? Let's look at four parameters that measure the size of the State.

Size Measured by Government Expenditure: Relatively Small

A government has three instruments at its disposal in any policy issue-area: produce, finance, and regulate. All three instruments require government expenditure. So, one way to judge government size is to measure public expenditure as a proportion of overall economic activity. The higher this parameter, the bigger the government.

In 2018, India's overall public expenditure as a proportion of its GDP stood at 27 per cent. The US was at approximately 38 per cent; Russia was at approximately 36 per cent GDP; Sweden was at approximately 49 per cent, and Pakistan was at approximately 21 per cent. Clearly, the Indian State is no outlier on this measure. Essentially, this parameter has been steadily rising for most countries across the world, ever since the welfare State became mainstream. Moreover, there is a strong correlation between government spending and income levels—the richer a country, the higher the government's expenditure.[3]

This is counterintuitive. The common perception is that because richer countries such as the US are capitalist, the government would have a smaller role to play in the economy. That's clearly not the case when measured on this parameter. As the country got richer, there were even higher demands to fulfil in the health, education, defence,

---

[3] This is known as Wagner's Law in public finance literature.

and infrastructure sectors. A capitalist economy doesn't
mean an absent State. It instead means a State that occupies
a larger portion of the economy but focuses on fewer areas
and does them well.

In reality, all economies are 'mixed'. They differ instead
in the way they intervene in the lives of citizens.

Size Measured by Government Employees: Small

Another caricature of the Indian State is that it is a bloated,
overstaffed organization with a large number of employees.
But the Indian State is relatively small on this parameter
too. Here are some statistics making this point from political
scientist Devesh Kapur's paper 'Why Does the Indian State
Both Fail and Succeed?':

In the early 1990s, the global average of government
employment as a percent of population was 4.7 per cent.
In countries of Asia, it was 2.6 per cent. In India, it was
2 per cent. Core elements of the Indian state—police,
judges, and tax bureaucracy—are among the smallest of
the G-20 countries. Indeed, while the absolute size of
government employment peaked in the mid-1990s, in
relative terms, the decline in size of central and local
governments began much earlier.

A comparison between the size of the civilian
workforce of the federal government in India with that
of the United States is instructive. Remember, India has a
large number of public enterprises and public sector banks
that are under the central government. Even so, the size
of the Indian federal government is half the size of its US
counterpart when normalized by population: specifically,

the US federal government had 8.07 civilian employees per 1,000 US population in 2014, down from 10.4 in 1995, while India's central government had 4.51 civilian employees per 1,000 population, down from 8.47 in 1995.[4]

The Indian State's people deficiency is the starkest in sectors where the State should've been the strongest, such as judiciary, law enforcement, health, and education. On this quantitative parameter, the Indian State is a relatively small one.

Size Measured by Competence: Too Small

Economists use the term 'state capacity' to describe the ability of a State to get things done. India's low state capacity has given rise to a cottage industry of papers and analyses. This line of research is backed by the daily choices of ordinary Indians. The Indian State's incompetence in fixing the most basic market failures, from law and order to public health and education, is apparent to its citizens. As soon as they can afford it, Indians prefer to stay away from government-run schools. The police instils fear rather than confidence. The judicial system is marred by poor quality and low throughput. Whether the Indian State is regulating, producing, financing, or procuring—low state capacity characterizes all these interventions. The competence gap has only widened over the years as many bright Indians now have the option of taking up a job outside the government, and outside India, with changing times.

---

[4] Devesh Kapur, 'Why Does the Indian State Both Fail and Succeed?', *Journal of Economic Perspectives* 34, no. 1 (February 2020): 31–54, https://doi.org/10.1257/jep.34.1.31.

Size Measured by Ambition: Too Big

This is really where the Indian State is overbearing. The aspiration of the Indian State has no bounds. Right from the outset in 1947, the Indian State sought to transform colonial India economically, politically, and socially. This revolutionary DNA meant that the Indian State set itself ambitious goals regardless of its capacity to achieve them. Over the decades, new goals were appended to this lofty project.

The Indian State is everywhere, and yet nowhere. This ambition extends along all three functions: producing, financing, and regulating. As a producer, there are nearly 1500 government-run companies in India, trying to manufacture everything from soaps to missiles and steel. As a financier, the State runs hundreds of programmes and schemes. At the height of its powers, the union government alone was running as many as 360 different central sector and centrally sponsored schemes. Most of these schemes fell squarely in the domain of India's state governments, but that didn't deter the expansion.

Finally, when the State isn't producing or financing, it tries to regulate every economic, social, and political activity through a plethora of rules, laws, and regulations. Regulators control rather than govern. For instance, a 2020 analysis suggests that a manufacturing firm needs to comply with 1536 laws that require 69,233 compliances and 6618 filings every year.[5]

---

[5] Manish Sabharwal and Rishi Agrawal, 'Reduce State-Level Regulatory Cholesterol to Aid Job Creation', *Mint*, 7 September 2020, https://www.livemint.com/opinion/online-views/reduce-state-level-regulatory-cholesterol-to-aid-job-creation-11599490648163.html.

What Does All This Mean?

So, the Indian State is big as measured by its own ambitions. The paradox is that on all other parameters, the State is quite small, neither possessing the capacity to enforce rules nor the ability to anticipate the consequences of policies beforehand.

Devesh Kapur writes that this 'precocious' nature of the Indian State has also skewed what Indians expect from their governments in three ways:

> One, precocious democracy tends to militate against the provision of public goods in favour of redistribution. Countries that experienced economic development prior to the transition to democracy also tend to adopt democratic institutions that constrain the confiscatory power of the ruling elite. However, when countries pursue democracy prior to economic development, the democratic institutions adopted enhance the redistributive powers of the state. Second, a precocious democracy with electoral mobilisation along social cleavages favours the creation of narrow club goods.[6] A central puzzle concerning the poor provision of basic public services in India is seemingly weak demand in an otherwise flourishing electoral democracy. Third, an imperfect democracy with noncredible politicians will tend to emphasise the provision of goods that are visible and can be provided quickly, like infrastructure,

---

[6] Club goods are a type of good in economics which are excludable and non-rivalrous. In this context, club goods refer to identitarian demands along community lines.

over long-term investments, like human capital or environmental quality.

Resolving this high-ambition versus low-capacity paradox is central to improving governance in India. It must choose to do fewer, more important things, and build the capacity to do them well. An omniabsent State is unacceptable.

5

The Right and the Wrong Question about the State

While discussing the inherent problems of the Indian State, we notice one question gets rarely asked while another is a favourite of the middle class. The one that's rare is why does the Indian State want to do so much? It is unlikely you will see a politician or a bureaucrat ever ask this. The question that comes up often is if we have too much democracy in India that stops us from unleashing our true potential? In this chapter, we will argue that we need to flip this argument around.

The Question Rarely Asked

In the second week of February 2021, something strange happened. While addressing the Rajya Sabha, PM Modi spoke about the Indian State being ineffective because of spreading itself too thin and the unfortunate demonization of the private sector in our polity. This wasn't usual. There's an implicit belief among people in India that *sarkaar* is the *maai-baap* (i.e., the State is the nanny). Despite decades of evidence to the contrary, we expect the State to intervene and set things right. From regulating taxi fares, pricing life-saving drugs to regulating content on television, we think the State has all the answers. Conversely, we are deeply suspicious of markets. There's a reason for it. We have seen a warped form of markets since the time it was championed during the British rule in India. The policies followed then were pro-business with a limited set of players who were given special privileges by the State. The core principles of a free market like open access, protection of intellectual property, restriction of monopolies, and an even playing field were conspicuous by their absence. Pro-business is different from pro-markets. But this nuance was lost because of the way business and capital established themselves during the Raj era. Our turn towards socialism in the 1960s and 1970s was driven as much by ideological conviction as it was by our misgivings about the horrors perpetrated by the market. This was a deeply held belief in society that was reflected in our films, literature, and in the public discourse. The usurious moneylender, the venal businessman, and the moral fallibility of those working for corporations were routine themes that have left a deep impact on our psyche. The counter to this emerged slowly in the mid-1970s when some of the finest economic minds trained in India and the West returned to India to see if they could impact policy. We will talk about the run-up to the 1991 reforms later in this book. Through the book we will talk about how markets have gotten a bad rap in India because we have created the most distorted form of markets on account of our muddled approach to them. The limited prosperity we have had since the 1990s because of freer markets, notwithstanding, we still think is zero-sum. Someone making profits translates to feeling cheated.

PM Modi was definitely going against the grain here. So, what exactly did he say?

The Print reported:

> While doffing his hat to the private sector on Wednesday for its contribution to the growth and development of the country, Modi questioned the 'power centre we have created in the country by handing over everything to babus'.
>
> '*Sab kuch babu hi karenge.* IAS *ban gaye matlab woh* fertiliser *ka kaarkhana bhi chalayega,* chemical *ka kaarkhana bhi chalayega,* IAS *ho gaya toh woh hawai jahaz bhi chalayega. Yeh kaunsi badi taakat bana kar rakh di hai humne? Babuon ke haath mein desh de karke hum kya karne waale hain? Humare babu bhi toh desh ke hain, toh desh ka naujawan bhi toh desh ka hai,*' Modi said.
>
> [Babus will do everything. By dint of becoming IAS officers, they'll operate fertiliser factory and also chemical factory, even fly aeroplanes. What is this big power we have created? What are we going to achieve by handing the reins of the nation to babus. Our babus are also citizens, and so are the youth of India.][1]

We don't know when words of this nature were last spoken in the Parliament. Maybe Minoo Masani made a few

---

[1] Sanya Dhingra, '"Babu Samjho Ishare" — Modi's Critique of IAS Evokes Shock but Many Also Call for Introspection', ThePrint.in, 12 February 2021.

speeches of this kind during the heyday of the Swatantra Party. But to have a hugely popular PM, one with the rare ability to make the public do his bidding, speak these words suggests a shift in direction that was long-awaited.

Anyway, that speech came on the back of weeks of protests against farm laws that had morphed into Ambani–Adani bashing. The names don't matter. A few decades back it was Tata–Birla. We also had the usual reports about how the pandemic has exacerbated inequality purely on the basis of notional wealth created by a rising stock market. And there were bizarre articles devoid of any economic logic during the pandemic that suggested we should make things free exactly during a time when we were supply-constrained. These are familiar grounds. This is often framed as the growth versus redistribution trade-off by economists. Our argument is India needs growth before worrying about redistribution. We aren't in some kind of a giant zero-sum game. Someone winning doesn't mean someone is losing. The pandemic hurt ordinary citizens, and they needed relief and support. This is undeniable. But this can be done without running down markets. Else, we risk going down the same path that kept us poor for decades in the name of *garibi hataao*. Growth is a moral imperative for where India is in its economic history as we will argue through this book. There will be temporary distortions while pursuing this. But that will be a smaller price to pay as the history of the past century has shown in India and elsewhere. Good intentions of prosperity for all and equality need the pie to grow. The horrors of pursuing an egalitarian utopia and ending up in a dystopian State-controlled regime are too recent to be forgotten.

Is that it? Or is there more that can be brought into this debate?

The State must aim to foster conditions in a society that advance the well-being and prosperity of its members. No one argues with this goal. The fundamental question of public policy then is what are the means it must adopt to create this environment?

Should the State aim for equality among its members through redistribution of its resources? There can be no harmony or stability in a society unless there's fairness and equality among its members.

Or should the State guarantee the fundamental rights of the citizens, provide for law and order that safeguards them against anarchy, and then get out of their way? People don't want the State to legislate for some notion of equality that's in its mind. They want freedom and security. That would do. Thank you very much.

This brings us to the old Rawls–Nozick debate. Rawls's landmark book *A Theory of Justice* (Belknap, 1971) argued for justice as fairness (the title of a later book of his) with two key principles. First, the greatest equal liberty principle that proposed people's equal basic liberties should be maximized. Rawls conceived of an artificial construct called the original position—a State where each one of us has to decide on the principles of justice behind a veil of ignorance. That is we are blind to any fact about ourselves; we are ignorant of our social position, wealth, class or any natural attribute. Behind this veil, Rawls asked how would we choose the principles of justice for society?

For Rawls, the logical choice for all of us would be what he called the maximin strategy that would maximize the conditions of those who have the minimum. Why? Because when the veil of ignorance is lifted, we wouldn't want to find ourselves to be the most disadvantaged in a society that doesn't care about such inequality. This gave him his second principle—the social and economic inequalities should be arranged only to provide the greatest benefits to the least advantaged.

Nozick agreed on the liberty principle with Rawls. But he had a strong disagreement on the idea of maximin. For him, any distribution of wealth (or holdings as he termed it) is fair if it comes about by a just and legitimate distribution.

He defined three legitimate means. First, where the acquisition of a property that is unowned is achieved through the enterprise of a person and this act doesn't disadvantage anyone else. Second, a voluntary transfer of ownership between two consenting entities. And third, a redressal of a past injustice in acquiring or transferring the holdings. Anyone who has acquired wealth or holdings through these means is morally entitled to them. An attempt by the State to redistribute based on any pattern it thinks is right would be a serious intrusion on liberty of citizens and, therefore, unjust.

So, the goal to reach a patterned distribution of wealth had a problem at its core. Once you achieve such a delicate balance, how do you maintain it? Every random economic act from there on will disturb the balance. And such random acts will be too many for the State to control. The State will then have to constantly meddle in the lives of its citizens to redress the balance. This meddling will spiral out of control soon till the State takes over the lives of its citizens completely. This is the communist totalitarian future. For

Nozick, the State can act to redistribute only with the consent of its citizens. If people voluntarily redistribute their wealth (means #2) to others and want to design a society on that principle, they are free to do so. But the State cannot impose it against their will.

To us, the first point of agreement between Rawls and Nozick is critical from an Indian context—the liberty principle or the basic freedoms that must be guaranteed to every citizen. These cannot be violated or the absence of such freedoms should not be tolerated even if doing so in some ways increases the aggregate prosperity of the society or helps the poor. Before we argue about redistribution, we must ask if we have created a society that satisfies the greatest equal liberty principle. That must be our first goal.

PM Modi must have been in a reflective frame of mind while delivering that speech about the State spreading itself thin. A bit of a segue and a personal reflection here might be useful. In an edition of our newsletter, one of us wrote about the changing nature of our relationship with the State. We have reproduced it here since it captures in spirit the disappointment with the State that's often felt by Indians of a certain generation.

> I don't remember when I lost my faith in the ability of the State to improve the lives of its people. Perhaps there wasn't an exact moment. Growing up, the State was all around me. I spent most of my childhood in what used to be called a 'colony'. One of the many that dotted the semi-urban Indian landscape in the 1980. A small industrial township whose heart beat to the rhythm of the government-owned factory at the centre of it. My

school, my playground, the hospital and even the temple
were all run by the State.

The State then subsidized a world-class higher
education programme for me. At the turn of the
millennium, I entered the workforce. If you had cut me
then I would have bled State.

Over the next two decades, I lost my faith. Gradually.
Two factors led to it. One, I understood the privilege
that allowed me to take advantage of the generosity of
the State. The accident of my birth—a savarna Hindu
male born in the mid-1970s to educated parents—
seemed to play a disproportionate role in my relative
success. I noticed the State could barely enable others
to do well who weren't born to privilege like me. They
didn't have the freedom that I took for granted. The
State was absent to those who needed it the most. Two,
the State had tremendous confidence in its capabilities
that, unfortunately, was inversely related to its actual
performance. This led the State to have its finger in
every pie, with poor outcomes. The State cast its long
shadow in everything I did. It was present everywhere.

The Indian State was simultaneously 'omnipresent'
and 'omniabsent' depending on who you were. One
thing was common though. The consequences of both
were terrible.

Once I saw through the nature of the State, I couldn't
'unsee' it. The sorry spectacle of the flailing State, as
Pritchett called it, was all around me. I wondered how
others couldn't see it. Why despite the overwhelming
evidence do we look for the State to solve problems
where there was no apparent market failure? Why
did the State not narrow its focus on things that really

mattered and build capacity in them instead of spreading itself too thin? Whenever I read about the argument for the State to get into further redistribution, I cannot help but ask what the end result of this patterned distribution looks like. Is there really any end to it? Why should we let it meddle even further into our lives trying to get the redistribution right? Why can't the State focus on ensuring that the privilege I was born with is made available to all its citizens? That would fulfil the first principle agreed upon by both Rawls and Nozick.

The rest is just criminal overreach.

The Question in Every WhatsApp Group

That brings us to the other question. Do we have a problem of too much democracy? In December 2020, a YouTube clip surfaced where the CEO of NITI Aayog was seen complaining about too much democracy in India. He later claimed he was misquoted. The usual brouhaha on social media followed. Memes appeared, Immanuel Kant was quoted, and Twitter had a field day.

To many Indians (especially the middle class), this was surprising. If you lived in India for long, you must have sometimes felt we have too much democracy. 'Nothing moves in India because everyone has a say.' 'You can't get anything worthwhile done because no one is willing to pay any short-term price for long-term benefits.' 'We elect goons and criminals because everyone has a vote.' 'Anything that's good for the majority can be hijacked by a minority that's vocal and organized.' 'We have all seen this. So, how can we outrage over the "too much democracy" comment when we know it is true?'

There are three aspects to consider while addressing this question. The first will clarify a few things about democracy and the State. The second part will be on the critique of democracy over the years. And at the end, we will talk about how despite everything, blaming 'too much of democracy' in the Indian context is meaningless.

To start with, democracy is a form of government—nothing more. There is an element of religious passion towards it by its adherents. This is particularly true in America and, possibly, stems from Walt Whitman, the poet of Democracy. Whitman elevated democracy to a mystical phenomenon. His poem 'For You O Democracy' (from *Leaves of Grass*, 1860 edition) is a hymn to it:

> I will plant companionship thick as trees along all the rivers of America, and along the shores of the great lakes, and all over the prairies,
> I will make inseparable cities with their arms about each other's necks,
> By the love of comrades,
> By the manly love of comrades.
> For you these from me, O Democracy, to serve you ma femme!
> For you, for you I am trilling these songs.

It is difficult to top that. Democracy is an end to itself, and it must be valued with passion. Whitman's spirit pervades the US polity to date. American exceptionalism over the last century has made democracy more than a mere form of government. It has come to be seen as an ideal for society. India too adopted not just a form of government following Independence, but this belief about the virtues of democracy, beyond a form of governance. This is one part of the problem.

But let's start with its definition itself. Democracy may not even be an ideal form to choose who will govern the State. But like that quote often misattributed to Churchill, it is the worst form of government except for all the others. Broadly, it means everyone has a share of the government and the majority view prevails. This is understood to recognize that every citizen has an equal opportunity in creating the legislature that will govern them. The State that has the monopoly of legitimate violence over its citizens has multiple arms to conduct its affairs. Not every arm of it is democratic in nature like the legislature. We don't elect our judges or our bureaucrats through popular mandate. In most cases, the process is designed to find the most qualified or the most appropriate person for the role instead of the most popular. Through an elaborate mechanism of checks and balances, these non-democratic institutions are subject to the will of the people. There are hardly any pure democratic institutions in any democracy.

Even the will of the people to determine the legislature isn't democracy in its purest form. Most modern democracies are representative in their form. This is a recognition that the rule can never be directly of all people but of 'typical members' who represent them. It tacitly acknowledges that those who represent the people are better suited than others to 'rule'. In that sense, every democracy still retains an element of aristocracy or the rule of the elite. It is important to remember here, this representative form of government while being partly elitist still can't be replicated in other spheres of society. No firm or enterprise can run on democratic principles. Nor can any team, guild, or community.

We shouldn't seek more democracy in society, probably striving for more inclusiveness and openness makes more sense. This means more forums to discuss and hear issues impacting the public in the normal course of governance than only during elections. A more transparent way of governing where the public has access to the decision-making process and the underlying trade-offs. The Scandinavian examples on democracy often quoted are not examples of better or deeper representation. They have succeeded in making the process of governing inclusive. Also, we should be striving for a better republic that strengthens the process of choosing the best representatives among the people who then wield the power of the State and use it to enhance the welfare of individuals.

There hasn't been any shortage of criticism of democracy over the ages. And we aren't including tyrants, despots, and dictators in this list. This is led by Plato and Aristotle who, it could be argued, lived in a society that was democratic (slavery notwithstanding). They viewed democracy as good in theory but difficult to put in practice. Aristotle clubbed democracy as a deviant constitutional form, clubbing it with tyranny and oligarchy. To him, the ultimate end of a State was neither to maximize wealth as oligarchs would believe, nor was it to promote liberty and equality in every public sphere, which is the aspiration of democrats. Instead, he argued, it was 'good life' that was the true end of the State. That requires a 'middle constitution' or a 'mixed government' of a numerous middle class that chooses a wise few to govern. If one were to be kind to Aristotle, the mixed constitution he bats for is the precursor to the modern republic.

Following the French and American revolutions in the late eighteenth century, the ideas of liberty and democracy were debated widely. Political philosophers from Ruskin, Carlyle, to Tocqueville were troubled by the exaggerated deference to the will of the majority. In their view, there was a qualitative difference among people and the idea to treat all of them as equal in their right to rule the State was terrible. The majority would be swayed by demagogues who would pander to their worst instincts, and the minority that was qualitatively better would lose the will to fight. James Bryce in *Hindrances to Good Citizenship* laid out the arguments of this school in detail. In a chapter entitled 'The True Faults of Democracy', he pointed out four flaws:

> First, a certain commonness of mind and tone, a want of dignity and elevation in and about the conduct of public affairs, an insensibility to the nobler aspects and finer responsibilities of national life.
>
> Secondly, a certain apathy among the luxurious classes and fastidious minds, who find themselves of no more specific account than the ordinary voter, and are disgusted by the superficial vulgarities of public life.
>
> Thirdly, a want of knowledge, tact, and judgment in the details of legislation, as well as in administration, with an inadequate recognition of the difficulty of these kinds of work, and of the worth of special experience and skill in dealing with them. Because it is incompetent, the multitude will not feel its incompetence, and will not seek or defer to the counsels of those who possess the requisite capacity.

Fourthly, laxity in the management of public business. The persons entrusted with such business being only average men, thinking themselves and thought of by others as average men, and not rising to a due sense of their responsibilities, may succumb to the temptations which the control of legislation and the public funds present, in cases where persons of a more enlarged view and with more of a social reputation to support would remain incorruptible. To repress such derelictions of duty is every citizen's duty, but for that reason it is in large communities apt to be neglected. Thus the very causes which implant the mischief favour its growth.[2]

Fairly prescient there. The criticism of democracy remained muted through much of the great wars of the twentieth century and the Cold War. However, the last twenty years have seen a revival of sorts. The question has been on new democracies that have sprung up without a fierce adherence to the notion of individual liberties. The earliest work on this was by Fareed Zakaria who in a piece titled 'The Rise of Illiberal Democracy' (*Foreign Affairs*, November 1997) wrote about the perils of democracy without the concomitant pursuit of liberalism. In an interview in 2017, Zakaria updated his warning about democracy:

The happy narrative we told ourselves was that there was an almost ineluctable path to liberal democracy, and the

---

[2] James Bryce, *The Hindrances to Good Citizenship* (Yale University Press, 1909).

evidence suggests that this is not how it works. Liberal democracy seems to be one of the many exits on which the democratic experiment could end, but there are others, like illiberal democracy, that are equally likely.

It appears this is what's happening in Turkey right now and in parts of Central Europe and in Russia. It's important to remember that despite all the repression, Putin is very popular. What we're learning is that authoritarian politicians have figured out how to achieve a balance between liberalism and illiberalism that keeps people satisfied. If they can give enough bread and circus to the public, they can maintain a stable working majority buttressed by a certain degree of repression of the press and political opposition.

And we have to reckon with the possibility that this model might become the most stable alternative to liberal democracy.[3]

All of the above is not to suggest there's a reason to applaud the lament of 'too much democracy' that springs among elite Indians. The reasons that have stymied India don't have much to do with the perceived flaws of democracy. Like we have pointed out earlier, it has more to do with an overextended State that's weak. Instead of being good in a few things (law and order, basic public services, and defence), the State has chosen to be bad in a lot of things.

---

[3] Sean Illing, 'Fareed Zakaria Made a Scary Prediction about Democracy in 1997—and It's Coming True – Vox', Vox, accessed 15 June 2022, https://www.vox.com/conversations/2017/1/18/14250364/democracy-liberalism-donald-trump-populism-fareed-zakaria-europe-fascism.

6

Democracy, Where Is Thy Sting?

'Bharat banana hai'

There is an old joke about this pious intent that many governments in India have had in the past. One way to read it is 'we have to build India.' The wicked way to interpret it is 'India is a banana (republic).'

There's a truth hidden somewhere in that joke.

What's the difference between building a nation or letting it slide to become a banana republic?

The answer lies in building inclusive institutions and developing state capacity in select areas. Areas where there are market failures like negative externalities (pollution, for example), natural market power concentration, public goods (clean air), or information asymmetry between providers and users of goods (regulations in finance, healthcare, etc.). These are specific areas where the markets fail in their primary duty of allocating resources efficiently and the State intervention is warranted. But this is easier said than done. How do we streamline the overbearing but flailing State that we have now to a leaner, more effective future?

Because where we are today or can be tomorrow depends on what path we took to reach here. Nations struggle to shed the legacy of their past. History is often destiny. Is there a way to change it?

In *Political Order and Political Decay* (Farrar, Straus and Giroux, 2014), Francis Fukuyama argues that successful societies stand on three pillars—a strong State, rule of law, and democratic accountability.

The key is to get the sequence right. A strong State must come first. States that democratize first, without building adequate State capacity, struggle. The government gets overwhelmed by competing demands from different groups. It either succumbs to majoritarianism or gets consumed by internecine strife. This explains the failures of democracy in many countries that won their independence post–Second World War. We often conflate a strong State with an overbearing one and worry about the consequences of its jackboots trampling the weak and the voiceless. This is a misplaced notion. A strong State and an overbearing State can never be in a stable equilibrium. The strength of the State as we argue through this book is in its effectiveness. The effectiveness comes in its ability to prioritize its focus. The state capacity should be chosen to be built in those areas.

Does that mean countries should hold off democracy till they build state capacity? That's difficult to sell to people who have been denied representation and share of power for ages. Also, how does a State become strong? We have countries that owe their state capacity to history. China has a long history of strong dynasties that centralized power to keep the many tribes in its periphery under check. South Korea and Japan built state capacity over years of monarchy or dictatorship before embracing democracy. There's a strong path dependence to building state capacity. History matters.

So, is history destiny like we asked earlier? Fukuyama believes States that got the sequence wrong—democracy first without a strong State—have needed shocks, like wars, to accelerate the building of state capacity. The Civil War and the reconstruction that followed helped the US, while the two World Wars built capacities in western European democracies.

How does India fare on the three pillars? Fukuyama contends India does well on democratic accountability and rule of law but lacks state capacity. This is not about big or small government. It is about a strong State that's effective and does things well regardless of the number of things on its plate. India has the sequence wrong. It became democratic while its history of fragmented princely states or a rapacious colonial ruling power didn't offer any legacy of a strong State. There are exceptions to this history that explains pockets of better governance like Kerala, southern Karnataka (Mysore region), Goa, and parts of north-eastern India.

Over the years, the State got bigger, not better, searching for that elusive capacity. It made matters worse with the license-permit raj of the 1960s and 1970s setting India back by decades. You know you have gone too far when you needed to wait for a decade to get a scooter or a telephone connection at home because the State had decided on the manufacturing capacity than letting the markets do it. India went through a period of reforms trying to get the State out of areas that markets could manage better. But this didn't mean a secular, planned retreat from many areas and diverting capacity to a narrow list of priorities. Instead, while the State weakened in areas it quit, regulators with untrammelled powers replaced it. In other areas, the State continued its overarching and ineffective hold.

The COVID-19 pandemic, like wars, could be the kind of shock that Fukuyama cites for building a strong State. Vijay Kelkar and Ajay Shah in their book *In Service of the Republic* also make a similar point:

> In the early history of many successful states, the leadership focused primarily on two problems: raising taxes and waging wars. Learning-by-doing took place through the pursuit of these two activities. State capacity in the early days in the UK and in Sweden was learned by building large, complex organisations which raised taxes and waged wars.
>
> The learning-by-doing that took place was not just about the narrow problems of raising taxes and waging wars. The learning-by-doing that took place was about larger ideas about how to organize the State. The general capability of public policy and public administration was learned in these two areas, which was then transplanted into other areas . . ,
>
> . . . If we live in a country with low state capacity, how does this change our thinking? In international experience, waging war was an important pathway to developing State capacity. That pathway is not open to India, given the nuclear deterrent.[1]

---

[1] Vijay L. Kelkar and Ajay Shah, *In Service of the Republic: The Art and Science of Economic Policy* (Penguin Random House, 2019).

For India, the war pathway has perhaps opened up with the pandemic. This could be a war-like opportunity to build effective state capacity that's long-lasting and widely accepted in society. So, how did we do?

The two years of the pandemic exposed the planning deficit of the union and the provincial governments. The severity of the lockdown, its duration, and the chaos in lifting it when the curve had anything but flattened and then the severity of the second wave, placed India in a league of its own. While it is easy to dismiss this line of criticism by asking for the counterfactual, there's growing evidence that we had the worse of both lives and livelihoods by the time we were done with it. Some part of this planning deficit can be attributed to the over-centralized governance model with a strong leader who trusts his instincts more than a planned approach. But there's no denying the large part played by India's poor administrative capacity. This has meant a series of failures—lack of a wider consultation before announcing the lockdowns leading to untold misery of migrant workers, poor availability of datasets, analysis and response mechanism, patchy coordination between the centre and the states, a bungling bureaucracy that flooded us with hundreds of circulars, clarifications, and retractions, and the usual distrust of seeking help from experts or the private sector in managing the response.

A State whose constitution leans towards centralization and a government with arguably the strongest PMO in history should have started with an advantage in planning and coordinating the emergency response. But it didn't. Simply because of the incentive mechanism that is set up in our democracy.

The incentives of State-run institutions often work at cross-purpose with the policy objectives, as was evident during the pandemic. For instance, the RBI and the finance ministry worked in tandem to cut rates, change reserve ratios, and infuse liquidity into the banking system. But the PSU banks that account for 75 per cent of the credit market didn't play ball. The excess liquidity remained parked at RBI at overnight repo rates. The fear of the '3Cs' (CVC, CBI and CAG)[2] over the years has distorted the incentive among bankers to take decisions like letting credit flow in the system. The bankers have seen the pendulum swing from what was once called the 'phone-banking' model of giving loans (receive a call from the ministry, clear the file, and disburse the loan without adequate underwriting) to being hounded by investigative agencies for even a legitimate decision.

Even after the union finance minister (FM) made specific assurances to the bankers and the ministry announced a package with government backstops, actual disbursements were meagre. Even that was more about older loans being renewed at newer rates instead of fresh disbursements to businesses affected by COVID-19. MSMEs, small businesses, and specific sectors like food, hospitality, and travel struggled through the pandemic for liquidity.

Banking isn't an isolated example of misaligned incentives. The inability of State-run organizations to scale the manufacturing of test kits in the initial days, the low level of testing in many provinces to keep the case numbers

---

[2] CVC: Central Vigilance Commission; CBI: Central Bureau of Investigation; CAG: Comptroller and Auditor General

low and project a sense of control, the blame game between the rail ministry and states on running the 'Shramik Special' trains meant to ferry the migrant workers, and the inability to support migrants because, as the FM said, the State has no database—all lead to a simple conclusion. State-run institutions don't have their incentives aligned to co-operate and solve problems during a crisis. When the second wave struck in April 2021, the whole pattern repeated itself with shortages of beds, oxygen cylinders, and medicines in the biggest cities across the country. The stark images of burning pyres and bodies floating in our rivers laid bare the poorly coordinated response between the union and the provinces.

While the government came up short on enabling its institutions, it outdid itself on stopping things and curbing liberties. Bans, curfews, fines, price caps, arbitrary rules to regulate interstate movements were all part of its arsenal. In Chapter 3 (*Mai-Baap Sarkaar*), we wrote about India being a 'Republic of No'. The performance of the State during the pandemic proved it decisively.

Fukuyama pitted his strong State argument against the 'orthodoxy' of the Chicago school of neoclassical economics that favours a limited role for the State. The Chicago school led by its high priest, Milton Friedman, has cast a long shadow on the US economic policy for the most part of the last four decades. The COVID-19 crisis, like many others in the past, has shown that the markets can't do all the heavy lifting. A strong State can intervene and move mountains at crunch time. A strong State is about an effective government that responds to a crisis with a plan and then implements it with close coordination among the different constituents of the State. We often confuse strong with big. A strong government knows it will only be effective if it focuses its efforts on a limited set of activities where it can spread its limited capacity for maximum benefits. It should leave the rest for others to do. In India, we have gotten bigger and bigger governments in search of the elusive strong and effective government. And the less effective a government, the more areas it involves itself in showing its power. You need to be strong to not be overbearing.

For Fukuyama, this is a balancing act that smart leaders have achieved—leaders who get most big decisions right and those who build consensus rather than polarize. Applying these conditions—strong State, smart leader, non-polarized polity—provides a good framework to understand which countries got their COVID-19 response right. The usual axes of authoritarian-democratic, welfare-market, or woman-led–man-led don't explain it. The countries that got the health and the economy response right were those that ticked all the three boxes—a strong State, a smart leader, and a society in harmony with its differences. The US, the UK, China (no propaganda can wipe away its failure in containing the pandemic), Russia, Brazil, and India fell short. South Korea, Germany, Japan, Vietnam, New Zealand, and Australia did well.

In the eighteen months of the pandemic, the government got bigger and more intrusive with quiet acquiescence from people. But not more effective. This is a pity. India doesn't tick the boxes on a strong State and a society in harmony. On smart leaders, let's just say, the jury is still out. The pandemic shock is still an opportunity for the leadership to build an effective and less controlling state capacity, free up markets, and unite the country. A smart leader with an eye on his place in posterity would not let this go. The other goals of *aatmanirbhar* (self-reliant) Bharat or being a *vishwaguru* would follow.

7

Aap Ka Neta Kaisa Ho?

Hindi films have a song for every situation. How about a politician walking the streets asking for votes during an election campaign, you may ask? The answer is *Aandhi* (1975), the Gulzar-directed film that was banned during the Emergency because the censor board thought Suchitra Sen's look and her character arc in the film seemed suspiciously close to Indira Gandhi.

That apart, Gulzar wrote some beautiful songs for the film that are now considered among the classics. But the song we are talking about here is the less-heralded *Salaam Kijiye,* a satirical take on a vote-seeking politician by a crowd of voters who follow him on the campaign trail. As the song goes:

हमारे वोट खरीदेंगे
हमको अन्न दे कर
ये नंगे जिस्म छुपा देते हैं
क़फ़न दे कर

ये जादूगर हैं
ये चुटकी में काम करते हैं
ये भूख-प्यास को
बातों से रम करते हैं

हमारे हाल पे लिखने किताब आये हैं
अरे भइ इसलिये, सलाम कीजिये
आली जनाब आये हैं
ये पाँच सालों का देने
हिसाब आये हैं

[They will give us food to buy our votes. They will cover in a shroud the sins of their past. These magicians can solve anything with their words. Hunger and poverty will disappear in a blink of an eye if you believe them this time. They are here to chronicle our hapless lives. They are here to account for the last five years of representing us. Let's salute these worthies.]

As you can see, by 1975, the Indian public had no illusions about the people who represented them. They were seen as an opportunistic lot, who dealt in rhetoric and promises and were removed from the reality of the people. This cynical view has dominated our politics. The representative is rarely seen as someone who is our own.

In this chapter, we will talk about the concept of representation and the notion of belonging to a political party. Does a politician represent her people anymore? Does membership of a political party trump all other identities and roles in a democracy?

The way things are, maybe MP should stand for Member of Party instead of Member of Parliament. The party line trumps the individual position, the likely interests of the constituents, and the opinions of the experts. The anti-defection bill introduced in the 1980s ostensibly to prevent the *Aaya Ram Gaya Ram* phenomenon made it difficult for an individual member to go against the party 'whip'. The centralization of power in political parties and the high command culture that every party has created for itself has rendered the members of legislatures powerless.

Even state governments behave more like state party units following high command diktats rather than serve their constituents' interests. On fiscal matters, state governments predictably fight among themselves along party lines over trifling issues. Their interests would be served better were they to unite and demand a better share from the union in a way the federal structure of the Indian State was meant to encourage.

So, the question is what happened here? How did we get here?

Let's hark back to the early phase of modern democracy. The core ideas that emerged from the enlightenment thinkers and political philosophers that powered both the American and French revolutions were about individual liberty and the formation of a State that reflected the 'will' of the people.

These built the foundation of a liberal democratic order as we know it today. This sounds simple but conceptually there was more happening. The Hobbesian model was that of human multitudes coming together to hand over power and authority to a sovereign through a political structure in abstract called the 'commonwealth'. In his book *Leviathan* (1651), Hobbes defined commonwealth as:

> One person of whose acts a great multitude, by covenants
> with another, have made themselves every one the
> author to the end he may use the strength and means of
> them all as he shall think expedient for their peace and
> common defense.[1]

For Hobbes, the people willingly transfer the power to
one man or to an assembly, agree on being united under
that power of commonwealth, and use the sovereign to
safeguard internal harmony and defend against external
threats. Once created, the sovereign could continue to
derive its legitimacy from this original covenant of the
multitudes or, over time, it could fall back on bloodline or
divine right. For Hobbes, the sovereign didn't need to be
representative as long as it used its authority and power like
it was designed in the social contract.

The Hobbesian ideas of commonwealth and sovereign
were great but there were two problems that later political
philosophers had with them. First, what circumscribes the
power of the sovereign? For Hobbes, it was absolute and
that was both good and necessary. Others weren't so sure.
The idea of balance of powers through natural checks and
balances was a consequence of that.

Second, what provides legitimacy to the sovereign?
Hobbes was only concerned about the multitudes living
in peace. So long as the sovereign assured that, it had
legitimacy. The later thinkers thought there had to be more
to it. That's how the design of the modern democratic
system came to be. There was to be a balance of power

---

[1] Thomas Hobbes, *Leviathan* (Penguin Books, 1968).

between the various arms of the sovereign or the State. The origin of this thought goes back to Montesquieu and his theory of separation of powers. And those controlling the levers of the State had to pass the test of legitimacy. Winning the mandate to represent the people offered legitimacy. And, therefore, elections became central to conferring this legitimacy to the State.

Now, let's see what's changed with elections since then?

First, there was an assumption that an average voter knows enough to make an informed and rational choice on who will represent her. This was possible in the pastoral world of the late eighteenth century. Like we have written in the introduction to this section, she is what Lippmann called the omnicompetent citizen. This is no longer possible in the modern world where the average voter only sees a narrow sliver of the world from her perspective. We have 'pictures in our heads' of the likely world outside. Political parties create narratives and offer themselves as the best choice by influencing these pictures in our heads.

Second, political parties themselves weren't a fully formed notion in the early years of modern democracy. There was a view that the citizens would choose from among them their best representative who would then legislate laws on their behalf. Political parties were viewed as a partisan coming together of vested interests. As early as 1796, George Washington was railing against political parties as factions motivated by 'spirit of revenge' were compromising on public good and allowing 'cunning, ambitious, and unprincipled men' to 'subvert the power of the people'.[2] But as Carl Schmitt would put in many years later, the concept of the political is reducible to the existential distinction between friend and enemy.[3] Therefore, the electoral battle for the spoils of power would make the party system inevitable. In fact, by 1942, E. E. Schattschneider, in his work *Party Government*, argued, '. . . that the political parties created democracy and that modern democracy is unthinkable save in terms of parties'.[4]

The political party was both useful and indispensable.

Third, the role of the representative of the people has undergone a change too. The usual question that comes up on this is whether the representative is a delegate of people or a trustee of their will and aspirations. In the delegate model, the representative is a mere mouthpiece for the will of her constituents and has limited autonomy of her own. In many forms of direct democracy (or council democracy), this is a norm. The representative was to be subservient to those whom she represents. This was also how many viewed representation in the initial years. This was contested by Burke in his famous 1774 speech to the electors of Bristol that laid the foundation of the trustee model of representation.

---

[2] Farewell Address 1796, George Washington Papers, Series 2, Letterbooks 1754–1799, http://www.loc.gov/resource/mgw2.024.

[3] Edward Fairhead, 'Carl Schmitt's Politics in the Age of Drone Strikes: Examining the Schmittian Texture of Obama's Enemy' *Journal for Cultural Research*, 2017.

[4] E. E. Schattschneider, *Party Government* (Holt, Rinehart and Winston, 1942).

Burke begins with this clear distinction of the role of the representative:

> Certainly, gentlemen, it ought to be the happiness and glory of a representative to live in the strictest union, the closest correspondence, and the most unreserved communication with his constituents. Their wishes ought to have great weight with him; their opinion, high respect; their business, unremitted attention. It is his duty to sacrifice his repose, his pleasures, his satisfactions, to theirs; and above all, ever, and in all cases, to prefer their interest to his own. But his unbiased opinion, his mature judgment, his enlightened conscience, he ought not to sacrifice to you, to any man, or to any set of men living. These he does not derive from your pleasure; no, nor from the law and the constitution. They are a trust from Providence, for the abuse of which he is deeply answerable. Your representative owes you, not his industry only, but his judgment; and he betrays, instead of serving you, if he sacrifices it to your opinion.[5]

He then goes on to argue why the conscience of the representative is important for a democracy:

> To deliver an opinion, is the right of all men; that of constituents is a weighty and respectable opinion, which a representative ought always to rejoice to hear; and

---

[5] 'Representation: Edmund Burke, Speech to the Electors of Bristol', accessed 28 January 2022, https://press-pubs.uchicago.edu/founders/documents/v1ch13s7.html.

which he ought always most seriously to consider. But *authoritative* instructions; *mandates* issued, which the member is bound blindly and implicitly to obey, to vote, and to argue for, though contrary to the clearest conviction of his judgment and conscience—these are things utterly unknown to the laws of this land, and which arise from a fundamental mistake of the whole order and tenor of our constitution.[6]

And goes on to clarify what a parliament is meant to be. The representative should neither be hostage to the views of his constituents nor of the interests of his party:

Parliament is not a *congress* of ambassadors from different and hostile interests; which interests each must maintain, as an agent and advocate, against other agents and advocates; but parliament is a *deliberative* assembly of *one* nation, with *one* interest, that of the whole; where, not local purposes, not local prejudices, ought to guide, but the general good, resulting from the general reason of the whole.

. . .

You choose a member indeed; but when you have chosen him, he is not a member of Bristol, but he is a member of *parliament*.[7]

The centralization of power in parties in India has meant we now follow neither the trustee nor the delegate model

---

[6] Ibid.

[7] Ibid.

of representation. The representative is beholden to the party alone.

There is another change as well. For years, the continued strengthening of identity politics meant it was more important for the representative to reflect the identity of her constituents than their aspirations. The selection of candidates by parties on caste, sub-caste, and community lines across constituencies was the dominant trend. This meant the individual representative could count on his local knowledge and alliances to be useful for a party. This meant she could still stand up as an independent voice of judgement like Burke envisaged when needed. But this is now being reshaped by the dominant party in India. The nationalist, Hindu, and resurgent India narrative is attempting to subsume the local identities and the natural balance of power that was available in the Indian polity. This has made the dominant political party today stronger than the sum of its parts and consolidated power in the 'high command' further.

This is an interesting time to contemplate on representation in a democracy like India. We chose universal adult franchise at the time of Independence much ahead of other nations. This was fundamental to the right of equality that the Constitution guaranteed. The social re-engineering phenomenon that dominated most of our politics between 1960s and the 1990s was an outcome of this right given to every citizen.

The representative might not have been a trustee in the way Burke thought of her. She might have toed the party line on most issues. But she 'reflected' the 'narrow' identity of the people she represented, and this mélange

of narrow identities coming together in the parliament
possibly made the democratic system more robust. What
we have now is a gradual shift to a more dominant single-
party system with a greater focus on what can be called
the One Nation, One 'X' philosophy. In recent times,
this algebraic 'X' can be substituted by a wide variety of
items—ration card, language, election, grid, and legislative
platform, to name a few. This sounds seductive in the
aggregate especially if your definition of the imagined
construct of Indian nation aligns with what's being
promoted. Will it make democracy stronger? The odds
are stacked against it if history is any guide.

8

An Encounter with the State

Vikas Dubey, a dreaded gangster with multiple cases of murder against him, was killed in an 'encounter' with UP police on a Friday morning in July 2020. In the week before, five of his associates who were involved in gunning down eight policemen were killed in different encounters or while they were in custody. In April 2021, an inquiry commission gave that very Indian of things, a 'clean chit' to the UP police because there was no material evidence to rebut the police version of the events.

A short version of the events that led to Dubey's encounter is useful here. Dubey was arrested on a Thursday at Ujjain. On the way to Kanpur in police custody, their vehicle overturned. Then Dubey did things that confirmed his legend as some kind of an extraordinary force of evil. In that overturned van, he freed himself from his handcuffs a la Houdini. He snatched a service revolver and bolted out of the van defying gravity (*Iron Man*). He then ran some distance despite having a steel rod in his leg that gave him a limp (*Forrest Gump*). After a while, he remembered he had a gun that could be used to shoot at the police (Gulshan 'bad man' Grover). But before he could use it, he was shot dead. While displaying such daredevilry, he kept his mask on all along. Guns didn't scare him. The coronavirus did.

Weber in his essay 'Politics as a Vocation' defined the State as a community that lays claim to the monopoly of legitimate use of physical force on its citizens. By definition, the State has the right of violence. The State is expected to use this power with responsibility. But expecting the leviathan to restrain itself is not enough. The State apparatus is designed so that there is what Montesquieu called a 'distribution of powers'. This is the system of checks and balances between the three branches of the State—executive, legislature, and judiciary—that is the basis for most modern constitutions.

Each branch of the State should have the power to limit the other two, thereby creating a balance between the three. This eternal state of constructive conflict between the three is the price to be paid to protect the citizens from an all-powerful centralized State. Often this isn't enough. The society creates its own medium to monitor the use of power by the State. The various rights organizations, civil society activists, and self-help groups are meant for the society to keep a check on the State.

The question of the use of violence by the State is central to the conception of the State. How much should it use, where, and under what conditions—these have to be clearly delineated with accountability identified for the society to be secure from the State. The Indian State has a patchy track record of the use of violence on its citizens. The many insurgencies and terrorist movements that have cropped up over the years have needed the heavy hand of the State to quell them. That apart there have been mafia dons, dreaded gangsters, and criminal overlords who have been a law unto themselves. The State, world over, often goes overboard in dealing with these elements at the risk of being seen as a violator of basic human rights. Things haven't been too different in India. A particular type of State violence that's unique to India is what is often referred to as 'encounters' where a terrorist or a criminal is killed in an apparent face-off with the police or the army where the option of arresting them was available.

Encounter killings aren't news in India. Yet the Vikas Dubey case was remarkable. Almost everyone had predicted that Dubey and his associates would be killed in an encounter. And the police followed the script. It was a chronicle of an encounter foretold. The public response to the killings was unsurprising. The 'nationalist' view of it was as a form of speedy justice that the due process of law won't guarantee. The argument was that these gangsters deserved what they got. So, what's to complain about? The 'liberal' view was aghast at the vigilantism of the State. This is a slippery slope, it warned. This isn't an isolated case of State vigilantism. Of late, there have been multiple instances of police shooting down suspects accused of rape or murder because they allegedly tried 'escaping' while in police custody.[1]

---

[1] Suchitra Karthikeyan, 'Explained: Police Encounters in India: Cases, Convictions and Court Orders', *The Hindu*, 3 June 2022, https://www.thehindu.com/news/national/explained-police-encounters-in-india-cases-conviction-court-orders/article65463140.ece.

These sordid events can be looked at from different perspectives, including an indictment of the lengthy process it takes to deliver justice in India. We are, however, interested in two specific things. First, the nature of the relationship between criminals and politicians in India. How do we understand it? Second, given the increasing allure of retributive justice delivered by the State in our society, what confers legitimacy to retributive justice and what are its constraints?

Let's paint a picture of the Indian State in broad strokes. Like all States, it has a legitimate monopoly over violence, and it uses it to manage law and order, among other things. India is a poor country and for most of its citizens the State is also the ultimate provider of resources and services. The Indian State is large in its remit and in its ambition but ineffective in translating them to action. On paper, it has a lot of responsibilities, but in reality, it doesn't have resources to discharge them.

There are three kinds of State behaviour that set the ground for criminality in society.

One, the absence of the State. This is quite common in India where the State has low capacity but high ambition. In many interior parts of India, the State can't fulfil its responsibility of providing law and order. Also, its role as the ultimate provider of resources and services is compromised by vested groups who corral them. In the absence of the State, a local enforcer takes over. This enforcer represents the interests of a specific dominant group (often, a caste), captures the resources of the State, and becomes the quasi-State in the region. But this capture of the State is not without 'contestation' from other groups. This leads to a cycle of crimes resulting in consolidation of power or a fragile peace between the groups.

The politicians find these enforcers useful because they hold sway over voting blocs. In a 'first past the post' electoral system with multiple parties in fray where a 30–35 per cent vote share is adequate to win a seat, these enforcers can swing the elections. In the 1980s, as the hegemony of the Congress weakened, many enforcers cut out the middleman (politician) and jumped into the electoral fray themselves. The growth in the Indian economy meant they got richer by capturing government contracts and branching out to other businesses. Over time, they had money, muscle power, and their loyal caste base—an unbeatable electoral combination.

This model has been replicated across India with minor differences. In regions where the Indian State has been able to make deeper inroads, the enforcer has become less a criminal and more a businessman. This applies to the more prosperous states in southern and western India. In the Hindi heartland, it is still the Wild West.

Two, the unwarranted interventions of the State with unintended consequences. Think prohibition, bad real estate or tenancy laws, high import tariffs, price caps and more. Each of these leads to the emergence of a powerful mafia that helps citizens circumvent these bad laws. The list of liquor dons, smugglers, water or coal mafia, and real estate goons is long in Indian cities. Since corporate political funding in India was banned for a long time, these criminals funded politicians in return for patronage. Over time, they morphed themselves into businessmen and joined political parties.

Three, the absolutist State. This is where the citizens have allowed the State to have unlimited power over them on ideological grounds. The ideology could be political, religious, or something contrived. The agents of the State have a free run and often turn into criminals. This is the worst form of criminality in politics. Barring a couple of years of emergency, India has not seen absolute State control. But there is a divide that's emerging where every issue is seen through a partisan political lens. The priority in framing any narrative is not the merits of a position but how it will help strengthen a political ideology or the other. The debate on the killing of Dubey is an example of this framing. Turkey, Hungary, the Philippines, and Brazil have seen more egregious versions of this play out in their polity. The institutional strengths of these countries have been no match to this capture. The US and the UK are in the midst of this battle where civil society is holding out. We should keep an eye out for any ideological capture.

The Indian State brought criminality in politics upon itself through its absence or injudicious interventions. The saga of Dubey's rise and his death is another instance of this. The solution to this is in narrowing the scope of the State and making it stronger and more effective within that. But we aren't heading towards that solution. The consensus being manufactured justifying Dubey's extra-judicial killing and the ease with which it is being accepted by people portends the start of the third kind of criminality. We will have agents of the State turning criminals because they have absolute power and the moral sanction of the public. This is dangerous. History has shown it singes everyone eventually. The guilty and the innocent.

This shouldn't go unchallenged.

There's an intuitive appeal to the notion of retributive justice. Someone commits a crime. They inflict pain on others without their consent. So, they need to be punished. This is easy to understand. There are philosophical disagreements over this though. There are other theories of punishment that focus on deterrence or incapacitation. But they have moral problems in them too. For instance, deterrence justifies using people as means for a larger good. This is the notion of punishing someone to set an example to others. This goes against Kantian categorical imperative or the supreme principle of morality.[2] Others find retributive justice puzzling. H. L. A. Hart, the famous British legal philosopher, once termed it as a 'mysterious piece of moral alchemy in which the combination of two evils of moral wickedness and suffering are transmuted into good'.[3]

Kant believed the law of retribution or *jus talionis* is the only way to determine the appropriate degree of punishment. The three claims of *jus talionis* are:

- Punishment is justified only if it is deserved.
- It is deserved only if the person has voluntarily done a wrong (that which is being punished).
- The severity of punishment is proportionate to the severity of wrongdoing.

---

[2] Immanuel Kant (1724–1804) argued that the supreme principle of morality is *a standard of rationality* that he dubbed the 'Categorical Imperative' (CI). All specific moral requirements, according to Kant, are justified by this principle, which means that all immoral actions are irrational because they violate the CI.

[3] H. L. A. Hart, *Punishment and Responsibility* (Oxford: Oxford University Press, 1968).

Among the most convincing arguments made in favour of retributive justice was Herbert Morris' appeal to fairness. Morris states that for us to live in a society and derive benefits from it, we must accept certain limits on our behaviour. If a person fails to exercise this restraint, he abandons a burden of constraint that others have taken upon themselves. In this way, he gains an 'unfair' advantage that others don't have. This advantage must be squared through a punishment.

The two questions that follow then are—who should be the punisher and what should be the quantum of punishment?

In the state of nature, the victim should be punishing the wrongdoer. This has many problems. The criminal might not be accessible to the victim to inflict punishment. Not all victims may also be in a position to punish. This world follows *matsyanyaya* and your ability to punish the wrongdoer is circumscribed by your relative power.

This is where the State steps in. The State has institutions to use its legitimate force. The institutions include the parliament to draft laws, the judiciary to determine guilt, and the police to enforce law. These institutions provide the victim with access to the wrongdoer, to argue for their punishment, and the courts decide on the quantum of punishment based on precedence, written laws, and jurisprudence. The severity of punishment should be proportional to the gravity of the wrong. The gravity of wrong can be tempered by factors like intentions, first-time offence, extenuating circumstances, or background. The scale of punishment is set with a few cardinal bands marked for certain kinds of crimes and then building an ordinal proportional scale between them. The State sets these laws.

Now, let's view the reactions to encounter killings from this perspective.

The citizens of India have transferred their right to use physical force to the State. This is important for people who argue—what about the rights of those eight policemen killed? The State has all the powers, physical and moral, to exact retributive justice. The system is designed for this. The State as a punisher has defined the norms for the use of this force to ensure it doesn't turn into a predator. This protects the ordinary, innocent citizens from the unbridled power of the State. These norms include the process for framing of charges, identifying the accessories, proving guilt, and delivering punishment. The State doesn't have any right to pick and choose among these responsibilities. Any compromise in this chain of checks and balances runs the risk of the State inflicting violence on the innocent. The encounter killings are acts of bad faith by the government because they violate this.

The institutions of the State work in tandem to deliver retributive justice. One arm of the State can't blame another for laxity and strike out on their own. So, the police can't implicitly blame the judiciary for delays in delivering justice. The failure is collective. In any case, judicial delays aren't the reasons why criminals like Dubey weren't behind bars. We have seen the State keep people in detention for long when it has so desired. The State has to find solutions to its problems. The State can't externalize its failures and plead that its hands are tied.

Retributive justice of the State is important to curb vigilantism in society. In its absence, vigilante groups would deliver justice without following any checks and disproportionate to the quantum of offence. When the State abandons due process, it becomes a private vigilante group exacting revenge. This can trigger a cycle of retribution and encourage vigilantism among other private groups. There's also the risk of criminals escalating violence against the State because there's a huge 'disincentive' to surrendering to the State. This will lead to more lawlessness in society hurting ordinary citizens.

The 'celebration' of encounter killings by sections of society and the media lets the State get away with its failures to deliver justice. The multiple holes in the story of the police suggest the State isn't even making a pretence of hiding its failures. In a perverse way, it has turned this failure into its success by playing to the gallery. Retributive justice shouldn't turn into revenge orchestrated by the State. The long-term repercussions of this kind of revenge will be terrible for society.

As George Fletcher wrote about retributivism in *Rethinking Criminal Law* (Little, Brown, 1978): 'It is not to be identified with vengeance or revenge, any more than love is to be identified with lust.' It is critical we know the difference.

II

Bazaar

9

India's Mis-Tryst with Markets

The US is a capitalist economy. The USSR is a socialist economy. But India is a mixed economy, carefully crafted to bring together the best of both worlds.

This was the central idea that most students learnt in their economics classes in schools for five decades after Independence. In this telling, the US economy is imagined as a place where *matsyanyaaya* reigns—rapacious businessmen run amok while the government is happy to sit it out. Goods and services are distributed among people, not on the basis of what people need, but on the basis of their purchasing power alone.

Like that song in the movie *Satta Bazaar* (1959) went:

Chandi ke chand tukdon ke liye, imaan ko becha jaat hai.
[For a few pieces of silver, the soul is bartered away in the market.]

In sharp contrast, the USSR is portrayed as a regimented economy where the State owns all means of production.

The government there knows best about what is good for its people; desires and preferences of individuals do not matter.

Finally, India is imagined as an economy where the government would bring together the best features of both capitalism and socialism to its citizens. This thinking meant that the State would be the driving force in most sectors of the economy, leaving the less important work to private enterprise. The State would strike a balance between control and freedom, redistribution and growth, planning and decentralization.

Such a classification ignores how big the State is in most Western economies (discussed in Chapter 4). Most western economies, including the US, have a large State. Spending by all levels of governments in the US makes up nearly 40 per cent of the economy compared to nearly 25 per cent in India. The US, like India, has a mix of free markets and government intervention, mix of private and public enterprise, and a mix of planning and laissez-faire. In reality, most non-communist States are mixed economies.

The critical difference between the Indian and the US economies then is actually in the mindset. In the US, the market and private enterprise are considered, first and foremost, as part of the solution. In such economies, amongst the three instruments of the State—production, regulation, and financing—the last two increase in size, while the private sector dominates the first. The State is very much present; it's only the nature of its interventions that differ.

Clearly, India isn't that economy. Economic freedom is relegated to being a 'good-to-have' feature in our conceptualization. While social and political freedoms are intuitively perceived as positive, economic freedoms are seen as something that benefits only corporations, not individuals. If we were to debate the idea of personal freedoms, two views often emerge. Those keenly tracking the richer countries will superfluously recount the benefits of the freedoms of expression, speech, and dissent. Those on the conservative end will argue that there is nothing like absolute freedom anyway—all freedoms are and should be circumscribed by societal perceptions and contexts. Either way, the casualty is economic freedom.

Why this narrative prevails in India is a matter of speculation. Perhaps, it is the colonial experience where a trading company later transformed itself into an exploitative ruler. Or perhaps, it is the post-colonial idea of a social revolutionary-State, where the private sector's role was limited to filling the small–little interstitial spaces the State chose not to occupy. Or maybe it's the lived experience of businessperson-politician nexus, an outcome of the license-permit raj. Perhaps, we took the Soviet propaganda about collectivism more seriously than we should have. Or maybe the reason is not ideological but a result of contingent realities starting with the balance of payments crisis in 1957–58.[1]

---

[1] Arvind Panagariya, one of India's foremost trade economists, writes in *India: The Emerging Giant* (Oxford University Press, 2008) that before the 1957–58 balance of payments crisis, 'licensing was limited to specific industries, and licenses were issued relatively freely. Foreign investment policy was broadly liberal, and even imports of consumer goods were permitted with ease'.

Whatever the reason, the consequence is a deep and instinctive distrust of private enterprise. This section narrates stories of how this distrust of markets plays out in our daily lives and discussions.

In any discussion on the government's role in the economy, the most common response you are likely to encounter is: should economic growth matter so much? It increases inequality on the one hand and crowds out the discussion on other important issues such as human capital development. Across the eight decades since Independence, this widely shared assumption keeps coming back, albeit in different forms. This backdrop gives the State the leeway to overextend itself in the name of achieving 'balanced' and 'inclusive' growth. So, the first chapter in this section discusses the idea of economic growth and how it relates to redistribution.

A consequence of the distrust of markets is a strong belief in the idea that any exchange is zero-sum. Whatever the economic logic of voluntary trade being a positive-sum game in which both parties stand to gain, we imagine every transaction as a duel. For one side to win, the other must lose, often brutally. This belief demands that the State must intervene in the name of justice even in the voluntary exchange of goods and services. Chapters 11 through 15 detail some such instruments that Indian governments are eager to deploy.

The perception of trade as an inherently exploitative activity also plays out in the way India sees brokers—better known as middlemen—of all kinds. Chapter 16 discusses this idea in detail.

Next, even when the Indian State chooses to loosen its control over the economy, it often picks up pro-business reforms over pro-market ones. The former means aiding specific companies and sectors, while the latter focuses on creating regulations to ensure fair competition. Pick up any newspaper and you will find reports on how governments are showering subsidies, promising single-window clearances, and offering tax rebates instead of fixing the underlying cost disadvantages that make running businesses difficult. Chapter 17 is about one such intervention that's become the buzzword in government over the past two years: production-linked incentives.

Another consequence of the mistrust in markets is how every asset sale by the government is anthropomorphized as a sale of the family silver. Chapter 18 looks at the common narratives surrounding the sale of public sector enterprises.

Chapter 19 posits that one of the reasons that many public policies fail in India is because of the attempt to achieve several objectives with one policy instrument. This chapter looks at a few cases of government intervention in markets emanating from this mindset of multi-objective optimization.

Chapter 20 investigates another popular lament in our policy discourse that goes something like this: 'Only in a crisis can our governments overcome policy inertia and status-quo-ist attitudes.' We posit that crises are no guarantee for good reforms. Moreover, some of India's best policies have come through incremental changes and are not induced by crises.

Broadly, in each chapter of this section, we reason why the government's noble intentions often end up in counterproductive policies.

10

The Evergreen Growth Debate

India is perhaps the only country in the world where while kids are named Vikas or Pragati (both Hindi terms for growth or progress). Economic growth by itself is viewed with suspicion by well-meaning intellectuals and by a large swathe of its population. Our default mental model of growth is that it is a zero-sum game. Someone growing means someone is losing out.

Therefore, we present a new philosophical razor of Indian public policy:

> Any sufficiently long discussion on Indian public policy ends up in the question: why care about India's GDP growth? There are other important things to do.

Despite India's lacklustre economic performance over the decades, the belief that India's economy has grown way too much finds widespread acceptance. Those who support a big State argue that India has pursued growth as an end in itself, ignoring the more important goals such as health and education. Across the aisle, many conservative Indians agree. They believe that spiritual well-being matters more than material prosperity.

Given this widely shared belief, economic growth finds very few unapologetic defenders in the Indian polity. Growth always needs to be couched in defensive language. By regurgitating moderating adjectives such as 'inclusive' or 'balanced', policy and political documents paint a picture of economic growth as an inherently elite, exclusive, and discriminatory project. Disambiguating 'economic growth' from 'human development' is also an outcome of this line of thinking. So, this chapter discusses a few ideas related to economic growth from an Indian perspective.

Growth as a Moral Imperative

The debate over economic growth has sharpened in the wake of the COVID-19 pandemic. The poor have been disproportionately affected; hunger and starvation have increased. On the other hand, the rich were able to socially distance themselves, continue working from home, and have online education for their children. Isn't this a failing of the growth-first narrative, and a consequence of the growing inequality in our society?

Indeed, the poor have been disproportionately impacted because of COVID-19. However, that's not a blinding insight. Virtually every disaster has the worst impact on the most vulnerable individuals and communities. Even in communal flare-ups, it's unfortunately the poor who get targeted.

However, the reason for this unfortunate situation is not inequality but *poverty*. The poor have no support system to fall back to in times of crisis. Even if Indian governments earnestly try to solve the problems of the poor, they just don't have the financial or intellectual resources to support every poor person. This is especially true during a crisis when the governments' attention is focused on averting the immediate crisis—a health emergency in the case of COVID-19.

The only long-term solution to this conundrum is to keep reducing the number of people in the most economically vulnerable cohort day after day. This would be true 'self-reliance'. We want to get to an equilibrium where all Indians at least earn enough so that they can avoid the worst outcomes of a calamity on their own, without having to depend on the largesse of the government in tough times.

And how can we do this? Through economic growth. The other option, redistribution, is necessary and unavoidable. But it alone won't work in the long run because the government will run out of people to extract from. The economic pie is just too small at present to be able to satiate everyone.

There's a thumb rule that highlights the importance of economic growth: every 1 per cent GDP growth in India can take nearly three million people out of poverty.[1] This is why economic growth is moral, not just instrumental.

---

[1] Pradeep Agrawal, 'Reducing Poverty in India: The Role of Economic Growth', IEG Working Paper no. 349, 2015, 33. In this paper, the author does an econometric analysis of growth and poverty. The result is striking: 'Increase in GDP per capita is strongly associated with decrease in poverty and a 1 per cent increase in GDP per capita should reduce poverty by about 0.78 per cent. These results imply that that higher GDP growth rate reduces poverty and confirms the international evidence that higher GDP growth is associated with more rapid decline in poverty is equally applicable for India.'

It's surprising that despite this moral imperative of growth, the term has gained negative connotations. Without sufficient economic growth, a discussion on inequality is moot. Every crisis will keep hitting the poorest in the worst possible way.

Should We Care about GDP?

Despite growth being a moral responsibility of the Indian State, it is only seen in vague, instrumental terms. Often, the whole idea of growth itself is questioned. In recent times, the Gross Domestic Product (GDP) has become a favourite whipping boy in political commentary and WhatsApp conversations. So, let's look at a brief history of this measure.

There wasn't a defined notion of GDP until the early part of the twentieth century. The governments kept themselves distant from the economy and there wasn't a need felt for a holistic national view of it. In the US, this changed with the Great Depression. As the government intervened to stimulate demand on the back of Keynesian principles, it became necessary for it to have a comprehensive view of the national income. The Department of Commerce called upon Nobel laureate Prof. Kuznets to develop the first set of national accounts. By 1942, this estimation of national income became an annual affair, and this helped the US government plan their wartime efforts. Soon another Nobel Laureate, Wassily Leontief, was drafted into the team and he built the first input–output account for the economy.

It is widely acknowledged that the development of the national income account and its segmentation helped the US calibrate its response to the Great Depression and mobilize war efforts in a planned way. The subsequent post-war boom strengthened the need for greater details on the gross national product and, over time, as data gathering became scientific and the economy more formal, GDP and its details became important tools for economic policymaking. Other countries followed suit and soon GDP became a widely accepted measure for the health of an economy.

Like any measure, GDP has its failings. For instance, it makes no distinction about the quality of growth. A government spending on war or investing in polluting industries will show an uptick in GDP though these may not be the right choices for its citizens. It also doesn't factor in non-market transactions like the food your dad makes for you or the happiness in your family WhatsApp groups because all of you have deleted TikTok. Also, GDP being a gross measure won't tell us how the income is distributed among the citizens or if the equity in the society is improving. Lastly, there's more to life than income; GDP doesn't measure the health, education, and well-being of society. It also says nothing about the environmental cost of growth.

However, here's the rub. Despite all of the above, it tells us a lot and at a regular frequency. More than any other measure, it gives a comprehensive view of inputs and outputs across sectors and their trends over time. Specific policy interventions in any area can be made using these measurements. The rate of growth in GDP is a shorthand for how the economy is faring and a useful way to compare different economies. GDP growth rate also helps the central bank in determining future interest rates based on what is called the Taylor rule instead of using the backward-looking rational expectations theory.[2]

Also, the complaint that GDP doesn't measure the environmental cost or equity or happiness is ill-informed. Do you measure Virat Kohli's worth by counting the number of goals he can score? You don't because that's not the game he plays professionally. GDP approximates national income, nothing more and nothing less. And we would argue, it is still the most important indicator to prioritize for a country like India where one in five are not able to earn enough to survive. That makes higher GDP a moral imperative for India, not just a good-to-have luxury that can be traded off for something else.

In summary, the GDP measure is like the report card of a kid at school. You can always argue the report doesn't measure her real knowledge, her potential and can't be a good predictor of her future success. These aren't always easy to measure objectively. Or, that it gives undue importance to tests and assessments. But you can't dispute it measures something important that gives you a good sense of the child's progress. Not having that measure would make things worse. GDP is somewhat like that.

Is Economic Growth Anti-Environment?

This is another argument we encounter often. The question came into sharp focus in 2020 when the draft Environment

---

[2] The Taylor Rule suggests that nominal interest rates should be based on two divergences: the divergence between the actual GDP and potential GDP, and the divergence between the actual inflation and target inflation.

Impact Assessment (EIA) notification was issued that year.[3] There were two contentious points in the notification that evoked strong reactions.

First, the notification allows the government to grant environmental clearance to projects after they have started work without an official clearance so long as the violators work on remediation and resource augmentation plan. This plan should correspond to one-and-a-half to two times the ecological damage assessed and economic benefit derived. Further, it states that violations can only be reported by the government or the sponsors of the project, not by citizens.

Second, there are about forty types of industries that are exempted from environmental clearance including projects that the government might term 'strategic'. There are other exemptions including road and pipeline projects in border areas (within 100 km from the Line of Actual Control [LAC]), construction projects of up to 150,000 square metres, and inland waterways and highways work.

Development versus environment is a trade-off even if this idea doesn't sit well with environmental activists. Taking an absolutist position on any side of this debate is impractical. We will come to two examples of why absolutist positions don't work at the end of the essay.

So, the question is how to think of this trade-off. We have four points to offer:

One, the way a $2000 per capita income country thinks about the environment can't be like that of a $50,000

---

[3] Draft Notification issued by the Ministry of Environment, Forests and Climate Change, Government of India, to be published in the *Gazette of India*, Extraordinary, Part-II, Section 3, Subsection (ii) http://environmentclearance.nic.in/writereaddata/Draft_EIA_2020.pdf.

per capita income country. Our state capacity is smaller, we have limited resources, and our people remaining poor doesn't help the environment either. There is also a moral imperative of saving lives here and now while weighing the long-term impact of environmental damage. So, merely imitating or benchmarking with the global standards of environmental clearance is fraught with risks. We won't help the environment because we won't have the capacity to manage a sophisticated law with many bells and whistles. And we won't help with the growth of the economy either.

Two, considering our state capacity, it is impossible to assess every single project upfront and clear them. This is the equivalent of wanting to scrutinize every single individual tax return. It doesn't make sense. It is useful to have high penalties for violations and have the ability to do a post-facto clearance. The debate can be on whether the penalties are stringent enough. So, this idea that post facto clearances are a complete anathema needs to be thought through. We have had the experience of clearances becoming either means of rent seeking or being hostage to policy paralysis in the early part of the last decade. It helps no one.

Three, the more exceptions in the law, the easier it is to be violated or abused. The number of industries exempted and the catch-all nature of the term 'strategic' should be debated. It has to be narrowed. Else, there will be a market for getting a project exempted that will negate the purpose of the law. A smaller list of exceptions is easier to monitor.

Four, the violations can be taken up in courts of law by individual citizens or environmental groups. To keep the door open for anyone to report a supposed violation that then needs to be investigated by a committee is impractical considering our state capacity.

Finally, we should learn from two of our experiences in the past decade.

First, environmental clearances all but stopped during 2011–14 for various reasons. In 2013, for instance, the union government received a total of 1538 proposals of which 372 were granted environmental clearances. There were 1128 projects that were waiting for clearances by the environment ministry in February 2014. This delay meant that the ministry achieved the dubious distinction of having the highest percentage of projects awaiting clearances, among all other union government ministries.[4] We aren't sure of the environmental benefits accrued to the society because of these delays. However, what it meant for our growth is clear, and there is data to show this. Private investments fell, infrastructure development slowed, companies who had taken debt to fund these projects suffered, banks ran up large NPAs, and growth faltered. Over a decade, we might have lost the opportunity to lift over fifty million out of poverty. There were other reasons too, but there's no denying this factor contributed in a large way.

Second, and we are admittedly stretching logic a bit here, the pandemic lockdown was seen to be good for the environment from an absolutist perspective. Remember in the initial days of pandemic we were inundated with

---

[4] Jyotindra Dubey, Anand Sinha, 'How Big a Hurdle Is the Minister for Environment and Forests', *Business Today*, accessed 23 February 2022, https://www.businesstoday.in/magazine/focus/story/minister-for-environment-and-forests-industry-hurdle-134939-2014-01-14.

pictures of some mountains that could now be visible clearly from Chandigarh or some birds that weren't seen in cities making a return. These pictures often carried the message 'nature is healing itself'. But what was the cost of such healing by shutting down economic activities? The humanitarian impact of the shutdown in a poor country like India is quite evident to all by now. Over 120 million Indians were impacted with most losing better-paying jobs in urban India and forced to migrate back to their villages. Another example of this is the decision of the Sri Lankan government in 2020 to switch to organic farming in a single swoop. In an economy already reeling from the pandemic, this was the last straw. Inflation flattened the economy, and Sri Lanka defaulted on its debt. The trade-off between growth and environment for countries like India is such that there cannot be absolutist positions taken that mimic more advanced nations. If anything, for the foreseeable future, the balance should tilt more towards growth.

When we think of our trade-off between growth and the environment, it is useful to keep these in mind.

What Creates (or Results in) Economic Growth?

In *India's Long Road: The Search for Prosperity,* veteran economist Vijay Joshi presents some astonishing numbers.

> From 1950 to 2010, there have been only three countries that have had 6 per cent+ growth for three decades or more on the run: China, South Korea, Taiwan. Only China has had a per capita growth rate of more than 8

per cent a year for thirty years. Another striking fact is that, apart from the above three countries, there has been no other country that has had per capita growth of 6 per cent a year for a continuous period of even two decades.[5]

Since we have sung paeans about economic growth, a good question to ask is what led to rapid growth in some regions of the world?

Four Reasons for Growth

We find there are four determinants (or clusters of factors) that have been used to argue why a country has seen rapid growth or, conversely, why it has failed.

Economic Freedom

In the post-Second World War era, we find a strong correlation between economic freedom and economic growth. Economic freedom here is represented by open and free markets and limited government. The specific policy initiatives include trade liberalization, labour market reforms, low tax rates, fiscal prudence (low debt to GDP ratio), open domestic financial markets, and ease of doing business. The works of Romain Wacziarg and Karen Horn Welch on trade liberalization,[6] Ross Levine

---

[5] Vijay Joshi, *India's Long Road: The Search for Prosperity* (Oxford University Press, 2017).

[6] Romain Wacziarg and Karen Horn Welch, 'Trade Liberalization and Growth: New Evidence', *The World Bank Economic Review* 22, no. 2, 1 January 2008, 187–231, https://doi.org/10.1093/wber/lhn007.

on domestic financial and banking reforms,[7] and Stephen Nickell on the downside of labour market rigidities[8] provide cross-country evidence of their impact on economic growth.

The success of the Washington consensus, the collapse of the authoritarian, State-run eastern bloc nations, and the emergence of the Asian tiger economies are used to support this argument. This became the standard prescription of the International Monetary Fund (IMF) to any developing economy looking for aid. While there are compelling arguments to support the economic freedom thesis, there have been two main criticisms of this.

First, the question of causality. Does economic freedom lead to economic growth or do countries that have seen economic growth tend to improve on economic freedom over time? In the 1960s and 1970s, South Korea and Taiwan used protectionist measures that restricted foreign players in their domestic market while promoting exports. The South Korean banking system was government-owned and they allowed conglomerates (*chaebols*) to emerge before they opened up their financial markets. Even Britain and the US rose in the periods they followed protectionist policies and then batted for free trade.

Second, the IMF prescription of fiscal tightening, structural reforms, and economic freedom hasn't worked in

---

[7] Ross Levine, 'Chapter 12 Finance and Growth: Theory and Evidence', in *Handbook of Economic Growth*, vol. 1 (Elsevier, 2005), 865–934, https://doi.org/10.1016/S1574-0684(05)01012-9.

[8] Stephen Nickell, 'Unemployment and Labor Market Rigidities: Europe versus North America', *Journal of Economic Perspectives* 11, no. 3, September 1997, 55–74, https://doi.org/10.1257/jep.11.3.55.

many countries across continents. A good example of this was following the Asian financial crisis of the late 1990s. Countries like Indonesia and South Korea that followed the IMF doctrine saw contraction and high unemployment. Malaysia refused the offer and imposed capital controls and forex curbs and fared better. The repeated bailouts of Argentina and Greece offer more examples of the failure of the prescription.

Political Freedom and Institutions

The role of individual liberty, property rights, limited regulations, and judicial effectiveness in enabling growth has been established through the works of the Chicago school of neoclassical economists including Milton Friedman, Gary Becker, and George Stigler and their intellectual forebears like Friedrich Hayek and James Buchanan. Francis Fukuyama in his influential work *Political Order and Political Decay* (Farrar, Straus and Giroux, 2014) makes a compelling case for a strong State (not the same as a large State), democratic accountability, and rule of law as the three necessary conditions for countries to be successful. He marshals facts from the Industrial Revolution to the present day to conclude that liberal democracy is the eventual evolutionary end state for all successful political orders.

Daron Acemoglu and James Robinson in their book *Why Nations Fail* (Crown Business, 2012) make a similar case for centralized power and inclusive institutions. States that create institutions that share power, focus on productivity and innovation, and improve over time have fared better over those who have extractive institutions that steal resources and benefits from the society for private gains of a few. Again, Acemoglu and Robinson provide cross-country comparison with data, stories, and history of institutions in different countries to highlight their role in economic performance.

However, these principles aren't as universal as their authors would like us to believe. China's rise is a strong counter to the notion of democratic accountability and inclusive institutions that privilege individual liberty and freedom. Taiwan, South Korea, and Singapore were under authoritarian rules when their economies took off. Going back into history, it can be argued that the periods of strong growth in Western colonial powers coincided with slavery, exploitation of women, and huge income disparity that were supported by the institutions and laws of that era. There's a stronger case for reverse causality. That economic prosperity led to greater empowerment of the masses and forced changes in institutions making them more egalitarian.

Geography

There are two ways to look at geography here. One is the natural resources available within a country. The other is the climate, lifestyles, and culture that have an impact on the type of society (individualistic or collective) and attitude to change (open or closed). Jared Diamond in *Guns, Germs and Steel* (W. W. Norton, 1997) proposed that the wide Eurasian landmass allowed humans to move along a latitude band over a huge area. This uniformity of climate and availability of land meant they could build large settlements, develop farmlands, and domesticate animals. This early adoption of agrarian life and animal husbandry meant they were better organized as a society and more resistant to germs. The scientific revolution that started in north-western Europe consolidated these geographic gains, and colonialism created a huge advantage whose benefits are still being reaped. Similar arguments have been made by people who have tried to explain why economic progress and distance from the equator are correlated for a number of countries and regions (the farther you are from the equator, the greater the prosperity).

In a later book *Collapse* (Viking Press, 2005), Diamond overweighs the environmental problem and climate change as the reason why societies collapse. He makes the case for 'carrying capacity' of the land and how overpopulation pushes this to the brink. The rapid growth among the oil-rich States of West Asia in the last fifty years is another instance of geography trumping all other determinants.

The problem with geography as destiny approach is twofold. One, there's not a lot of policymaking you can do to alter the geography of a country (except annexing other countries). Two, it is easily falsifiable because so many countries with similar geography have different growth trajectories (Russia with any western European country in the last century, for instance) and many great civilizations of the past thrived in geographies quite different from where prosperous countries of post-Industrial Revolution era are located.

Investment (Physical and Human Capital)

Robert Solow showed that given similar institutions and structural parameters, a country with a low base of capital investment can have rapid economic growth by increasing investment. Over time, countries will converge in terms of their per capita income as diminishing returns to reproducible capital plays out. Paul Romer showed this holds true for human capital too. But he added an additional variable of ideas through which he showed countries can go beyond the inevitable slowing down of the rate of economic growth.

So, investments in physical infrastructure, technology, and human capital helped countries to catch up with others over time while innovation and ideas helped them avoid diminishing returns and jump curves.

There are two challenges to this argument. First, it is difficult to control the quality of institutions and structural capabilities so that they are the same across countries. A country wanting to accelerate its growth cannot switch to similar institutions as a developed country overnight. A transition of this kind takes time, and it is fraught with political and social risks. Two, there's research to show that not all kinds of investment have a positive correlation with economic growth. It is important to know the trade-offs involved. Also, development economists have shown that a significant investment in the quality of human capital has to be done over a sustained period of time as a prerequisite for growth to take off. There is a lot of fog here, and a lot of retrofitting of evidence has been done to prove a point on which investment should come first.

Cross the River by Feeling the Stones

It is clear there's no single answer to the question of why countries experience a period of rapid economic growth. Context matters and as does luck. This doesn't mean there's nothing to learn from others or from our own history. We are only suggesting the need to keep an open mind, follow sound reasoning and titrating policy recommendations to arrive at what suits us best based on evidence. However, what's also clear is there are a set of negative variables that emerge from the above that we should learn to avoid. These are quite obvious—weak rule of law, poor accountability, lack of a performance-driven culture among institutions, and entrenched corruption.

Lastly, there's no permanent cycle of growth and rising prosperity. The Minsky Cycle holds true for countries and empires too.[9] Within each boom, there's a seed of bust already sown. Any rise is followed by a fall. It is inevitable. History stands witness to it.

---

[9] A Minsky moment is a sudden, major collapse of asset values that marks the end of the growth phase of a cycle in credit markets or business activity.

11

When the State Owns What's Yours

A typical scene in those old Bollywood films with a rural setting was that of the zamindar standing with his 'not-so-smart' (*naalayak*) offspring on the terrace of their haveli and telling him:

> *Yahan se jahaan tak tumhari nazar jaati hai, woh saari zameen hamari hai!*
> [All the land that you can see from here belongs to us.]

In reality, the only zamindar who can make such a claim in modern India is the Indian State.

A fundamental concept underlying economic reasoning and public policy is the property rights system. To an Indian, the phrase 'right to property' conjures up the image of a rapacious zamindar exploiting peasants. This narrative has fostered a zero-sum perception—owning property is assumed to have occurred in the context of the violation of someone else's human rights. This perception has, in turn, meant that the enforcement of property rights has always been weak in India. Once a fundamental right, the right to property under the Indian Constitution was deprecated to a constitutional right by the 44th amendment. Now the State can go about violating an individual's right over their property, as long as it can couch this takeover is being done under vaguely defined 'public interest'.

Why Is a Functional Property Rights System Necessary?

A property right is an exclusive authority to determine how a resource is used. This applies not just to land but to any physical or intellectual property such as your phone, your water bottle, or your innovation. Such a right can be held by a person, a group of persons, or the State.

When this exclusive authority over someone's resources is protected—by the State or society—the owners can be confident of deploying and improving the quality of their owned resource instead of spending their energy in feverishly protecting the resource from being stolen by another entity. Moreover, giving an exclusive authority to someone to enjoy the use of a resource changes the nature of competition itself, bringing it into the realm of social acceptability. For example, without property rights, entities might compete over a common resource by resorting to means such as intimidation, denial, and distancing. But once it is demonstrated that the authority over a resource will be protected, competition shifts to owners improving their offering to win more buyers. Finally, a strong property rights system also enables the exchange and sharing of resources, as resource owners can be confident that their ultimate ownership is secure.[1]

Now this sounds quite theoretical and straight out of an economic reasoning textbook, which this book is not. So, to understand how pivotal the concept of a well-functioning property rights system is, we turn to an Indian story of violation of these rights. By understanding what happens when property rights are denied, we might better appreciate their importance.

Daastaan-e-Sandalwood

The story of sandalwood production in India is as intriguing as it is frustrating. The wood is used for its timber. The oil extracted from its roots is used in perfumes, incense, soaps, and medicines. In India, sandalwood has a special religious significance as well.

As hopeful consumers, many of you would have heard about the astronomical costs of this wood. Many of you would have also heard about brigands such as Veerappan who gained Robinhood status by smuggling sandalwood. Some of you might have been duped into buying ordinary scented wood being passed off as sandalwood. But few

---

[1] Read Armen A. Alchian's foundational work on Property Rights for a detailed (and readable) discussion. Armen A. Alchian, 'Some Economics of Property Rights', *Il Politico* 30, no. 4, 1965, 816–29. Another good resource is this article by Peter J. Boettke. 'Why Did Armen Alchian Have to Teach Economists About Property Rights?', *Econlib*, accessed 23 February 2022, https://www.econlib.org/library/Columns/y2020/BoettkeAlchian.html.

of us realize that the strand that connects these stories is misguided State action.

Generally, the price of a commodity is indicative of its natural scarcity, but that's not the case here. Nearly 90 per cent of the world's sandalwood resources are available in the three Indian states of Karnataka, Tamil Nadu, and Kerala. And yet, the production of sandalwood in India has declined sharply. In 1965–70, annual production stood at 4000 tonnes.[2] By 1999–2000, it had decreased by half. And by 2019, it had become just 200 tonnes. Other countries supplied a total of 400 tonnes in the same year, while the total global demand is estimated to be nearly 6000 tonnes a year. This massive demand–supply gap has made sandalwood so costly that it is often referred to as 'red gold'.

The drastic fall in sandalwood supply from India can be explained by a long history of denial of property rights. In fact, State interference in growing, producing, and selling sandalwood has a history of nearly 230 years in India. Here's how the story goes.

Sandalwood was in huge demand even during colonial times, especially in China. The East India Company— never one to miss a trading opportunity—aimed to exploit the resources in southern India and export them to China. The problem was that a lot of the sandalwood-growing area fell under the kingdom of Mysore, led by Tipu Sultan. Recognizing the commercial value of this resource, Tipu Sultan forbade his subjects from trading in the wood with

---

[2] Aparna Pallavi, 'Return of Scented Wood', *DownToEarth*, 28 February 2015, https://www.downtoearth.org.in/coverage/forests/return-of-scented-wood-48569.

the Britishers in 1786. To take this idea further, he decreed sandal as a 'royal tree', monopolizing sandalwood trade in 1792.[3] Thus began, out of good intentions, the story of sandalwood's decline.

Eventually, this sandalwood trade blockade became one of the primary causes of the Anglo-Mysore Wars. Once the Britishers took control, they were only happy to continue the sandalwood trade monopoly. The conception of sandalwood as a source of government revenue strengthened. Fast forward to Independence and we see that such was the lure of the scented wood that subsequent Indian governments followed the same policy of denying property rights to sandalwood growers. Even when the tree was located on private land, it belonged to the state government, and the owner of the land was required to make a declaration of the number of trees on his land. The forest officer could enter any private land and cut the trees and the range forest officer was supposed to give 75 per cent of the value as decided by the officer. Landholders were to be held responsible for damage or theft of any tree even though they had no exclusive authority over it. Violators could be imprisoned and fined. Further, in Karnataka and Tamil Nadu, it was necessary to get a licence to store, sell, and process sandalwood. Possession of sandalwood in excess of twenty kilograms was made an offence.

Unsurprisingly, the complete disregard for property rights meant that no one was interested in growing

---

[3] Ezra D. Rashkow, 'Perfumed the Axe That Laid It Low: The Endangerment of Sandalwood in Southern India', *The Indian Economic & Social History Review* 51, no. 1, January 2014, 41–70, https://doi.org/10.1177/0019464613515553.

sandalwood on their land. It became a liability to be gotten rid of rather than an asset to be invested in. After all, who would want to be accountable for a resource whose fruits of labour they cannot enjoy?

The result was a steep fall in production. But the story didn't end there. Given that the demand for wood was still high, a thriving black market emerged. With supply from cultivators choked off by government policy, smuggling the wood growing in government-controlled forests became a lucrative opportunity. Such were the profits to be made that the government could not protect sandalwood smuggling from these forests. When governments created armies of forest guards and personnel to 'protect' the forests, many forest staff colluded with smugglers, further causing the depletion of the resource. Eventually, this smuggling business paved the way for the likes of Veerappan, who moved away from the riskier 'business' of killing elephants to the far-more profitable sandalwood smuggling.

After decades of this failed policy of denying property rights, governments recognized their mistake in 2001, when the Karnataka government allowed private players to grow and own sandalwood. Tamil Nadu followed suit in 2002. But this recognition of exclusive authority remains incomplete. The government continued to monopolize demand, which meant that farmers could only sell the sandalwood back to the government. Realizing that this was still a major stumbling block, the Karnataka government further liberalized sandalwood policy in 2009. Now, the growers could sell their wood directly to semi-government corporations such as Karnataka State Handicrafts Development Corporation (KSHDC) and Karnataka Soaps and Detergents Limited (KSDL). Apparently, KSDL offers a non-negotiable sum of Rs 3500 per kg of sandalwood. The company then turns around and sells the product for nearly Rs 16,000. Even today, farmers are not free to sell to other private players or export their produce.[4]

Meanwhile, Australia, which had its own native sandalwood, shifted to the Indian variant in 1998, introduced genetically engineered high yield varieties, and beat India at its own game. So much so that India now imports Australian sandalwood for the sandalwood oil industry!

The Takeaway

The sad sandalwood story illustrates that denial of property rights took away a shot at prosperity for thousands of ordinary farmers. One of the key components of liberty is economic freedom. Denial of this core freedom to individuals by the State or the society is a cruel act that perpetuates poverty. The State shouldn't be let off easily when it abridges this basic right.

The hope is that learning from the mistakes of previous generations, many states in India have now adopted liberal policies for sandalwood production. This shouldn't be seen as isolated policy reform. The principle that needs to be internalized is that the State should focus on the protection of property rights of individuals instead of usurping them.

---

[4] Akhil Kadidal, 'Sandalwood Growers Demand Free Market Trade', *Deccan Herald*, 26 February 2019, https://www.deccanherald.com/city/sandalwood-growers-demand-free-720363.html.

12

The Sun Hasn't Set on the Empire Yet

Pan Singh Tomar was a soldier in the Indian army who won steeplechase golds at many national and international athletics events in the 1960s. He returned to his village after his retirement and soon found himself in the middle of a property dispute, caste oppression, and an overbearing system. He rebelled, formed a gang of dacoits, and went on an extortion and murder spree. His story was immortalized on screen by Irrfan Khan in an eponymous film made by Tigmanshu Dhulia in 2012. One line stood out in the film. When asked why he had turned a dacoit, Irrfan (playing Tomar) deadpans:

> *Beehad mein baaghi hote hain; dakait milte hain Parliament main.*
> [There are only rebels in the ravines; dacoits are found in Parliament.]

Mancur Olson, an American economist and political scientist, made significant contributions to the field of institutional economics in the last quarter of the twentieth century. The type of governments and how their nature influenced the provision of public goods, the system of taxation, and the freedom for collective action were his areas of interest. In his oft-quoted paper, 'Dictatorship, Democracy, and Development' (1993), Olson introduced the concept of the 'roving bandits' and the 'stationary bandits' while discussing the nature of government.[1] Roving bandits, as the term suggests, are constantly on the move, looking to find the next settlement to pillage. They have no long-term view of the village they have in control now. Maximize the loot, slash and burn down the place, and move on. Call it the Gabbar Singh model of running political affairs.

Olson suggests if the bandits gave this lifestyle choice a bit more thought, they would rather opt to become 'stationary bandits'. That is setting up a kind of permanent system that would monopolize looting, but balance it with the growth and prosperity of the village. They would guarantee law and order and protection from external threats and support all efforts that would increase the productivity of the settlement. A stationary bandit is a bandit with a long-term plan.

For Olson, anarchy is when a State is overrun by roving bandits. Autocracies tend to act like stationary bandits but soon turn into roving bandits because no autocrat lives forever. Democracies are run by stationary bandits who monopolize and rationalize theft in the form of taxes, and in return, deliver order, peace, and public goods.

---

[1] Mancur Olson, 'Dictatorship, Democracy, and Development', *The American Political Science Review* 87, no. 3, 1993,: 567–76, http://dx.doi.org/10.2307/2938736.

This might sound somewhat callous, but there's no denying the truth underlying this view. This is a useful construct to apply to India from the time it came under the direct control of the British Crown. The colonial British government saw themselves as roving bandits. One could argue they did some good for India—modern education, railways, irrigation, and basic healthcare—but nobody was under the illusion that they did this for the long-term welfare of Indians. The intent was to maximize the returns from India while not completely ruining it. The Indian State that replaced it could have modelled itself on stationary bandits. But the system was set up for roving bandits. And seventy-five years since, the State hasn't been able to make the transition to becoming stationary bandits. Like we will see below, this manifests itself in many strange processes that are still followed by the government.

For the rare capitalist-minded young boys growing up in the 1980s, Hindi films presented two viable career options—becoming a smuggler or an industrialist. It was easy to give up on the smuggler option early. It involved a lot of unnecessary running (is there any other kind?), staying awake at night, unloading *sona* (gold) at Madh Island (lucrative but with a requirement of insomnia), and having a pesky, upright, uniformed younger brother breathing down your neck (Shashi Kapoor).

But industrialists? Well, that looked swell. You wore safari suits, carried a briefcase that had lots of loose paper, drank an occasional Black Dog, and went around in nice cars. The only work that looked real and kept you busy involved bidding for government contracts. A bit of bribing, some kindly threats, or a minor kidnapping—the whole *saam, daam, dand, bhed* (request/cajole, bribe, punish/threaten, exploit) arsenal—was all you needed to get the civil servant or the minister on your side to help you undercut your competition. This seemed all quite doable. What's more, you had a palatial house with two spiral stairways and an agreeable name like Ahuja, Singhania, or R. K. Gupta. The only downside was having a college-going progeny with a dubious academic record who was prone to singing '*Gapuji gapuji gam gam'* (Poonam Dhillon in *Trishul*).

Well, into each life some rain must fall, as some Longfellow had said.

Anyway, let's narrow our focus down to the government contracts that exercised R. K. Gupta (Sanjeev Kumar) in Yash Chopra's *Trishul* (1978). The procurement of goods and services by the government of India is still largely governed by the Contract Act, 1872 and Sale of Goods Act, 1930, and General Financial Rules (GFR) that are amended periodically. The most prevalent mechanism of awarding a contract in government departments and PSUs over the last century has been the L1 system, also called the Least Cost Selection Method. There is a bit of history to this. The colonial government (roving bandits) wasn't too keen on spending a lot on infrastructure and development projects in India. A minimal threshold of quality was all that was needed. Nothing long-lasting. So, the search was always for the lowest cost bidder who would just about get the job done.

Though alternatives like the Quality and Cost Based System (QCBS) and Quality Based System (QBS) are gradually being adopted, the L1 system still holds sway after seven decades. We love our colonial past a lot that way. So, you could lie your way through the technical bid claiming excellent capabilities. Once you crossed that threshold, all you needed was some friendly insider who tipped you about competitive bids so that you could price your bid marginally lower than your closest competitor. Voila, you are in business.

Three problems cropped up on account of this. First, since technical bids didn't have a weightage, the projects were often won by less competent firms who couldn't either complete the project or did a shoddy job. Examples of this are visible all around us in government infrastructure and road projects. We keep repairing the same roads every year because we just cannot get roads built that could last a few years.

Second, it encouraged rent-seeking behaviour among public servants who had information about rival bids. In the cult classic *Jaane Bhi Do Yaaro*, municipal commissioner D'Mello played off two builders (Ahuja and Tarneja) against each other to maximize his benefits till one of them bumped him off. This wasn't far from the reality of how government contracts were awarded.

Third, it led to the crowding out of honest, competent players from the government tender market because they wouldn't play ball. Bad money drives out the good. Soon, all you are left with are low quality bidders and the terrible outcomes follow.

In Yash Chopra's *Trishul*, these issues come to a head. Vijay, who runs Shanti Construction, is an upstart who has no experience in large construction projects. In a couple of pivotal points in the film, he either bribes the civil servant or uses inside information about his rival (Gupta

Constructions) and outbids them marginally. By marginally, we mean the very definition of the term—for one tender, he bids one rupee lower than Gupta Construction. In no time, Shanti Construction drove Gupta Construction out of business. Of course, we felt bad for R. K. Gupta. He was a victim twice over—of Vijay in the present and of roving bandits from the past.

13

How Many Bans Will They Enforce Before Bans Are Forever Banned?

A Ban in the Time of COVID-19

In May 2020, the Union agriculture ministry issued a draft gazette notification to ban twenty-seven generic pesticides because of their biohazards.[1] Fertilizer companies and other stakeholders could give their objections within forty-five days before the final notification was to be issued.

This move was during the first COVID-19 lockdown. The severity of the lockdown was already hurting the economy. When the numbers would come in later, we would know that the economy had shrunk by over 20 per cent over the same quarter of the previous year. Since the pandemic then seemed to be limited to urban centres, the rural economy was expected to be the saving grace.

---

[1] Extraordinary Gazette Notification CG-DL-E-18052020-219423 in *The Gazette of India*, issued by the Ministry of Agriculture and Farmers Welfare.

Agriculture was still expected to show growth, though marginal, for the year.

There was a small problem involving locusts though. From the beginning of 2020, a swarm of locusts of biblical proportions was moving from the eastern coast of Africa towards the middle east and the Indian subcontinent. These swarms could destroy thousands of square kilometres of cultivated land area in a single day. By May 2020, they were at the western border of Rajasthan and in a few weeks, they were destroying crops in northern India.[2]

That's when the proposal for the ban on pesticides came in.

Only three among the twenty-seven pesticides listed were in the red triangle category (highest level of hazard). These should have been phased out years ago. The remaining twenty-four have been used by farmers for decades without demonstrable downstream environmental or health risks. The domestic agrochemical industry was manufacturing these pesticides at prices that could be afforded by the small Indian farmers. Their revenues could be impacted by up to Rs 8000–9000 crores.[3] Also, the banning of these products would have led to the import of patented products into India,

[2] 'Locust Attack Tracker: Where the Hoppers Are Headed and How States Are Preparing for Battle', *The Indian Express*, 29 May 2020, https://indianexpress.com/article/india/locust-attack-tracker-india-rajasthan-punjab-uttar-pradesh-maharashtra-haryana-6431893/.

[3] Sharad Dubey, 'Government's Proposal to Ban 27 Pesticides Will Hurt Agrochemical Firms and Farmers, Analysts Say', *Bloomberg Quint*, accessed 12 February 2022, https://www.bloombergquint.com/business/governments-proposal-to-ban-27-pesticides-will-hurt-agrochemical-firms-and-farmers-analysts-say.

which were likely to increase the per acre cost of pesticides for the farmer by two to three times.[4] It was not the best of times to burden the farmer. Also, the list of banned pesticides includes Chlorpyriphos and Malathion. Their primary use?

Killing locusts.

To be fair, the gazette stated that these chemicals could be used for desert locusts but not for agriculture. But how would you determine end-use when someone is buying it? Also, we had a situation where the locusts were already on agricultural land across most of north and central Indian states. Any use of pesticides on locusts meant it would be used over agricultural land. Yet, the government put these two locust-killing pesticides on this list. For context, only two countries had banned Malathion—Syria and Palestine. We were the third. In a separate move, a few days earlier, the Union government had been busy procuring an additional stock of 53,000 litres of Malathion to control the locusts before the sowing of Kharif crops began.[5]

The same pesticide it wanted to ban after forty-five days.

India Loves a Ban

Barely a week passes without the State banning something. Sometimes we wonder if the more appropriate national anthem should be 'ban gan man'.

---

[4] Ibid.

[5] 'Government Steps Up Measures to Control Locust', *The Economic Times*, accessed 12 February 2022, https://economictimes. indiatimes.com/news/economy/agriculture/government-steps-up-measures-to-control-locust/articleshow/76045316.cms.

Stripped to its core, a liberal democracy has two core propositions for its citizens. It offers them the liberty to make their choices. And it seeks consent from them for any action that will impact them with a few identified exceptions. Simply put, the Constitution offers citizens freedom and guarantees them 'negative rights', i.e., the right not to be coerced.

Governments in India often don't see things this way though. There's always a feeling that citizens cannot handle this freedom and need to be protected from making wrong choices. This perhaps stems from the colonial hangover of seeing citizens as subjects who are illiterate and uninformed. The real solution of informing and empowering them so they can make their own choices appears like real work. Who wants to do that? The better option is to curtail choices or even eliminate them. Like the Hindi proverb goes, '*Na rahega baans, na bajegi baansuri*' (to treat the problem at its root). This is where bans come into play in our public policy. It is among the most favoured tools of the governments in India. Alcohol, food products, books, films, chemicals— we ban with abandon.

There are two perspectives we use here to think about the consequences of a ban. One, a ban stifles the freedom to act or speak for a citizen and eventually reduces the choices available to society. When you ban a book, the voice of the author is muzzled, and society loses the opportunity to hear that opinion. Two, a ban rarely eliminates a problem. Instead, it drives the market underground, turning ordinary citizens into criminals as they look for the banned object to satisfy their curiosity as to the reason for the ban.[6] This creates new incentives for rent-seeking by the State. Administering a ban diverts state capacity, which is already low in India from more important tasks. It is a lose-lose on all counts.

Yet, we have a long history of using bans. The ostensible reason is that the greater good will be served. A book might create social unrest. Alcohol will corrode the character of the society. These are all noble intentions but eventually yield bad outcomes. We rarely pause to weigh what we lose as a society when we ban something.

Tujhko Mirchi Lagi Toh Main Kya Karoon

Let's take the banning of a book or a film. This is quite common in India. The most famous instance of this was the banning of Salman Rushdie's *The Satanic Verses* in 1988. As the story goes, Khushwant Singh, the editor of the *Illustrated Weekly of India*, suggested the banning of the book in his review. This was taken up by Lok Sabha MP, Syed Shahabuddin, who petitioned the government to ban the book. The Rajiv Gandhi government promptly banned it. The book wasn't even released by then in India. Nobody, barring a handful of media people, possibly had read the book then. This Indian ban snowballed into a global controversy and in February 1989, Ayatollah Khomeini of Iran called

---

[6] It might seem like a black comedy but the ban of alcohol in Bombay mean that some entrepreneurs started manufacturing ear drops and eye drops with a large percentage of alcohol. Refer to Rohit De, *The People's Constitution* (Princeton University Press, 2018) for more details.

upon Muslims around the world to execute those involved with the book. Rushdie then went into hiding with the help of the British government. Over the next two years, there were riots, arson, and bombings across major cities in the world, all committed by people who had probably never read the book.

Over the past thirty-three years, the banning of *The Satanic Verses* has been used by various groups for their ends. It has been cited as an example of repression of free speech, of Muslim appeasement in India, and for seeking bans on books written about Hindu deities. With the benefit of hindsight, it is clear that the long-term impact of the ban has been bad for society. Yet we persist in banning books and films because we believe our people are emotional and unreasonable who cannot just ignore a work of art that isn't to their liking.

There is a conundrum here. Everyone believes free speech is the foundation of our liberty. It therefore follows that we all have the right to offend. But we don't want others to offend us—'my right to free speech is precious but yours is problematic.' How and why have we arrived here?

Before we proceed, a point of clarification. We are talking about free speech limitation in the context of the State or the government here—that is to what extent the government should intervene on freedom of speech and expression. This is different from the conduct of private people or entities. A publishing house is free to drop an author or a book if it deems fit. Some other publishing house will pick it up. Similarly, you are free to not read a book that offends you. There are many other books in this world.

John Stuart Mill's classic text *On Liberty* (1859) is a good starting point for a discussion on free speech. He makes a compelling moral argument for free speech and its benefits to society. Mill argues:

> If all mankind minus one were of one opinion, and only one person were of the contrary opinion, mankind would be no more justified in silencing that one person than he, if he had the power, would be justified in silencing mankind.[7]

Mill offers three reasons to support this argument. First, human beings aren't infallible. We can or should never be certain about our truths. Second, there's a possibility that the contrary opinion of that one person was the truth. Society will be better off hearing that truth. Socrates and Galileo were holding blasphemous opinions during their time. Silencing them didn't help society. Third, even if the contrary opinion is false, it gives another kind of benefit to society. The airing of that view allows others to refute it. This strengthens the truth.

However, Mill understands this freedom can't be absolute. This is where the problem starts. Mill puts a condition on free speech:

> . . . the only purpose for which power can be rightfully exercised over any member of a civilized community, against his will, is to prevent harm to others.[8]

---

[7] James Stuart Mill, *On Liberty (1859)* (Batoche Books, 2001), 18, https://socialsciences.mcmaster.ca/econ/ugcm/3ll3/mill/liberty.pdf.

[8] Ibid., 13.

This is called the harm principle. In other words, your freedom to swing your fist ends where my nose begins. So, the question is what kinds of speech can cause harm? Mill considered this to be a narrow sliver restricted to any speech inciting a mob to harm someone. He stated:

> An opinion that corn-dealers are starvers of the poor, or that private property is robbery, ought to be unmolested when simply circulated through the press, but may justly incur punishment when delivered orally to an excited mob assembled before the house of a corn-dealer, or when handed about among the same mob in the form of a placard.[9]

For Mill, there's a context to free speech as seen above. If it leads to harm to others, there is a reason to curtail it. The problem is that the definition of the harm threshold and the context have changed over the years.

Three kinds of exceptions have arisen:

Hate speech: Any speech that targets a specific group and threatens to undermine the social structure should be limited. This is how the first-ever amendment to the Indian Constitution came about. A series of cases on freedom of speech were upheld by different courts, allowing organizations as diverse as the Rashtriya Swayamsewak Sangh (RSS) and its publication *Organiser* and *Cross Roads*—published by diehard communists—to express their views freely. Nehru and his cabinet amended Article 19 and

---

[9] Ibid., 52.

included 'reasonable restrictions' to freedom of speech
and expression in the interests of the State, public order,
decency, or morality.

Blasphemy: Any speech that hurts the core religious
beliefs of a group that could incite them to violent acts
have been placed under restriction. There is no clear line
here. Some groups tend to be more sensitive, and others
have started mimicking them. States have followed up
with laws placing restrictions on such expressions against
religious beliefs.

Psychological harm: Over time, the notion of psychological
harm caused by a speech or by words has crept into the
definition of harm. The libel laws of the UK where the truth
is secondary to the psychological harm (loss of reputation)
of a person was an early example of this tendency. The
current trend in college campuses in western democracies
where certain topics have been taken off the curriculum
because of complaints by students of being 'triggered' is a
manifestation of this harm.

The rapid spread of social media and smartphones have
compounded the problem of context. These platforms
programmatically nudge people to inhabit echo chambers
that reinforce their 'truths'. This makes them less sensitive to
any contrary opinion. The radically networked groups find
it easy to turn into online or offline mobs to go after their
opponents. The speed of information in these networks is
faster than the response time of the State, leading to real
harm in society. Also, the majoritarian trends seen in many
democracies in the past few years has exacerbated this

problem. The definition of the harm threshold is now held to ransom by the majority.

So, where does that leave us? First, we don't have to be free speech absolutists of any kind. But considering how far we have slipped on the definition of the harm principle, we must bat for free speech with rigour today without any kind of intervention by the State. Any nuance of harm can be accepted only after we start with the axiomatic belief that free speech is a virtue under all circumstances. Else, it will be a series of compromises all the way.

Second, the anxieties about social media platforms and fake narratives and their harms are valid. But to choose what's fake or real and to let the State, which is an interested party in this debate, decide this is fraught with more risks. The counter to them must emerge from challenging them with truth and increasing public awareness. Censoring will cut both ways.

Third, we underestimate the long-term preference of society for decency, etiquette, and truth. We haven't legislated to ensure we don't abuse our neighbours in daily conversations or behave rudely in public. For instance, there's no law prohibiting the usage of the n-word in the US. But no decent person uses it. We maintain a decorum because most of us have an intrinsic understanding of the limits of the right to offend. Those who don't understand this tend to fall in line over time through the social mechanism.

Free speech is under threat from both sides of the ideological spectrum. There's the right-wing lynch mob, fake news farms, and abusive trolls on one end and the easy-to-get-triggered, check-your-privilege, de-platforming mob on the other. This is the slippery slope we have gone down once we started broadening the definition of the harm principle. It has hurt all of us.

Gangajal

But a ban is not just a restriction of our freedoms. It often is just a bad policy move whose unintended outcomes play out over time. We have taken an everyday example of a ban below to unspool this for you.

This is what the Union government proposed to ban in July 2020—Reverse Osmosis (RO) purifiers that demineralize water. As long-time connoisseurs of the language in government notifications, we reproduce excerpts below from the twelve-page document from the Ministry of Environment & Forest (MoEF) including Schedule 1 (section C, subsection 2). The prose is incandescent. And we also learnt from it what flocculation is. No, it is not what it sounds like:

> Installation or use of Membrane-based Water Purification System (MWPS) shall be prohibited, at the Point of Use or at the Point of Entry for purification of supplied water which is subjected to conventional flocculation, filtration and disinfection process or is from any sources which are in compliance with acceptable limit for drinking water prescribed by Bureau of Indian Standard 10500:2012.
>
> . . .
>
> BIS shall develop system and procedure to monitor, assess, certify the type and process integrity of the MWPS for compliance of provision of Schedule – I in consultation with CPCB. The validity of the certificate shall be as

prescribed in the guidelines prepared by BIS. The certificate shall have mention of date of certification, its validity, treatment technology used, recovery efficiency, and other terms and conditions as specified by BIS. BIS shall develop such system and procedure within a period of six months from the date of publication of this notification in official gazette.[10]

The draft notification had twenty-five items of definition and a list of fifty-nine responsibilities spread across eleven different players (Port Authority also featured among them). We tried understanding the rationale for the ban.

RO purifiers reduce total dissolved solids (TDS) in water. This process leads to water wastage. Some estimates suggest for every 100 litres of water purified, about 80 litres of water is wasted.

In locations where the TDS in piped water is already below 500 milligrams per litre (mg/litre), RO water purifiers might demineralize the water. This isn't good. Some minerals in water are important for the human body. Taking them out leads to mineral deficiency with long-term health implications. Hence the ban on RO water purifiers in locations where TDS is below 500 mg/litre. The notification has the usual quota of coercion applied to every stakeholder in the ecosystem—domestic and industrial users, manufacturers, importers, and water supply agencies. The National Green Tribunal (NGT) had given the government until the end of 2020 to implement the

---

[10] Draft Notification issued by the Ministry of Environment, Forests and Climate Change, Government of India.

ban. In a previous hearing, NGT had sent out a tough message to the Ministry of Environment & Forest (MoEF) to implement the ban. It had warned:

> . . . failure of the concerned officers to comply with directions of the tribunal can lead to punishment under Section 26 of NGT Act, 2010 also by the way of imprisonment, and that December 31 is the deadline for MoEF to comply else from January 1, concerned officer in charge will not be entitled to draw salary and further coercive measures may be considered.

There. You can draw some solace. The ministry is getting coerced too.

The fifty-nine responsibilities outlined in the notification include a bewildering array of inspections, permissions, reports, licenses, standards, monitoring mechanisms, and deadlines. To wit, this will need enormous state capacity across agencies to implement.

Like we said earlier, we have a ban in India almost every week. But once in a while, there comes a ban so perfect for explaining what ails policymaking in India that we can actually light three *diyas* (always in triplicate) at the altar of our public policy *kul-devata* to express our gratitude. This was that kind of a ban.

On the surface, it appears like the right thing to do. Anyone who has an RO purifier at home (and who hasn't one?) is aware of the water that's wasted. The intention of the ban seems good.

But as we never tire of emphasizing, intention counts for nothing in public policy. We will see why in this case.

Shankkar Aiyar's book *The Gated Republic* has a self-explanatory subtitle—'India's Public Policy Failures and Private Solutions'. The book begins with making a case for the role of the State in providing for education, health, security, water, and electricity. Aiyar quotes Adam Smith from *The Wealth of Nations*:

> . . . the sovereign or the government has three duties of 'great importance' to attend to. First, the duty of protecting the society from violence and invasion of other independent societies; secondly, the duty of protecting, as far as possible, every member of the society from the injustice or oppression of every other member of it, or the duty of establishing an exact administration of justice; and, thirdly, the duty of erecting and maintaining certain public works and certain public institutions which it can never be for the interest of any individual, or small number of individuals, to erect and maintain; because the profit could never repay the expense to any individual or small number of individuals, though it may frequently do much more than repay it to a great society.[11]

Aiyar has two central arguments in the book. First, the Indian State has 'flailed or failed' in the 'third duty' outlined by Adam Smith above. The history of independent India is dotted with public policy failures in delivering basic governance. Second, the citizens of India have normalized these failures and the moment they can afford it, they

---

[11] Shankkar Aiyar, *The Gated Republic: India's Public Policy Failures and Private Solutions* (HarperCollins Publishers India, 2020).

check out from the State. They find private solutions for education, water, electricity, and security while paying their taxes to a State that should be providing these. Aiyar calls it a 'ceaseless secession':

> The voice of the average Indian is not heard and the wait has been too long. And so Indians are desperately seceding, as soon as their income allows, from dependence on government for the most basic of services—water, health, education, security, power—and are investing in the pay-and-plug economy.[12]

Aiyar starts his book looking at the promise of clean, drinking water to every Indian. He is unrelenting in his analysis of many policy failures, unfulfilled promises, and the sheer incompetence of the State in managing water and its supply in India. There are delightful stories on how private solutions like bottled water, RO purifiers, and overhead water tanks emerged to fill in for the State. But these have further exacerbated the class divide, leaving a large section of the population in abject 'water poverty'. The NITI Aayog's Composite Water Management Index 2018 report that the book quotes sums up the water crisis in India:

> India is currently suffering from the worst water crisis in its history. In its review of states across nine broad sectors of water management, it found 60 per cent of the states, home to over half the 1.3 billion populace, performing poorly. Elaborating on the crisis, it presented

---

[12] Ibid., 6.

a shocking parade of facts—600 million people face high to extreme water stress; about two million people die every year due to inadequate access to safe water; twenty-one cities, including Delhi, Bengaluru, Chennai and Hyderabad, are expected to run out of groundwater by 2020, affecting 100 million people; 75 per cent of households do not have drinking water on premise; 84 per cent of rural households do not have piped water access; 70 per cent of our water is contaminated; India is ranked 120 among 122 countries in the water quality index.[13]

Now think of the proposed RO purifier ban. Instead of using the scarce state capacity that we have to solve the acute water crisis described above, we are going to expend capacity by regulating a water purifier ban. Does the ban address the reason why we have the biggest market for water purifiers in the world? The answer is no. Yet, instead of solving the root cause of the problem, we are redressing the symptoms. This is the kind of misguided overreach that has rendered the State ineffective in solving the problems of basic governance. The State spreads itself so thin that it has no agency, and it becomes invisible to people.

Let's give this good-intentioned policy the benefit of the doubt. Assume the whole of India stops using RO purifiers. Would we have solved India's water problem? The answer is no. Look at the chart below.

---

[13] Ibid., 58.

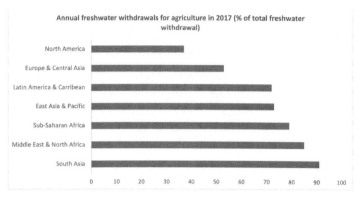

Source: World Bank[14]

Domestic consumption accounts for 2 per cent of all freshwater consumption. A minuscule amount of that 2 per cent would be 'wasted' by RO purifiers. Imagine, we are trying to put in a regulatory mechanism to fix this minute problem. You will now appreciate what the idiom 'missing the wood for the trees' means.

A few of you may argue that we shouldn't conflate the two problems and that two wrongs don't make a right. We should still support a ban on RO purifiers. We disagree. The ban won't be effective because the weak State won't be able to enforce it. It will create newer problems. The problems of implementation are staring at us.

The first problem is in defining which locations have TDS of less than 500 mg/l in our cities and towns. Almost every city or town in India now depends on private water

[14] Tariq Khokhar, 'Chart: Globally, 70% of Freshwater Is Used for Agriculture', *World Bank Blogs*, accessed 12 February 2022, https://blogs.worldbank.org/opendata/chart-globally-70-freshwater-used-agriculture.

tankers run by the 'tanker mafia' for its water needs. So, you might live in say, Koramangala, Bangalore that might have TDS below 500 but the tanker supplying to your housing complex might be sourcing its water from a location that has TDS above 500. So, what should you do? Trust the tanker water and drink it directly because RO purifiers are banned in your locality? This will just add more misery to citizens.

Second, manufacturers will continue to make RO purifiers because there's a market for them in areas with TDS greater than 500 mg/l. So, these purifiers will be available in the market. Will the government then do a house-to-house inspection to find who is installing these purifiers in a location where it is banned? Or will the manufacturer or the retail outlet ask you for a home address proof before selling a purifier? Who will monitor them? This Russian nested dolls of one entity monitoring another which in turn is monitored by a third is a never-ending spectacle in Indian public life. Airport security checks are a great example of this.

Third, in locations that have a TDS greater than 500 mg/l, the RO purifiers will continue to be used and the water wasted. How does a partial ban help? What's the net water savings here?

This brings us to the next set of questions. Why then do we have this ban? Who mooted it? And how could it have been passed?

Shruti Rajagopalan and Alex Tabarrok in their paper, 'Premature Imitation and India's Flailing State' offer some answers. They argue that Indian elites love to imitate the more developed countries in adopting sophisticated policies that have limited benefits in a country at India's stage of development. This leads to an already weak State saddled with a premature load. They write:

> As a result, the Indian elite initiates and supports policies that appear to it to be normal even though such policies may have little relevance to the Indian population as a whole and may be wildly at odds with Indian state capacity.
>
> This kind of mimicry of what appear to be the best Western policies and practices is not necessarily ill-intentioned. It might not be pursued to pacify external or internal actors, and it is not a deliberate attempt to exclude the majority of citizens from the democratic policy-making process. It is simply one by-product of the background within which the Indian intellectual class operates.[15]

The efforts by the NGOs to ban RO water purifiers seem to be animated by these imitation instincts. It is well-intentioned but irrelevant.

So, what we will end up with is that the State will struggle to regulate the ban, domestic and commercial users will find private alternatives to circumvent the ban, manufacturers will struggle with additional State intervention, and there will be newer opportunities for rent-seeking by officials who will monitor, inspect, certify, and apply fines.

---

[15] Shruti Rajagopalan and Alexander Tabarrok, 'Premature Imitation and India's Flailing State', *The Independent Review* 24, no. 2, 2019, 165–86.

Nothing will change—the amount of water wasted in India, the scarcity of water for people who can't afford bottled water or a purifier, the continued dependence in cities on the water mafia who have political patronage, and the annual cycle of droughts and floods in India. Citizens will continue to secede from the State to their gated mini republics.

All because the State loves to solve problems it can. Instead of those it must.

How did the story pan out on the pesticides ban we wrote at the start of this chapter?

Shortly after the notification, in June, the chemicals ministry wrote to the agricultural ministry calling the ban sudden and highlighting its negative impact on exports. The agricultural ministry lifted the ban on the exports of these pesticides. It also extended the date to submit comments on the notification from forty-five days to three months. Then the Association of Sustainable and Holistic Agriculture (ASHA) accused the chemicals and fertilizers ministry of selling out to the industry lobby.

So, what did we learn? First, the ban on the pesticides in May 2020 was based on an expert committee report of December 2015. It took four and a half years for the recommendations to be turned into a policy. A fine example of speed in policymaking. After all these years when the guidelines were put out, another ministry of the government objected to it immediately. Was the ban decided by one ministry without consulting the most obvious ministry? In four and half years after the expert committee report, did no one in the agricultural ministry think—since we are banning pesticides, maybe we should ask the chemicals ministry what they think about it? Also, if they missed consulting the most obvious ministry, what are the odds that other stakeholders outside of the government were sought for their views? Is there such a thing as stakeholder mapping among the policymaking tools used by the government?

Plus, we also got a well-meaning advocacy group into the mix. This will go down the legal path and, who knows, another four and half years might pass before we see the end of this.

14

The Tyranny of Fixing Prices

In Vedanta philosophy, God is *sarvagna* (all knowing), *sarv-vyapak* (omnipresent), and *antaryami* (an inner witness of your thoughts and actions). By this definition, the modern conception of God in line with our Vedic tradition will be the Indian State. It is *sarv-vyapak*, and it struts around like it is *sarvagna* and *antaryami*. Nowhere does this become more apparent than how the State randomly fixes prices based on a vague notion of 'public interest'.

In Chapters 2 and 3 of the book, we discussed how We, the People, think of the State as the primary troubleshooter for all our problems, even though the Indian State doesn't have the capacity to perform the very functions explicitly meant for it such as law and order, policing, and public service provision.

This acceptance of an expansive State means that it intervenes often in the lives of ordinary Indians. By projecting itself as acting in a vaguely defined 'public interest', governments can get away with proverbial murder.

Of the many tools at its disposal, price-fixing is close to the Indian government's heart.

Price-fixing refers to administering the prices of goods and services. From movie tickets to air tickets, and from house rents to the paracetamol tablet in your medicine cabinet, India's governments over the years have developed a knack for price-fixing. Like the salt in your biryani, 'prices should be neither too high nor too low but just perfect' is a widely shared belief within and outside the Indian State.

Now, let's take a step back and think about what prices do. You'll realize that there is something truly magical about the price system. A well-functioning price system is actually a decentralized coordination mechanism. This was the argument of Friedrich Hayek's seminal paper 'The Use of Knowledge in Society'.[1] In an era when the idea of central planning was the dominant narrative, Hayek argued that a well-functioning price system can do what a centrally planned economy can't. Merely knowing the price of a commodity—and nothing else—acts as a signal for both consumers and suppliers to change their behaviour in important ways. For example, high prices signal the consumer to regulate consumption but also provide an opportunity for suppliers to increase their production. One price that communicates the underlying scarcity of a good can optimally coordinate the actions of all the participants in that good's market. This is an incredible insight.

---

[1] Friederich A. Hayek, 'The Use of Knowledge in Society', *The American Economic Review* 35, no. 4, 1945, 519–30, https://doi.org/10.1257/aer.98.5.i.

Recollect what happened in the early days of the COVID-19 pandemic. There was a sudden increase in the demand for cloth masks. This spurt caused the prices of masks to rise. Soon enough, garment manufacturers sensed the opportunity. Shirt and trouser manufacturers started making masks instead. With new suppliers in the market, the variety and quality of masks on offer improved. By the time the second wave hit, masks were available at multiple price points at your local street corner. All this happened without any government company entering the market.

Now imagine how this would've worked if the government had tried to control the prices on cloth masks in the supposed interest of the public. With prices being capped, garment manufacturers would have had no incentive to change their assembly lines for producing masks. Next, there would be no incentive to manufacture masks that might provide additional features at higher costs—like the masks that now have strings going around the head instead of the ones that gnash against the ears, or the washable 'N95-like' masks that are a better alternative than cloth masks.

However, the price system is rarely allowed to operate this well in India. Our movies are filled with instances of high prices as evidence of something evil that must be rectified through price control. The idea that governments must regulate prices of all things important is deeply ingrained. No wonder surge pricing by taxi aggregators is met with calls for government action.

So, in this chapter, let's look at examples that can help us explain why price-fixing, not a high price, is evil.

Example 1: The Case of the Delhi Smog

The infamous Delhi smog makes its unmistakable presence felt every year. There are many reasons for this phenomenon, an important one being the burning of crop residue in neighbouring states. Of late, the dominant narrative has turned to blaming unthinking farmers who carelessly burn crop residue instead of disposing it in less-polluting ways. However, few of us stop to think that the buck stops with a price-fixing tactic that's been central to Indian governments—the Minimum Support Price (MSP).

Let's trace the causal chain for the smog backwards to understand the connection.

First, we now know that the Delhi smog is caused at least partially by crop residue being burnt on many farms *simultaneously* over a short time period so that farms can be cleared up to sow wheat in the first week of November.

That should make us ask, why can't the burning of crop residue be staggered in time? Turns out, that's not possible because the kharif crop (paddy) is sown only after June 15. This leads to a delayed output leaving farmers with very little time to clear the field for the next crop. Hence, crop burning.

That, in turn, leads us to the next question: why can't the paddy crop be sown earlier? That's where our favourite protagonist—the government—comes in. The government of Punjab passed a Punjab Preservation of Subsoil Water Act in 2009 that prohibits paddy transplantation before June 15. If this rule is violated, paddy nurseries can be destroyed. Repeated violations can also lead to disconnection of electricity supply of offending farmers, which given that farmers have to use electricity for tube wells, can be a huge inconvenience.

That should spark another question, what explains these rules prohibiting paddy cultivation before June 15? Turns out, this ban is intended to save water during the peak summer season. Paddy farms apparently need 4500 litres/hectare water in April as against 3000 litres/hectare in June because of evaporation in the summer months.

That, in turn, should make us ask: why are farmers growing rice in a water-scarce area? To which the answer is a price signal known as the Minimum Support Price (MSP). The MSP is a government-assured minimum price guarantee on the sale of particular crops. Assured procurement of rice by the government on behalf of the Food Corporation of India (FCI) incentivizes over-production of rice even in areas not well-suited to the crop.[2]

We can't be too smug in uncovering this connection. The MSP was introduced at a time when India was struggling with food shortages. So, the government thought it would be a good idea to incentivize farmers by promising a minimum procurement threshold price. Given the limited capacity of the government to procure grains, it only meant that a few farmers in some states were able to take advantage of this policy.

---

[2] We came across this linkage between MSP and the smog in this article by well-known agriculture economist, Ashok Gulati, 'From Plate to Plough: Sowing Paddy, Reaping Smog', *The Financial Express* (blog), 11 November 2019, https://web.archive.org/web/20201116033518/https://www.financialexpress.com/opinion/from-plate-to-plough-sowing-paddy-reaping-smog/1760567/.

This is not to say that the government should've done nothing. Through a focus on high-yielding varieties of seeds, irrigation facilities, fertilizers, and mechanization, the Green Revolution significantly improved the productivity of Indian agriculture and helped India overcome food insecurity to a large extent. Where the government went astray was in deploying a highly interventionist tool like MSP that is partly responsible for the current environmental and economic concerns with Indian agriculture. The lesson: it's prudent to be careful before changing incentives of millions of producers and consumers by setting prices.

Example 2: The Evils of Rent Control

Next, we turn to a case where prices have an upper threshold. Economists call it the price ceiling. There's popular support for capping prices across sectors. Despite economists telling us that price ceilings lead to poor product quality, shortages, or both, we support government policies that set an upper limit for the prices of commodities *we* want.

One of the oft-repeated tropes in many movies centred on Mumbai covers one kind of price ceiling quite well—rent control.

The Bombay Rent Control Act of 1940 is a tourist attraction that you can't miss when you go around the southern end of the maximum city. Almost every building is a living ruin. It is like Rome except people still live in those ruins. The Act froze the rental rates for about sixty years. All kinds of distortions followed. The supply of rental accommodation went down; landlords had no incentive to repair, paint, or maintain their properties; tenants lived in fear of a building collapse during monsoons; sub-tenancy and black market flourished; and legal cases multiplied, dragging on for years. The cascading impact of this led to supply shortages of housing in Mumbai and drove up the real estate rates over the years.

Saeed Mirza's 1984 film *Mohan Joshi Haazir Ho* (MJHH) narrates one such story of rent control. Like many other takes on this issue, he gets the story right, but the diagnosis is totally wrong. Bhisham Sahni and Dina Pathak play an old Mumbai couple who sue their landlord (Amjad Khan) for letting their building fall into complete disrepair. The landlord isn't a great moral specimen of the human species. But he is also a victim of the Rent Control Act. He couldn't care less for the upkeep of the building considering his rental income. The old couple hires a pair of not-so-honest lawyers (Naseeruddin Shah and Satish Shah chewing up the scenery) while the landlord brings on Rohini Hattangadi. The lawyers quickly form a cartel and drag the case for years, milking their clients dry. Finally, the court official goes for a physical examination of the property that has been temporarily spruced up by the landlord. The court dismisses the case. In a memorable final act, Sahni bangs his head against the props that are holding up the building till they give away and the whole structure collapses on him.

You'd think the landlord and the lawyers were the villains of the piece. But as we know, they were only playing to their incentives. The real culprit was the State. It had blood on its hands.

Instead of bringing down rents by allowing more supply of housing, the rent control has not only hurt Mumbaikars, but it has also capped the promise the city held for millions.

Example 3: Airfare Caps

You might think an elite service like air travel can surely have prices set only on the basis of available demand and supply. You would be wrong.

If you tried to book flight tickets during the pandemic in 2020 and 2021, you would have noticed a strange and unpleasant phenomenon—not only were the ticket prices high across the board, but all airlines seemed to be charging exactly the same high price.[3]

It's likely that you would've shrugged this occurrence off by blaming the government for raising taxes on fuel and shelled out the ticket money anyway. But you would only be half-right. Turns out, a few restrictions on prices that the Ministry of Civil Aviation had imposed since May 2020 were in place for nearly a year and a half. These restrictions played havoc with the consumers, airlines, and airports. Here's how.

Airline ticket prices in normal circumstances are determined by demand and supply considerations. Price broadly reflects the scarcity of the seat you occupy. That's why you would have encountered significantly higher prices closer to the travel date when fewer seats are left. This situation changed in the wake of the first wave of the pandemic when the union government intervened in both the pricing and capacity of airlines.

Specifically, the government put three restrictions in place.

---

[3] One of us (Pranay) wrote about this convoluted policy. Pranay Kotasthane, 'Why the Govt Shouldn't Decide What You Pay for an Air Ticket', *The Times of India*, 15 August 2021.

One, it put a cap on the total capacity that airlines can deploy. Note, this didn't mean a restriction on the number of passengers in a flight but a restriction in terms of the total number of flights that an airline can operate. The stated intent of this capacity restriction was to discourage discretionary travel.

Two, the Ministry of Civil Aviation imposed a ceiling on the ticket price depending on the sector and travel time. This was apparently done to protect consumer interest so that airlines don't charge higher prices to compensate for the capacity restrictions.

Three, the government also imposed a price floor on the ticket meaning that tickets couldn't be sold below a particular price even if the airlines wished to do so! The stated intent of this restriction was to protect financially weaker and smaller airlines.

What began as a COVID-19 emergency measure to discourage travel took the shape of a hydra-headed policy aiming to solve many problems at the same time.

An unintended consequence of this intervention was rent seeking. Rent-seekers often distort government policies to serve their own interests. And that was the real reason behind these three-fold restrictions. The capacity restrictions and price floors appeared to be a clientelistic policy to clip the wings of the larger players in the market and give breathing space to the financially weaker airlines.

Public policy analysis differentiates pro-business policies from pro-market ones. The former means aiding specific companies while the latter means that the government's role should only be limited to ensuring fair competition.

These restrictions were pro-business and anti-market. They should worry us for three reasons.

First, the direct cost of price regulation was borne by the consumer—ticket prices of most airlines conveniently settled to just below the price ceiling regardless of how early you booked your tickets. Moreover, these restrictions further damaged the fiscal position of the then government-owned Air India, which was losing nearly Rs 20 crores of Indian taxpayers' money every day.

Second, these restrictions established a precedent for the government to intervene in the interests of 'financially weaker' players, even if that comes at the expense of the consumer. The government that starts setting prices to protect weaker airlines might as well extend its 'protection' to weaker players in other sectors, further harming consumers.

Third, these restrictions prevented an already beleaguered sector from bouncing back. Not just airlines but airports faced higher losses due to lower footfalls. Airport Council International, a global trade body representing airport interests, calculated a loss of $129 billion in 2020 and an estimated $108 billion in 2021.[4] There were job losses across the globe in this sector. In an already dire situation, these restrictions further depressed recovery in India.

Once testing and vaccination were available, the goal of preventing spread through air travel could have been achieved by mandating COVID-19 detection test results or

---

[4] 'The Impact of COVID-19 on the Airport Business and the Path to Recovery', *ACI World* (blog), accessed 15 February 2022, https://aci.aero/2021/07/14/the-impact-of-covid-19-on-the-airport-business-and-the-path-to-recovery-2/.

fully vaccinated certificates for air travel. Price bands and capacity caps did not serve this purpose. The government stuck with price controls anyway.

Example 4: Stent Pricing Caps

In 2017, the National Pharmaceutical Pricing Authority (NPPA) slashed the prices of high-end stents by nearly 85 per cent. People cheered; this price reduction will make stents more accessible, or so they believed. The long-run effects of such drastic price impositions are still underway, but the trends are clear.

As one can easily anticipate, this has led to a change in the basket of suppliers. The companies supplying specialized imported stents, costing far above the price cap, have drastically reduced imports. The result is lower consumer choice for all Indians. While the rich can still afford to fly to another country to get a better-quality stent, ordinary Indians have been left to contend with lesser choice and inferior quality. Moreover, while the higher quality suppliers have bowed out, Chinese stent makers have rushed in to fill the gap.

While some reports suggest that more Indians opted for stents in 2017 once prices were slashed, such analyses do not account for the long-run harmful consequences listed above. If providing cheap stents was a policy priority, the better alternative would've been for the government to procure stents in bulk using competitive bidding, as China did. Instead, by imposing price controls, the government washed its hands off and left heart-ailment prone Indians worse off.

Example 5: Schooling in Profits

The education sector is even more prone to price controls. Not only is for-profit education not allowed in India, but governments also never miss a chance to fix the fees of private schools. For instance, the Karnataka education department 'slapped' show-cause notices on 164 schools for increasing fees for the academic year 2020–21.[5] The Department of Public Instruction (DPI) had prohibited private school managements from increasing tuition fees by the usual 15 per cent because of the financial crisis faced by families in the lockdown.

Let's unpack this example a bit. In the first two months of the COVID-19 pandemic, the schools must have saved a bit on electricity, water, and some consumables (chalks, markers, chemicals, lab instruments, housekeeping, etc.). Based on the spending large corporate offices have on utilities and housekeeping, it's difficult to see them saving anything more than 5–7 per cent on these items. In those two months, schools also digitized a lot of their content, bought licenses of a learning management platform, linked it to a videoconferencing platform and trained all their teachers in online teaching. These things, unfortunately, do cost a bit. Moreover, schools will have to reconfigure classes to adhere to social-distancing guidelines, sanitize the school more often, possibly hire more teachers (because the class

---

[5] Ralph Alex Arakal, 'Bengaluru: Over 900 Complaints Filed against Private Schools over Fee Hike', *The Indian Express* (blog), 22 May 2020, https://indianexpress.com/article/cities/bangalore/bengaluru-private-school-fee-hike-6422381/.

size has shrunk), and spend more on any snacks or drinks they give at school once the schools reopen.

Should the schools compromise on these areas because the fees are capped now? Or, should we bring up that familiar Indian argument—they should make lesser 'profits'? Who determines what's the right level of profit? The ministry or the market?

Example 6: 'Market-Based Pricing' with Government Characteristics

Did you know that the price of a paracetamol tablet in your medicine cabinet is capped at approximately Rs 2 by the government? Nearly 200 companies produce paracetamol under different brand names in India and such levels of competition would've kept the price of paracetamol low in any case.[6] What then explains the price cap?

Turns out that not just paracetamol, nearly 14 per cent of drugs by value and 25 per cent by volume in India fall under price controls.[7] Not only are their prices capped, but the mechanism used for capping is disingenuously labelled 'market-based pricing'. Essentially, the government

[6] Prabha Raghavan and Anil Sasi, 'Short-Supply Covid Vaccines Outliers in Govt's Spirited Price Cap Push', *The Indian Express*, 16 May 2021, https://indianexpress.com/article/india/short-supply-covid-vaccines-outliers-in-govts-spirited-price-cap-push-7316704/.

[7] Viswanath Pilla, 'Explainer: How Drug Prices Are Regulated in India', Moneycontrol, accessed 15 February 2022, https://www.moneycontrol.com/news/business/explainer-how-drug-prices-are-regulated-in-india-4606751.html.

is actively distorting market prices and yet is successful in passing the blame on markets for the resultant price rise!

Market-based pricing of pharmaceuticals here obviously doesn't mean that a drug can be priced on the basis of demand and supply alone. Instead, it just means that the price cap will be calculated by averaging prices of brands that hold at least a 1 per cent share of the market for the formulation.

Anticipating the unintended consequences of such a policy is not difficult. One, price caps disincentivize differentiation and innovation. Why would any new company invest in creating a new formulation when it cannot reap the benefits?

Two, price caps foster collusion and rent-seeking. With new entrants impeded from disrupting the sector, incumbents can benefit by colluding with each other. By collectively and incrementally increasing the price of their brand, the price cap threshold can still be pushed up.[8]

And three, the engineered market-based pricing deepens the scepticism Indian consumers have with the price system. No wonder that an ordinary Indian intuits that market-based price is just a euphemism for unreasonable price hikes.

Another sector where the government passes off its active price distortion as a market-based mechanism is in fuel pricing. Since 2010 and 2014, the prices of petrol and diesel have been deregulated respectively. If the markets

---

[8] Rhea Reddy Lokesh, 'The Anti-Competitive Effect of Price Controls: Study of the Indian Pharmaceutical Industry', *World Competition* 43, no. 2, 1 June 2020, https://kluwerlawonline.com/journalarticle/World+Competition/43.2/WOCO2020014.

were truly allowed to operate, petrol and diesel prices should have hit an all-time low over the last few years because of the excess supply. More recently, the COVID-19 pandemic even depressed the demand. And yet, petrol prices hit a century because the government more than compensated for the drop in market prices by increasing the tax rate on the two fuels.

So, the next time you see sticky high prices, poor quality, or both, first investigate the government diktats on pricing in that sector. Distorting prices costs lives.

The Takeaway

Imposing price controls is a sign of both government hubris and sinisterness. Hubris because the government is pretending that it knows what price is just right, ignoring consumer demands or supplier incentives in the process. Also, because price control relies on the government having the capability to first enforce the price range. As we are all used to witnessing, with limited state capacity, the more likely outcome is that the price-controlled commodity finds its way to an underground, unregulated market at far higher prices. Price controls are sinister because their imposition indicates that the government is serious about consumer or supplier welfare but wants to get there without doing the tougher job of better procurement or increasing market competitiveness for the self-correcting processes to kick in.

15

Aatmanirbhar Is Everywhere

One of the many imprints the colonial experience has left on the Indian State and society is the mistrust of international trade. Every few years, import substitution returns with a bang in the policy discourse, albeit with a new name. The latest version goes by the name *aatmanirbharta*.

Self-Reliance in Facepalm Style

It is apt to start the discussion on *aatmanirbharta* by paying our respects to the original dramatic prophet of self-reliance and swadeshi *jagran* of post-independent India. Over seven years of what can mildly be described as frenzied creative itch, Manoj Kumar wrote, directed, and starred in four hugely successful films that were a cocktail of socialist nirvana, swadeshi self-sufficiency, nationalism, and intermittent bashing of western civilizational values and capitalism. That he did all of these with a persistent facepalm on the screen that may or may not have been ironic, added to his legend.

The most watchable of these is the *Jai Jawan, Jai Kisan* drama, *Upkar* (1967) where Bharat (Manoj Kumar) is the salt-of-the-earth-farmer working hard (and singing harder) on his fields while fending off the usual evil forces of agrarian capitalism—money lenders and middlemen.

He sends his younger brother (Prem Chopra) to *vilaayat* (abroad) for further studies but the *ahsaan-faraamosh* (ingrate) returns home 'de-sanskritized' and demands his share of the *zameen* (land). There's a *bantwaara* (land division), and some great overacting by Pran and a Manna Dey song later, Bharat is left distraught. That's when there's a *jung* (war, not the Swiss psychoanalyst).

Bharat trades his plough for the self-loading Ishapore rifle and is off responding to the call of duty. Prem Chopra meanwhile is doing what all agents of capital did in Hindi films—selling fake stuff, black marketing, and hoarding. Eventually, Bharat returns triumphant from the war and sets everything right. While *Upkar* was a celebration of the honest and hardworking kisan and jawan, it trained its guns firmly on the enemy outside.

The physical aggression of the neighbour and the cultural invasion of the West (in the form of Chopra) were viewed as inimical to our swadeshi ideals. This idea of the West being inferior in civilizational values was driven home with the subtlety of a sledgehammer in Manoj Kumar's next venture *Purab aur Paschim* (1970). The central plot revolves around reforming Saira Banu who, while living in London, has taken on Western values. No, she isn't shown reading Aristotle, Adam Smith, and Bertrand Russell while quoting Shakespeare and Keats. Instead, she smokes and drinks in short skirts and has a bunch of sexually liberated friends. This was the *pashchimi sabhyata* (Western civilization) problem. Manoj Kumar (Bharat) eventually brings her to India, and she is 'reformed' by Bharat—the man and the nation.

Almost half a century later, there's still a huge undercurrent of these sentiments in India. Don't believe us? Watch Akshay Kumar movies. This notion of being culturally superior but having been robbed of our due place in the world is quite strong. Every single achievement of the people of Indian origin is seen as a validation of this. Any acknowledgement of namaste, yoga, or ayurveda by the West is regarded as a belated testament to our glorious past. This revanchist belief in our superiority is then used to drive half-baked ideas around self-reliance, localization, and eschewing 'liberal' Western values.

There's some merit in using the past (real or imagined) to rally a nation around. This has to be channelled towards nation–building and societal progress that's substantial and equitable. It is easy to overdose on the past and to use it to settle current political scores instead. Self-reliance is a worthy goal to pursue but blended with excessive self-worth, it can lapse into a pursuit of a utopian autarky. That's the real danger of this mindset.

The world will acknowledge India as a worthy power through its actions and their outcomes. The evangelizing of our cultural strengths is best achieved through a strong economy and an open, transparent, and diverse society that stands apart from others. There's a film somewhere in there that needs to be made and deserves to be seen by us all.

Films aside, let's return to the question of self-reliance. To what extent does it make sense?

What Is '*Aatmanirbharta*'?

Fundamentally, there's no reason why we shouldn't aim to be more self-reliant by making more products domestically. But like most things in life, we should be careful about how far we go with this philosophy. Taken to an extreme, this will lead to autarky.

Let's first look at what happens if we stretch self-reliance beyond economic reason. Consider your family as an economic unit. Maybe you run a company that manufactures solar panels and your spouse works for an IT services company as an engineer. You have school-going kids who are dependent on you for their needs. You employ a cook and domestic help at home. You and your spouse like spending time in your kitchen garden during your leisure hours. As your garden blooms with herbs, vegetables, and flowers, you realize the price you pay for them in the market is exorbitant compared to what it takes to grow them at home. You are soon questioning everything you buy from the market—milk, juices, clothes, soaps, food grains, your kids' tuition, and entertainment. Everything would be cheaper and safer if you made them at home. You can see where this is going. Would you start making all of them at home?

We are sure you find the question absurd. The obvious answer is no. Why? First, you don't have time to make all of them at home even if you devote all your spare time and consider putting your kids to work on them too. Also, you won't be good at raising cows, tailoring, or growing paddy in your garden. Lastly, you and your spouse are good at your jobs. If you spend your time learning more about your work, you will get richer rewards. In the language of economics, you enjoy a comparative advantage in doing your jobs well rather than growing paddy in your garden. So, it just doesn't make sense for you to make everything at home. Sure, you will still do a few things predominantly at home. For instance, you can't imagine eating restaurant food every day. So, you will cook food at home on most occasions. Or, maybe you will always use herbs from your garden rather than buying them from outside. But these will be limited based on your priorities.

It is actually not a huge leap of imagination to extend this model to a nation-state. There are natural resources, climate, land, technology, and people that any country is endowed with for it to use productively. A country gets better at producing a few goods or services over time while it either doesn't have the resources or the expertise in making others. So, it buys them from other countries that are good at making them. Now, it is possible that the country has spare resources (people or otherwise) that it can put to use to make a whole lot of things within its boundary. The question is which of these things should the country start making at home rather than buying from outside? The country can't indiscriminately decide to make every single product at home. The criteria to decide this could include—what it might be good at making based on its assessment of its capabilities, what it could make in large volumes so that it might even sell it to others and profit, and what could be high on priority for the safety and security of its citizens.

You will realize we have to carefully choose the areas we want to be self-reliant in. This will yield a smaller basket of products and services that we can target in being world-class producers.

We must not forget if we start closing our doors to others indiscriminately, they will start doing the same to us. This will be a zero-sum game. Specialization and comparative advantage are real constructs. They help everyone gain. It is obvious to us when we apply that to our daily lives at homes. It can seem a bit non-obvious when we think of it for a country as large as ours. But it is no different.

Consider another recent example. The FM, Nirmala Sitharaman, spoke for crores of Indians when she said, 'Ganesha idols made of clay have been traditionally bought from the local potters during Ganesh Chaturthi festival every year. But today, why even Ganesha idols are imported from China . . . why such a situation . . . can't we make a Ganesha idol from clay, is it the situation?'[1]

It is indeed 'the situation'. Let's think through this argument. China didn't start making Ganesha idols because they heard an *aakashvani* (voice from the sky) about Indians wanting Ganesha with Chinese characteristics.

It is important to remember here—countries don't trade between themselves; people do. Some years ago, a trader in India asked if China can make so many things cheap, can't they make Ganeshas too? This trader knew his market. Clay Ganesha idols costing Rs 1000 each would draw 200 customers who could afford them. That's a market size of

[1] '"Why Import Even Ganesha Idols from China": Nirmala Sitharaman in Push for Self-Reliance', *Hindustan Times*, 26 June 2020, https://www.hindustantimes.com/business-news/why-import-even-ganesha-idols-from-china-nirmala-sitharaman-in-push-for-self-reliance/story-zAbQw4b8vzH4GgM9ega6UI.html.

Rs 2 lakhs. But if Ganesha idols were priced at Rs 200, he reasoned, 2000 customers would buy them. That would double his market to Rs 4 lakhs.

Lord Ganesha will forgive us for saying this but demand for his idols is elastic in this great land of ours. So, the trader placed his order with his Chinese partner who started making Ganesha idols with Indian characteristics. If there are Indian makers of Ganesha idols today who can match China's prices, this trader will go to them. Else, if he is forced to sell only clay idols that are made in India at Rs 1000, the market will shrink back to Rs 2 lakhs because the demand for Ganesha is elastic. That will be bad for the trader and also customers who can't afford a clay Ganesha costing Rs 1000.

Now, you will ask the obvious question. If we support our makers of clay Ganesha, won't they become competitive over time? The answer is not quite. First, clay-Ganesha making is a labour-intensive process unlike the mass manufacturing of moulded Plaster of Paris (PoP) Ganesha. This means a single worker in China can produce a thousand Ganeshas every hour while a worker in India will struggle to make ten. Second, our laws don't encourage scale. We love small-scale industries in the mistaken belief they are good for small manufacturers. They are not. Ganesha, *diyas*, *agarbattis* are all categorized in the *laghu udyog* (small-scale industries) category.

If we have to compete with China, we have to reform every single factor of production (land, labour, and capital) and simplify our laws. The industry needs *Vighneshwara* (another name of Ganesha; the remover of obstacles) to help solve the Ganesha problem. If we did that, we would have a comparative advantage on many of these products.

So, the answer to the problem of Ganesha with Chinese characteristics is with the finance minister, not with the traders. The traders should be asking questions to the finance minister about Ganesha.

China is no longer interested in making low-value goods at scale. They are moving up the manufacturing value chain that improves factor productivity and gives better realization. We should be competing with them there rather than trying to make Ganeshas and *agarbattis* at suboptimal scale.

Coming back to *aatmanirbhar*, there's a paradox in pursuing the goal of self-reliance for any country. One can be self-reliant at multiple levels. The highest level (level 1) of self-reliance is when an economic unit can produce and consume everything by itself. No country in the world has reached this level.

The slightly relaxed condition of self-reliance (level 2) is when one can afford to buy what they want irrespective of who produces it. This level can be achieved by becoming rich. If you are a rich country, you can pay to buy any service you want. Even if the service provider asks for more, you have the wherewithal to buy.

The lowest level of self-reliance (level 3) is when you cannot produce what you want and neither do you have the economic wherewithal to afford everything you wish. However, you do have enough diversified relationships with many producers of items that are really critical for you. So, you get what you want in your time of need from at least one of them.

India seems to aspire to reach level 2—the slightly relaxed condition of self-reliance. Fair enough. To get there, we need to become rich. To get rich, we need investment and expertise from abroad. In other words, India needs to rely on others. Just like Japan, China, Taiwan, and South Korea did on their journey to get rich. So, and this is important for us to understand, how we proceed towards becoming self-reliant is just as important as the goal. If we close our economy to the world in our search for level 1 self-reliance, we will fall short of achieving even level 3 self-reliance.

How *Aatmanirbharta* Might Play Out: Exhibit A

Mosquito-killing electronic racquets are ubiquitous in India. You will find them at homes, in shops, and with anyone who works outdoors in the evenings (watchmen especially). It's a lovely little contraption. Priced between Rs 200 and Rs 300, these can last a few months and once charged can be used for a few days uninterrupted. Importantly, they can be used outdoors, which makes them popular among those who work outdoors in the evenings. Indian traders mostly import these racquets (at a likely import price below Rs 120) and incur the import duties, costs of storing, and distributing these racquets far and wide.

But, the Directorate General of Foreign Trade (DGFT) in a notification dated 26 April 2021, prohibited the import of 'mosquito killer racquet' (their words) if the C.I.F. (cost, insurance, and freight) value is below Rs 121 per racquet.[2]

---

[2] Amendment in import policy and incorporation of a Policy Condition under HS Code 85167920 and 85167990 of Chapter-85 of ITC (IIS), 2017, Schedule-I (Import Policy), Ministry of Commerce & Industry, Government of India https://content.dgft. gov.in/Website/dgftprod/f42639ef-fe8b-4eb9-8558-435bf44f09ac/ Notification%20No.2%20english.pdf.

Of course, the process that led to the threshold being precisely Rs 121 is something we want to study when we grow up.

Anyway, the general idea appears to be to become *aatmanirbhar* in making these racquets and not allow cheap imports dumped in India. The unintended consequences of such steps are easy to anticipate.

Jugaad (improvization) will set in quickly. Traders will ask importers to increase the prices of their racquets above Rs 120 and over-invoice them. The same racquets will now cost more.

Once this jugaad is noticed, we might prohibit any import. There will then be a short-term shortage in the supply of racquets as we won't be able to up our domestic production capacity to meet demand. The price of racquets will go up.

In the absence of imports, there won't be an incentive for domestic manufacturers to compete with the best. This could lead to poor quality of racquets and a permanently higher price for them in future. In any case, there is a price floor set now of Rs 121. We have seen this film play out all through the 1960s–1980s across sectors.

Unfortunately, the poor will suffer the most. The short-term supply shortage will hurt and then the elevated prices will bite (apart from the mosquitoes whose karma is to bite). There's a lot that 'mosquito killer racquets' and their import prohibition tells about our public policy over the past seven decades.

The *'aatmanirbhar'* programme is turning into a case for higher import barriers, import substitution, and a desire to level the trade deficit. Colour TV import licenses are back. Swadeshi toys are the flavour of the month. There's even a plea to adopt dogs of Indian breed over their foreign counterparts.

How *Aatmanirbharta* Might Play Out: Exhibit B

As *aatmanirbhar* Bharat became the showpiece of India's economic package to combat the pandemic, the FM and the commerce minister repeatedly assured the nation that self-reliance isn't about closing ourselves to the world but dealing with it on our own terms.

But the reality is not very far off from the import substitution regime of the 1960–80s. In July 2020, the Directorate General of Foreign Trade (DGFT) announced restrictions on the import of colour TVs, rolling the clock back to more than two decades. Nostalgia is good but not of this kind. Importers of colour TVs had to seek a licence from DGFT. Another news report suggested that the government plans to increase tariffs and trade barriers on 300 imported products:

> The government document showed feedback had been sought from various Indian ministries to arrive at the list of around 300 products. India has increased duties on more than 3,600 tariff lines covering products from sectors such as textiles and electronics since 2014.[3]

[3] 'India Plans Extra Tariffs, Trade Barriers on 300 Imported Products: Sources', *The Economic Times*, 19 June 2020, https://economictimes.indiatimes.com/news/economy/foreign-trade/india-plans-extra-tariffs-trade-barriers-on-300-imported-products-sources/articleshow/76447119.cms.

Then came a notification from the ministry of commerce regarding the revision to the Public Procurement Order, 2017.[4] There have been significant changes to the government procurement policy based on this notification. It's a work of art.

- Each supplier will be categorized into either Class-1 local supplier, Class-2 local supplier, or non-local supplier based on the percentage of local content in their end product or service. Those with more than 50 per cent local content will be Class-1, between 20 per cent and 50 per cent will be Class-2, and the rest will be non-local suppliers.
- Each nodal ministry or department will have to now assess the domestic manufacturing capabilities, supplier base, and available capacity. This is to ensure they are able to assess the local capacity and competition for a good or service.
- Once the nodal ministry is convinced local capacity exists, only Class-1 suppliers will be eligible for the bids.
- In case local capacity doesn't exist, the L1 (the lowest-priced) bidder will be checked for local content. In case they are Class-1, the bid will be awarded to them. In case the L1 bidder isn't a Class-1 supplier, the closest-priced Class-1 bidder will be invited to match the L1 price up to a limit called the 'margin of purchase preference'. This is set at 20 per cent or above in the notification.

4 Public Procurement (Preference to Make in India), Order 2017, Revision, Ministry of Commerce & Industry, Government of India, https://dpiit.gov.in/sites/default/files/PPP%20MII%20Order%20 dated%204th%20June%202020.pdf.

It can't be lowered below this without approval from the minister.

In simple words, a Class-1 local supplier has the option of bidding at 20 per cent higher than the price of L1 bidder. If they do so, they win the bid. There's an additional wrinkle on whether the contract is 'divisible' or not, but you get the gist. The Class 1 local supplier gets an option to win the bid away from L1 while being priced 20 per cent higher.

There are other interesting bits in the notification. In case there are countries that bar Indian companies from bids in their domestic markets, the ministry plans a quid pro quo. Also, there are multiple provisions to fine and debar suppliers, random audits, and other usual list of definitions in the notification.

Looking at the above notification, it feels that we are moving towards the already tried and failed regime of import substitution for all goods and services. There's a sizeable section of the society and the State that believe our path to prosperity lies in being *aatmanirbhar*. We have a history of following such policies through the decades of 1960s–1980s. The slow growth rate of that era, the dismal quality of our products, and the long waiting time for products is still fresh in some of our memories. Maybe the new generation wants a taste of it. There's no reason why this time the outcome will be different.

We should make our firms competitive to take on suppliers in global markets. Instead, we are giving them crutches in the domestic market. The only way to win is for our firms to benchmark themselves to global standards and exceed them. It would have made some sense if the Class-1 local supplier was given the mandate to match the L1 rates and quality standards within two years of winning the bid or some clause of the kind that spurs global benchmarking. An uneven domestic playing field is just fooling ourselves about our capabilities.

Also, such guidelines further increase the load on state capacity and its discretionary powers. Nodal departments will decide on whether there's sufficient capacity in a particular sector for it to qualify for local content guidelines. There is no objective measure to arrive at this decision. Instead of competing with a foreign firm, domestic firms will lobby with the department to classify their sector differently and eliminate foreign competition. The determination of the percentage of local content and its audit and inspection will open up another window of rent-seeking among officials.

There are other practical challenges. It is possible for a supplier to certify they will have more than 50 per cent of local content at the start of the work. But it is anybody's guess if they struggle to keep local content above 50 per cent during the course of the work. The supplier might be debarred from future bids but will the current project be stopped and rebid? It is quite likely there will be an escalation of government costs because the local supplier will take time to become cost-effective in many sectors. This is an additional strain on an already bad fiscal situation.

Lastly, it is difficult to understand why we have included all goods, services, and works under these guidelines. We have limited availability of technical talent, trained resources, and capital. Instead of producing world-beating champions in a few selected sectors, we will end up producing a large number of mediocre suppliers who will compete locally and end up being subscale. They will deliver low returns on capital employed and stall labour productivity and wage increases.

There doesn't seem to be strong economic voices advising the government about the long-term implications of such moves. Or, maybe, the government knows about it but continues to pursue this course for short-term gains and for the inherent emotional appeal of such steps. The government and the people want to repeat history. Who are we to get in the way?

16

Aap Party Hain Ya Broker?

That line from Dibakar Banerjee's sleeper hit *Khosla Ka Ghosla* (2006) sums up our attitude to middlemen. We have an instinctive distrust of business or 'corporate'. But that's small change compared to our almost visceral antipathy to broker. We use *dalal* (literally, middleman) as a pejorative in polite conversations—it is someone who gets in the way of an honest transaction between two willing parties and takes a 'cut'. The Indian State and its governments follow this cue. From the trader at the Agricultural Produce Market Committee (APMC) mandis to agents representing companies that make defence equipment, the middleman is the easy policy target whose elimination is seen as necessary. Nobody can see what they produce or the labour they put in, yet they seem to corner most of the profits.

Take the case of the trader in the APMC mandis. The farm laws had an explicit goal of freeing the farmers from the *arhtiyas* (middlemen). These *arhtiyas* were seen to be exploitative agents who benefitted by using the existing laws to their advantage without adding any value in the process. If this were true, the farmers would have accepted the new laws. Instead, the farmers and *arhtiyas* got together and got the farm laws repealed. Were there mere vested interests of rich farmers at play here? Or, is there a value that the much-maligned broker or *dalal* brings to the table? What explains this behaviour?

India might be an extreme case but elsewhere in the world too, the intermediary isn't the most welcome of sights. For every business that has middlemen bringing the buyers and sellers together, there are scores of entrepreneurs building platforms to make them irrelevant. The billion-dollar start-up idea to disrupt any industry is to take out the intermediaries, drive the costs down, reduce 'friction', and offer customers a wider array of choices for free.

There are two questions that should interest us:

- Why did we have intermediaries in the first place if they add to friction, make a cut by buying low and selling high and, in general, are viewed unfavourably by everyone?
- Is real disintermediation possible in any marketplace?

The Economic Case for Brokers

The usual arguments made for an intermediary are quite intuitive. There is the market-making role, to begin with. Take flowers for example.

There are customers looking to buy flowers but who don't know flower-growing farmers. Even if they knew a few, those farmers might not be growing the variety of flowers the buyers need. In the same vein, the farmers won't know their likely buyers beyond their immediate vicinity. The 'transaction costs' of finding out each other for every individual farmer or buyer is just too high.

Brokers step in to create a market. They understand the demand of the customers located in a specific area, search for farmers who grow those types of flowers, take the risk of buying them, then transport them to a market close to the buyers, and provide an assortment of flowers as choices to the customers. There are various costs the broker incurs in this process—search, transportation, storage, and risk capital. The broker makes the market 'liquid' and the transactions follow from there. Without these costs, there's no market. Without a market, there's no trade between the farmers and customers. No trade satisfying the needs of two parties is a net negative for society.

There's more to this though. Once the broker repeats the transaction over time and attracts other brokers who compete for the same buyers and sellers, we have two additional benefits for the ecosystem. One, every broker looking to increase her business works to optimize the transaction costs, which then translates to lower prices for the customer. This dynamism of price discovery ensures there is a continuing relevance of the broker. Two, over a period of time, the broker is able to differentiate between the output of various farmers, rate them on quality, and provide additional service of 'certifying' the product. This deepens the market with customers willing to choose their desired quality of product and paying a price for it.

However, even this example doesn't quite capture the fundamental role of a broker in society. Why? Because the above example is a win–win kind. Everyone benefits at the end of it. But what about instances where the size of the pie is fixed?

That brings us to R. A. Radford's seminal paper 'The Economic Organisation of a P.O.W. Camp' written in 1945.[1] This eleven-page paper is a deep sociological study of life in a prison camp, and from it emerges a truth that's simple and profound.

The camp had over 2000 prisoners who received food parcels from the Red Cross. The parcels were exactly the same for everyone containing tinned milk, jam, butter, biscuits, beef, chocolate, sugar, etc., and cigarettes. The prisoners of war in the camp were from various ethnicities and religions. It isn't difficult to imagine what happened next. The prisoners had different preferences for the goods within the parcel. The non-smoker had no use of the cigarettes, many didn't want the milk, and the Sikhs didn't want the beef. Soon trading began.

Radford writes:

At once exchanges, already established, multiplied in volume. Starting with simple direct barter, such as a non-smoker giving a smoker friend his cigarette issue in exchange for a chocolate ration, more complex exchanges soon became an accepted custom.

Stories circulated of a padre who started off round the camp with a tin of cheese and five cigarettes and returned

---

[1] R. A. Radford, 'The Economic Organisation of a P.O.W. Camp', *Economica* 12, no. 48, 1945, 189–201, https://doi.org/10.2307/2550133.

to his bed with a complete parcel in addition to his original
cheese and cigarettes; the market was not yet perfect.[2]

There are two fundamental truths here. First, the gift
economy doesn't stay that way for too long. People like
to trade. Second, a broker (like the padre mentioned) can
go around enabling exchange among prisoners because he's
seen to be trustworthy and could end up with more than
what he started. This is a very powerful point. Everyone
who traded with the padre did so of their own volition.
All transactions were voluntary. They traded because they
thought they were better off with that transaction. Yet
after all the trades were done, the broker (padre) made a
tidy profit of a complete extra parcel. This was a classic
case where the size of the pie was fixed. The total parcels
remained the same. The padre merely rearranged them on
the basis of individual preferences. The prisoners ended
up with less than what they had, yet everyone felt they
benefitted.

Differential preferences and different perceptions of
value drive trade among people and anyone facilitating that
will make a profit even in a 'zero-sum' scenario. This was a
remarkable insight.

Also, over time as the prices were 'discovered',
preferences became more varied and barters got more
complex, a full-fledged exchange developed in the camp:

. . . there was a lively trade in all commodities and their
relative values were well known, and expressed not in

---

[2] Ibid.

terms of one another—one didn't quote bully (beef) in terms of sugar—but in terms of cigarettes. The cigarette became the standard of value. In the permanent camp people started by wandering through the bungalows calling their offers—'cheese for seven' (cigarettes) and the hours after parcel issue were bedlam. . . .

The inconveniences of this system soon led to its replacement by an Exchange and Mart notice board in every bungalow, where under the headings 'name', 'room number', 'wanted' and 'offered' sales and wants were advertised. When a deal went through, it was crossed off the board. The public and semi-permanent records of transactions led to cigarette prices being well known and thus tending to equality throughout the camp, although there were always opportunities for an astute trader to make a profit from arbitrage. With this development everyone, including non-smokers, was willing to sell for cigarettes, using them to buy at another time and place. Cigarettes became the normal currency, though, of course, barter was never extinguished.[3]

This isn't easy to comprehend. Nothing was being produced by anyone in the camp. Yet a market developed and some middlemen made profits. Radford writes:

It is thus to be seen that a market came into existence without labour or production. . . .the articles of trade—food, clothing and cigarettes—as free gifts—land or manna. Despite this, and despite a roughly equal

---

[3] Ibid.

distribution of resources, a market came into spontaneous operation, and prices were fixed by the operation of supply and demand. It is difficult to reconcile this fact with the labour theory of value.[4]

Despite all of this, the middleman still got a bad rap:

More interesting was opinion on middlemen and prices. Taken as a whole, opinion was hostile to the middleman. His function, and his hard work in bringing buyer and seller together, were ignored; profits were not regarded as a reward for labour, but as the result of sharp practices. Despite the fact that his very existence was proof to the contrary, the middleman was held to be redundant in view of the existence of an official Shop and the Exchange and Mart. Appreciation only came his way when he was willing to advance the price of a sugar ration, or to buy goods spot and carry them against a future sale. In these cases the element of risk was obvious to all, and the convenience of the service was felt to merit some reward.[5]

There is no getting away from this. The broker adds value, even in zero-sum scenarios, while being simultaneously despised. This is hard-wired into us. In some cultural contexts, like in India, this is deeply entrenched.

What makes it worse in India is the idea that the State can play the role of the broker and eliminate the profits

---

[4] Ibid.

[5] Ibid.

made by them for the betterment of the market. Multiple problems stem from this. One, the State is a monopoly. It doesn't have the incentive like that of an individual broker to lower transaction costs and keep price dynamic. Over time, the cost of this lethargy is borne by both the buyers and sellers. The agents of the State who wield the power of the broker without the attendant risks turn into rent-seekers. The buyers and the sellers are at the mercy of the broker who sets the terms of the trade.

Lastly, the market gets distorted. The price loses its value as a signal. Side deals are struck. Licenses are scarce and get auctioned in informal markets. Black markets emerge. And the liquidity is held to ransom by a few people. This is exactly what happened in India when the government played the role of intermediaries controlling the APMC mandis. The government didn't eliminate middlemen. Quite the opposite, it metamorphosed middlemen into odious, profiteering rent-seekers. A free market of brokers with regulations that prevented cartelization would have served the farmers and customers better.

Is Real Disintermediation Possible?

That brings us to the question of disintermediation. The internet has reduced the search and information costs down to zero. This gives the impression that real disintermediation is possible like that done by Uber, Airbnb, or TripAdvisor. But there are three flaws in this argument.

Many of these platforms have turned into intermediaries themselves with almost monopoly powers in certain markets. Come to think of it, even Google and Facebook are intermediaries who turn in enormous profits every year in their roles as market-makers. The one disintermediating an industry eventually becomes an intermediary.

These platforms disintermediated by offering more choices directly to the customers. Over time the choices available on them multiplied to an extent that it paralysed the users. Anyone looking to choose a restaurant in an unfamiliar city knows of this problem. Soon enough you will need an intermediary to sort through the many highly rated restaurants all around.

There are intermediaries whose role is the exact opposite of what traditional brokers do. They keep parties apart to enable a transaction. Investment bankers and sports agents are examples of this. The intermediary keeps things on balance and doesn't let a deal fall through by keeping the parties from directly interacting with one another. As search and information costs fall, this role of keeping parties away from one another continues to remain relevant.

So long as there is trade and there are differential preferences, the broker won't go out of business. The poor image they suffer is on account of a deeply held Marxian belief that visible labour is the real thing of genuine value and anyone trading only in information or whose labour is invisible is a mere opportunist. This gets compounded when the State intervenes to intermediate themselves or allows for cartelization of brokers.

A free market where a broker competes on equal terms to drive transaction costs down, provide choices, and keep the market liquid benefits all. Intermediaries came into play to reduce friction in transactions. Eliminating them won't make things frictionless. The solution is not to eliminate brokers but to let many brokers operate.

17

Pro-Market, Not Pro-Business

In September 2019, the Union government modified the Income Tax Act, reducing corporate tax rates for domestic manufacturing firms. As a result, the revenue foregone on account of this tax reduction was estimated to be nearly Rs 1,45,000 crore. This move was met with criticism on two counts. One, this reform helped the larger companies more than the smaller ones as the latter were already paying a lower tax rate. And two, the tax reforms left a huge gap in the government revenue bucket. How should we as ordinary Indian citizens think of such tax reductions? Instead, is it better—as it is commonly believed—that governments should help businesses through subsidies, incentives, and rebates to achieve higher growth rates? These two questions get to the core of the State–market relationship in India.

In reality, there is no dearth of incentives, subsidies, and rebate schemes by the government. Often, these schemes keep getting *evergreened* under new acronyms, as frequently as terrorist groups in Pakistan change their names. And despite this visible, possible intent on behalf of the government, India's economic prospects have slowed down over the last decade.

To understand why, we need to appreciate that the distinction between 'pro-market' and 'pro-business' reforms is critical. This difference was first made in the Indian context in a paper titled 'From "Hindu Growth" to Productivity Surge: The Mystery of the Indian Growth Transition' by Dani Rodrik and Arvind Subramanian in 2004. A pro-market policy refers to removing impediments to all economic activity. For example, the substantial dismantling of the 'license-permit-quota' raj through economic liberalization in 1991 was a pro-market reform as it reduced entry barriers for new, old, and yet-to-be-born firms in the market alike. Such reforms are pro-competition as they level the playing field for newer entrants against established players who have the 'blessings' of the government. A pro-business policy on the other hand favours the incumbents. Allowing capacity expansion for existing players, incentives for increasing production, and tax rebates for specific sectors are all examples of policies that mainly help existing businesses scale up their operations.[1]

As you can imagine, it is easier for governments to come up with pro-business policies rather than pro-market ones. The losers are the consumers who incur dispersed costs and the businesses that are yet to start operations and hence lack a voice. The winners are existing businesses that get concentrated benefits in the form of higher profits and

---

[1] Dani Rodrik and Arvind Subramanian, 'From "Hindu Growth" to Productivity Surge: The Mystery of the Indian Growth Transition', Working Paper, Working Paper Series (National Bureau of Economic Research, March 2004), https://doi.org/10.3386/w10376.

lower operating costs. It is hence not surprising that most industry bodies and companies bat for similar government support—tax rebates, production incentives, input subsidies, and suchlike.

Keeping pro-market, pro-competition policies on the back burner is harmful to the economy. While incumbent businesses might benefit from band-aid fixes, governments are responsible for a different and tougher task of ensuring there is economic dynamism in the market. Raghuram Rajan and Luigi Zingales make this point eloquently: the society must 'save capitalism from the capitalists' by limiting concentration of ownership of productive assets, providing a social security net for the economically disadvantaged, and supporting free trade to maintain competitive pressure on domestic firms.[2]

However, this pro-market, pro-business distinction remains an underappreciated point in Indian public policy. This chapter discusses two such policies that have helped a few businesses but have been harmful to the market in the long run.

Items Reserved for Manufacture Exclusively by the Small-Scale Sector

At the height of the licence raj, to boost employment growth in India's small manufacturing establishments, only firms considered to be small-scale industries were allowed to manufacture a reserved list of items. In 1967, forty-seven

[2] Luigi Zingales and Raghuram G. Rajan, *Saving Capitalism from the Capitalists: Unleashing the Power of Financial Markets to Create Wealth and Spread Opportunity* (Princeton University Press, 2004).

items were put on this list. By 1978, this pro-business policy had expanded its scope to 504 reserved items. And by 1997, this number had reached over 1000, and even included many electrical and electronic goods!

Notably, despite the pro-competition economic overhaul of 1991, this reservation policy couldn't be dismantled. The incumbents mounted a strong resistance. It was only in the last decade that the list was pruned significantly. The last twenty items on this list were removed as late as April 2015.

To answer how this policy hurt the economy, we need to assess the *opportunity cost* of this policy. In other words, what did we lose in protecting the interests of a few businesses? The overt policy objective was to boost employment growth in the small-scale sector. But in an article titled 'How did de-reservation of small-scale industry affect employment?', economists Ann Harrison, Leslie Martin, and Shanti Nataraj write that:

> . . . once a product was de-reserved, the number of establishments making that product increased by nearly 15%. In addition, employment increased by 50%, output by nearly 35%, capital by 45%, and wages by 6%.

Further:

> Contrary to the expectations for such policy, we find that eliminating the policy was in fact associated with increases in overall employment and that these increases were driven by entrants into the de-reserved product space. Our findings are also in keeping with

the evidence on the relationship between establishment size and growth in India. We find that it is young establishments, not small establishments, that exhibit high employment growth. The removal of small-scale reservations increased overall employment by encouraging the growth of younger, larger establishments—those that are most likely to pay higher wages, create more investment, be more productive, and generate growth in employment.[3]

Apart from failing to meet its intended policy objective, this pro-business policy also derailed India's chance of developing a competitive manufacturing sector, the implications of which afflict us even today. Jairam Ramesh in his book *To the Brink and Back: India's 1991 Story* (Rupa Publications, 2015) explains the consequences in these words:

> Besides, what this reservation had done, was kill India's chances of emerging as a global supplier of consumer goods, garments, sports goods, toys and many electrical and electronic items—all of which became areas of China's manufacturing leadership in the 1980s and thereafter.[4]

---

[3] Ann Harrison, Leslie Brown, Shanti Natraj, 'How Did De-Reservation of Small-Scale Industry Affect Employment?', Ideas For India, accessed 28 January 2022, http://www.ideasforindia.in/topics/money-finance/how-did-de-reservation-of-small-scale-industry-affect-employment.html.

[4] Jairam Ramesh, *To the Brink and Back: India's 1991 Story* (Rupa, 2015).

The de-reservation happened because of a report of the Expert Committee on Small Enterprises under the chairmanship of Abid Hussain (1997), which pulled no punches in exposing the lacunae.[5] The lesson still remains relevant. Not only are brilliant sounding pro-business policies often ineffective, they also damage the overall economic health.

The Production-Linked Incentive Scheme

Another kind of pro-business policy category popular in India is production incentives. The idea sounds simple. Governments promise businesses a cashback to encourage them to produce more in India. There have been many versions of this policy across sectors but we zoom in on the latest iteration in the manufacturing sector that goes by the name of production-linked incentive (PLI).

The idea seems elegant on paper: the government will reward companies for additional sales of manufactured goods with a cashback. The more the sales (either domestic or exports), the more the cashback. The intent seems sound too: encourage companies to up their manufacturing game.

First introduced for the electronics sector in 2020, reports seemed to indicate that the government was focusing on a narrow list of five sectors where India has a comparative advantage. But as can be expected from a pro-business policy, soon every other sector started demanding a PLI. Sure enough, the Union Cabinet had announced PLIs worth Rs 2 lakh crore for thirteen disparate sectors

---

[5] Abid Hussain, 'Report of the Expert Committee on Small Enterprises', Department of Small-Scale Industries and Business Enterprises, New Delhi, 1997.

over the next five years by October 2021. These include automobiles and auto components, pharmaceutical drugs, advanced chemistry cells (ACC), capital goods, technology products, textile products, white goods, food products, and telecom and speciality steel.

Let's assume that the size of the incentive is big enough to attract new investment. Even if that happens, it is easy to anticipate the anti-competitive nature of this policy.

One, there's a risk of important business decisions being left to government officials and committees. Consider, for example, the PLI scheme for the electronics sector has specific eligibility criteria both on incremental investment and incremental sales a company needs to commit over the next five years. This is supposed to be cross-checked by a Project Management Agency (PMA), a government body formed under the Ministry of Electronics and Information Technology (MeitY).

The PMA must further submit its recommendations to an Empowered Committee (EC) composed of CEO NITI Aayog, Secretary Economic Affairs, Secretary Expenditure, Secretary MeitY, Secretary Revenue, Secretary Department for Promotion of Industry and Internal Trade (DPIIT), and Directorate General of Foreign Trade (DGFT), which will make the final decision. The EC is also empowered to revise anything—subsidy rate, eligibility criteria, and target segments.

In short, more bureaucracy and predictably unpredictable delays. The speed of incremental investments might get decided by the speed of government decision-making. EC's powers to make any changes to this policy in the future are also filled with possibilities of regulation becoming *overregulation*.

There's one more gap. In order to increase innovation, the PLI scheme will not consider incremental investments towards land and buildings as towards the eligibility criteria. Only investment towards plant, machinery, equipment, research and development is allowed. This might incentivize companies to fudge their land dealings and government officers verifying the real quantum of incremental investments to cut deals for themselves.

Two, the cost of the subsidy is being borne by the ordinary Indian. The thirteen sectors chosen by the government might see a crowding-in of investment at the cost of other sectors. Are these thirteen industries strategic for India while others aren't? We don't quite know the basis of this selection. Every policy move has an associated opportunity cost. It's a bane of Indian policymaking that policy decisions are rationalized solely by looking at projected benefits and ignoring opportunity costs. In the context of PLIs, the government needs to pay up Rs 2 lakh crore over the next five years to a few companies in these thirteen sectors. The government will most likely rake in this revenue in the form of taxes. The scheme would make sense if the benefits are projected to be higher than this number. Whether an analysis of these costs has been taken into account, we don't know.

Third, rent-seekers often distort a policy programme to serve their own interests. Companies that benefit will seek to modify the eligibility criteria to suppress competition, thus leading to more market concentration. They might even try to extend the sunset clause of this scheme in order to keep benefiting from the discount. This phenomenon has already taken shape. Mobile device manufacturers eligible for the PLI scheme asked the government to invoke the clause of 'force majeure' to declare FY2020–21, the first year under the policy, a zero year. They cited disruptions due to COVID-19 and the fallout of India–China tensions as reasons for the request.[6]

In short, goalposts start shifting. Excuses follow. Businesses block competition. We have decades of experience proving the futility of such industrial policy measures.

Which Pro-Market Policies Does India Need?

Glorified subsidies for a few sectors won't transform manufacturing in India. Simpler tax, policy, business, and trade environments would. The chairman of the India Cellular and Electronics Association (ICEA) explained this well when he said, 'The disability stack runs deep in the economy. For example, the taxes on fuel. Second, electricity is not subsumed under GST (goods and services tax). So how do you become competitive?'[7]

India's restrictive trade policies are another significant barrier. Increasing import tariffs in the name of protecting domestic companies leads to not just higher costs for all

---

[6] Surajeet Das Gupta, 'Mobile Device Makers Press for 2021 as Zero Year under PLI Scheme', *Business Standard India*, 27 March 2021, https://www.business-standard.com/article/companies/mobile-device-makers-press-for-2021-as-zero-year-under-pli-scheme-121032700064_1.html.

[7] Goutam Das, 'Inside the Plan to Mobile-Make in India', Mint, 28 October 2020, https://www.livemint.com/industry/manufacturing/inside-the-plan-to-mobile-make-in-india-11603895399056.html.

Indian consumers, but also Indian manufacturers. With imports of parts becoming costlier, exports by Indian manufacturers are unable to compete at the global level. For instance, a recent comparative study analysing import tariff regimes of India, Thailand, Vietnam, China, and Mexico by the ICEA tells us that:

> The main difference in their policy approach is the tariff policy of India compared to others. India has relied heavily on higher tariffs whereas other countries have not done so. Higher tariffs orient the approach of investors and domestic producers away from global markets and towards the domestic market. Notably the exports for India compared with others have remained low as has been examined in this report.[8]

In fact, there is evidence to suggest that higher import duties are now negating all the benefits provided under the PLI schemes.[9]

This is the key point. Perhaps PLIs are a much-needed band-aid solution for a wounded economy but they cannot transform manufacturing in India. We also need to reduce import tariffs so that domestic firms can import raw materials cheaply on one hand, and compete with global businesses on the other. Finally, there are a host of labour laws that

---

[8] IKDHVAJ Advisors LLP and India Cellular & Electronics Association, 'A Comparative Study of Import Tariffs in Electronics', accessed 23 February 2022, https://icea.org.in/wp-content/uploads/2022/01/Report-by-ICEA-on-Detailed_Tariffs-Drive-Competitiveness-and-Scale_06022022.pdf.

[9] Ibid.

prevent the easy entry and exit of businesses in India. Rationalizing them is another pro-competition measure India desperately needs.

In other words, the Indian economy needs a bold Reforms 2.0 agenda that protects markets, not a few hand-picked businesses. Keeping aside the economics, there's a political angle here as well. The spate of pro-business policies such as tax rebates and subsidies that Indians have got used to over the years, justifiably lead to charges of unfairness and crony capitalism. At a macro-level, this inspires a general aversion towards businesses, profit-making, and markets.

It is in this light that we should assess the corporate tax reduction for manufacturing firms. For India, lowering the highest tax rates while broadening the tax base has been advocated as a pro-market measure by public finance specialists. However, lowering the tax rate still does not mitigate the several other cost disadvantages of doing business in India such as the difficulty of entry and exit, high import tariffs, and uncertain policy environment underlined by the infamous retrospective taxation cases in the last few years. To spur competition, an overhaul of these mechanisms is imperative.

18

Why Mortgage 'Family Silver'?

Bhaad mei jaaye Sensex *aur* disinvestment.
[Let the stock market and disinvestment go to hell.]

> —A. B. Bardhan, General Secretary of the Communist
> Party of India, after the 2004 national elections

We Indians are a melodramatic bunch. A popular trope in Indian cinema of the pre-1991 era was unsuspecting commoners falling into the debt traps of evil moneylenders. This would often involve a scene where the poor had to mortgage their valuable possessions to usurious badmen. Such is the power of this imagery that 'selling India's family silver' has become a metaphor that gets deployed every time a government-owned company is put on sale.

There are two problems with this metaphor. Firstly, government-owned companies are hardly a family matter. Take the instance of Air India. By the time it went on sale in 2021, Indian citizens were paying nearly Rs 20 crores a day for the government to run a full-service airline that only the richest Indians could afford. If this is a family, it sure is an extractive one. Secondly, most government-run companies when put up for sale end up in the hands of private Indian citizens. How this transfer implies a *sale* of family silver is incomprehensible.

Be that as it may, the phenomenon of government-run companies illustrates two critical lessons for public policy: opportunity cost neglect in public policy and the marginal cost of public finance.

Opportunity Cost Neglect

While the slogan 'Government has no business to be in business' is liberally deployed in our policy discourse, the number of public sector undertakings (PSUs) have been on a steady rise. Starting from five in 1951, the Union government had a majority stake in 348 companies by 2019. Adding the 1100-odd companies that various state governments run, there are now nearly 1500 government-run firms in India covering a broad scope from real estate holdings to sandalwood soap manufacturing to defence equipment production.

How do we decide which of these functions are suitable to be run by governments? When this question is raised, the instinctive response is to take a moral standpoint—if something is good, it must be made the government's job. Since the list of all good things in life is inexhaustible, this trajectory leads to an 'omniabsent' State, which is chasing wishful desires instead of providing the necessities that only it can.

From an economic standpoint, it is useful to consider one central concept that every public policy action must evaluate: opportunity cost.

Kuch paane ke liye kuch khona bhi padta hai.
[No pain, no gain. There are no free lunches.]

There are countless versions of this aphorism, and yet it is an incredibly difficult concept to grasp in public policy. What these statements suggest is that when there's scarcity, trade-offs are inevitable. When resources are deployed in pursuit of one particular policy direction, the same resources are not available for other use. This forgone alternative use of any resource due to a policy choice is referred to as the opportunity cost.

This concept forces us to think beyond counting the benefits of any policy action and ask a tougher question: is this policy the best use of the limited resources available with the government? Even the worst possible public policy measure will most likely have some benefits and winners. Remember how demonetization was supposed to have reduced insurgent and terror activities in Kashmir? Even if we assume it to be true, does it justify demonetization?

Though the answer is obvious in this example, this kind of reasoning is commonplace in public policy in India. Corporate Social Responsibility (CSR) laws are justified on the grounds that they created some good assets, and prohibition is justified because it supposedly protects rural Indians from alcoholism.

Sound public policy would be based on different questions. Was the opportunity cost of making CSR mandatory more than the benefits that were realized? How do the costs incurred on enforcing prohibition and the lives lost due to spurious liquor deaths compare with the benefits of reducing alcoholism?

This seems intuitive. After all, we do such trade-offs all the time in our private lives. Turns out though, opportunity cost neglect is quite common in public policy. A research study showed that while people make opportunity cost trade-offs in private consumption, they fail to do so while thinking of public spending.[1]

A plausible reason for this dichotomy is that we as individuals do not feel connected to the actual expenditure of government money even though it's we who pay for the expense in the form of taxes. Another explanation the study finds is that 'politicians rarely explicate what they do not spend public resources on. Rather they focus on what they do spend resources on, further harnessing opportunity cost neglect in public policy.' Finally, some of us are prone to thinking about spending in terms of specific categories such as health, education, defence, or airline services, and are thus reluctant to even consider alternative uses of money in areas outside our favourite category.[2]

This familiar phenomenon of opportunity cost neglect leads to a problem characteristic of the Indian State. It spreads itself too thin, trying to do lots of things and ends up doing virtually nothing well enough.

---

[1] Emil Persson and Gustav Tinghög, 'Opportunity Cost Neglect in Public Policy', *Journal of Economic Behavior & Organization* 170 (February 2020): 301–12, https://doi.org/10.1016/j.jebo.2019.12.012.

[2] Ibid.

How do we check this bias? That's where the second concept comes into play.

Marginal Cost of Public Funds

A useful thumb rule to consider government expenditure is this: the cost to Indian society for every rupee of government spending is around Rs 3. Therefore, the government should only spend an additional one rupee when the gains to society from that action exceed Rs 3.[3]

This powerful insight comes from *In Service of the Republic: The Art and Science of Economic Policy* by Vijay Kelkar and Ajay Shah. The concept behind this thumb rule is known as Marginal Cost of Public Funds (MCPF), which measures the loss incurred by society in raising additional revenues to finance government spending.[4] In an ideal world, an additional Re 1 public spending would require an additional tax revenue of Re 1, which would in turn impose a cost of Rs 1 to the society. Alas, taxation is not frictionless. Taxes lead to deadweight loss i.e., some trade disappears because of the price rise inflicted by the tax. Raising additional taxes also increases the cost of compliance for all taxpayers. The government also incurs costs on administering new taxes. Consequently, the MCPF ranges from 1.25–2 in OECD countries. But this problem is especially severe in India because we have too many bad taxes, exemptions, and distortions. Together, they impose

---

[3] Kelkar and Shah, *In Service of the Republic.*

[4] Bev Dahlby, *Marginal Cost of Public Funds: Theory and Application* (Cambridge, MA: MIT Press), p. 1.

an immense cost to the society, increasing the MCPF to around 3.[5]

So next time someone says that the government should continue to run Air India or Bharat Sanchar Nigam Limited (BSNL), ask them to think about MCPF. The key learning is that the government should spend only on areas where marginal gains to society exceed the MCPF. This means increasing spending on correcting key market failures such as defence, law and order, public health as the benefits from these areas will far outweigh the marginal costs on the society.

Back to Public Sector Undertakings

The story of PSUs in India showcases both opportunity cost neglect and MCPF neglect. It wasn't always supposed to be this way.

After the Second World War, most newly independent underdeveloped nations opted for a developmental path known as Import Substitution Industrialization (ISI). Under ISI, trade and economic policy measures were designed with the explicit aim of replacing foreign imports with domestic production. India went for one of the most extreme versions of ISI. High import tariffs were supplemented by non-tariff barriers, restraints on foreign investment, regulation of

---

[5] Ajay Shah, 'Marginal Cost of Public Funds: A Valuable Tool for Thinking about Taxation and Expenditure in India', The Leap Blog (blog), accessed 23 February 2022, https://blog.theleapjournal.org/2016/08/marginal-cost-of-public-funds-valuable.html.

private investment, and most importantly State-control of all important industries.[6]

The reason behind the policy to build PSUs in the early days is interesting. Nehru's economic vision was to reduce dependence on foreign markets in the shortest possible time. This meant that the creation of a domestic machinery sector became an important policy goal, to ensure that future investments didn't come from outside India. Given that India's private firms were too small to make mega investments, the government took up the mantle of building a heavy industry sector.[7] By 1951, there were five union government-owned PSUs, which grew to 84 by 1969. Most of these investments in these early days were of the greenfield type, where the government built new companies from the ground up.[8]

The opportunity cost of a new, poor State investing its scarce time and resources in building heavy industries was significant. Nevertheless, this policy did have some benefits in terms of creating a new industrial base.

It was the next phase of PSU-creation where things went out of control. Beginning 1969, the Indira Gandhi government started nationalizing existing private firms in

---

[6] Tirthankar Roy, 'The Origins of Import Substituting Industrialization in India', *Economic History of Developing Regions* 32, no. 1, 2017, 71–95, DOI: 10.1080/20780389.2017.1292460.

[7] Arvind Panagariya, *India: The Emerging Giant* (Oxford University Press, 2010), p. 31.

[8] Devesh Kapur, 'India's Public Sector Enterprises: Where Do We Go from Here?', The Print, 14 November 2018, https://theprint.in/opinion/indias-public-sector-enterprises-where-do-we-go-from-here/149208/.

banking, insurance, coal, and many other sectors for reasons that were political rather than economic.[9] By 1980, the number of PSUs had risen to 179.

This expansion came at a tremendous opportunity cost. The already-limited government capacity was diverted to running these industries. Indian Administrative Services (IAS) officers were parachuted into leadership positions of nationalized firms, diverting resources and attention from core responsibilities such as law and order, defence, foreign policy, and public service provision. For all this cost, these companies had little to show. Inefficiency and corruption became the norm. Their role in employment generation has kept falling steadily, even as salaries of PSU personnel have risen way faster than the per capita income of Indians.[10]

From an MCPF lens, the proliferation of PSUs continues to inflict serious costs on society. Some erstwhile inefficient private companies that would have melted away on their own became national burdens to be supported by taxpayers after nationalization. Take the case of recapitalization of PSU banks. In 2017, the union government had to infuse Rs 2.11 lakh crores to keep them afloat. Then in 2019, a further Rs 70,000 crores of Indian tax payers' money was given away to these banks. Given that the MCPF for India is estimated to be 3, recapitalization cost to the Indian society over the last five years is of the order of Rs 9 lakh crores!

---

[9] Mihir S. Sharma, 'The Day India's Banks Died Because of Political Priorities of a Populist PM', *Business Standard India*, 19 July 2019, https://www.business-standard.com/article/finance/the-day-india-s-banks-died-because-of-political-priorities-of-a-populist-pm-119071900251_1.html.

[10] Kapur, 'India's Public Sector Enterprises'.

Over time, the mounting losses eventually brought a shift in the narrative on PSUs. The 1991 economic reforms gave an opportunity for a change in the official stance, and 31 PSUs were identified for disinvestment in 1991–92. A Disinvestment Commission was formed in 1996 to gradually privatize some PSUs. The Department of Disinvestment was set up in 1999. It was upgraded to a Ministry of Disinvestment in 2001. After showing some initial promise, the disinvestment agenda was again put on the backburner starting 2004.

Over the next seventeen years, there was a lot of talk but little action on disinvestment. The approach has remained ad-hoc, with PSUs being chosen for disinvestment primarily to raise revenues. In every budget, governments set a disinvestment target for itself with the aim of reducing its fiscal deficit. This focus on a revenue target from disinvestment led to perverse incentives: when it couldn't find genuine buyers, the government coaxed other PSUs like Life Insurance Corporation to purchase government-run companies on sale. This 'sale' showed up as revenue in the government accounts even though the government's stake did not reduce in reality. Passing the burden from this hand to the other cannot reduce the opportunity costs of government control.

Another ad-hoc approach that governments adopted was to consider the sale of only those PSUs that incurred consistent losses. For example, the argument that Air India made a loss of 'Over Rs 20 Crore Per Day' was repeatedly (and successfully) used to rationalize Air India's sale. This approach implied that it was okay for governments to run businesses as long as they were profitable. This is another demonstration of opportunity-cost neglect—governments devote their limited capacity in running businesses regardless of the profit & loss statement of the PSU. This line of thinking also implicitly implied that the sale of a PSU first required running it down into an incorrigible loss-making entity. A sale became politically feasible only after the government passed on the loss burden to taxpayers. And remember, because the MCPF is 3, the Indian society incurred thrice the cost.

Is There a Way Out?

The 14th Union Finance Commission, a constitutional body, proposed that the only way to resolve the PSU mess was to create a prioritization framework. Public ownership should be a goal only in a few narrowly defined areas such as:

(a) activity assessed as strategic in terms of public interest;
(b) the enterprises having earmarked or assigned natural resources with sovereign or quasi-sovereign functions;
(c) the enterprises required to cater to market imperfections;
(d) enterprises where returns on investments are higher than any alternative investment by the government; and (e) public utilities, where some presence of public enterprises may be desirable as a reference point for getting more reliable information for the regulators.[11]

Outside this reduced set, the government should sell all businesses. The focus in this approach is on the reduction of

---

[11] 'Fourteenth Finance Commission', Volume 1, p. 221.

overall government equity in non-strategic sectors, and not as much on the revenues raised by the sale of government assets. This approach acknowledges the importance of tools like opportunity cost and MCPF. It confronts trade-offs and focuses government attention to areas where it is needed most. Without this anchoring point, the omniabsence of the Indian State will keep rising.

19

Can Crises Dissolve Policy Inertia?

There's a familiar trope in old Bollywood films when someone is terminally ill. A grim-faced doctor (sometimes the veteran actor, Sapru) walks out after examining the patient and then announces to those waiting outside—'*Ab inhe dawaa ki nahin, dua ki zaroorat hai.*' In other words, this is the time for prayer. The time to act is gone.

The usual course of action after this line is for the female lead or the mother of the protagonist to head to the nearest temple while the old family retainer (often a Muslim) begins his '*sajda*'. This collective persuasion to the Almighty usually works.

While this is what our society apparently does during a crisis, not so the State. The State often rouses itself from slumber during a crisis and becomes unusually hyperactive. Many experts weigh in with a solemn line: a crisis should never be wasted. Apparently, the mental model about the crisis for them is that of policymakers sitting around with lots of time on their hands. So, they should get up and use the crisis to some kind of advantage. Should we be bathing our crises in this stream of positive light? Is solving anything while dealing with a mortal threat a good way to find long-term answers?

What the COVID-19 Crisis Tells Us[1]

At the peak of the pandemic, we found many public policy opinion pieces that advanced one narrative: the economic and humanitarian crisis unleashed by COVID-19 was the perfect opportunity to undertake long-pending reforms in everything from agriculture, labour, health infrastructure, education, and administration. Inherent in this view was a strongly held belief that only a crisis can jolt India to resolve seemingly intractable politico-economic constraints. Come a crisis and we can somehow convince key stakeholders on deeper reform.

In this perspective, incremental reforms are for the faint-hearted. The route to real change is to first stumble into a crisis and then turn it around. Let's investigate if this crisis-induced reforms model has any instrumental value.

John W. Kingdon's public policy classic *Agendas, Alternatives and Public Policies* (HarperCollins, 1984) can help us understand the crisis–opportunity paradox better. Kingdon argues that just a crisis does not ensure reform. Instead, his schema says that an issue surfaces at the top of the decision-making agenda of the government only at the opportune moment when three distinct streams

[1] This essay first appeared in *Deccan Herald*. Pranay Kotasthane, 'Coronavirus: Turning a Crisis into a Policy Opportunity', *Deccan Herald*, 24 April 2020, https://www.deccanherald.com/opinion/coronavirus-turning-a-crisis-into-a-policy-opportunity-829310.html.

converge—the problem stream, the solution stream, and the politics stream.

Look at the *problem stream* first. Without an acknowledgement at the highest political levels that a problem really exists, the issue won't even be considered by the government. A crisis often turns out to be a type of problem that forces the government to acknowledge the issue. But it cannot, by itself, cause change. For that to happen, two other streams need to be met simultaneously.

In comes the *solution stream*. This refers to the entire solution set available to the decision-maker. government is unlikely to pick up a policy problem for decision-making during a crisis unless there is a range of pre-existing solutions in place already. Climate change, for example, is an issue where the problem itself is now well acknowledged. However, given that the solutions are still heavily contested, it is not one of the highest policy priorities for the government.

For the solution stream to be in place requires the availability of data and the presence of a policy community that systematically converts ideas into solutions, weighing the costs and benefits of each action. Then comes the expert committee process. Though often seen in derisive terms, expert committees perform the key task of thinking through various policy solutions and string them together into a coherent whole. This entire process needs to have been in place even before the problem becomes urgent and important.

The third stream is the *political stream* that comprises the public mood, dominant societal narratives, election results, and global trends. Change in governments is often interpreted as a go-ahead for the incoming government's manifesto. It isn't surprising therefore that the most challenging reforms are often picked up earlier in the term.

The idea of 'political will' is relevant to the alignment of the political stream. Visionary leaders can change the dominant social narratives. In fact, major crises can even make it easier for a political actor to convince their constituents about reform. This was the idea put forward by Robert Putnam in his landmark paper 'Diplomacy and Domestic Games'. He argued that the politics of many international negotiations can be thought of as a two-level game. At Level 1, the national governments negotiate with international players such as the IMF, World Bank, or the US. At Level 2, the national governments negotiate with domestic groups that pursue their interests by pressuring the government to adopt favourable policies.[2]

The key insight here is that dynamics of negotiations at one level can be used as points of leverage on the other. Take the case of the 1991 Indian economic reforms. P.V. Narasimha Rao and Manmohan Singh were able to use the rationale of external pressure at Level 1 (conditionalities imposed by the IMF) to water down opposition in Level 2 (domestic actors benefiting from the status-quo). The economic reforms were good for India in and of themselves but the balance of payment crisis provided a political opportunity to execute them using the excuse of World Bank conditionalities.

---

[2] Robert D Putnam, 'Diplomacy and Domestic Politics: The Logic of Two-Level Games', *International Organisation* 42, no. 3, 2006, 427–60.

The situation during the pandemic was different in that there was no international agency at the other end of the negotiating table. Instead, it was a global pandemic that crippled livelihoods. The world seemed to head towards a recession or at least a K-shaped recovery that would hurt low-income economies and families disproportionately, reducing their chances of playing catch-up with the rest of the world.

In that sense, an entrepreneurial leadership could still use that moment to convince their own Level 2 constituents about reforms that we anyway needed. For instance, there were efforts by companies to reduce their dependence on China as their sole global manufacturer after COVID-19. The conditions required for relocating these global manufacturing to India could be used as a point of leverage to drive few domestic economic reforms in labour and capital investments.

Luckily, during the pandemic, on the economic front, both the problem and solution streams were already aligned. The problems were well-known over the last two decades. Reforms 2.0—comprising the liberalization of land, labour, and capital—too were well-known. Whether the government did enough of that is a question that the future will answer.

Finally, hope can never be a policy. Similarly, expecting a crisis by itself to spur reforms is foolishly hopeful. It's like saying that Team India should always put itself in a follow-on situation in a Test match so that we can replicate the heroics of the 2001 Kolkata Test. Don't forget that moment also needed a V. V. S. Laxman, a Rahul Dravid, a Harbhajan Singh, massive public support, and lots of luck.

20

All I Wanted Was Everything

If you travel in suburban trains in Mumbai, you will notice that ads for a certain 'Baba Bangali' and his ayurvedic cures appear on walls beyond Andheri station as you head northwards. Baba Bangali and his ilk are found all over India in small roadside tents selling all sorts of herbal concoctions for the poor who cannot afford modern medicine or are gullible enough to fall prey to magic cures. Among the many wonder drugs that Baba Bangali has in his *jhola*, the one that's most potent and a near panacea to all ills is the *Rambaan aushadhi* (literally, the medicine akin to Lord Ram's bow implying its all-conquering nature). The ultimate solution to all ills.

Turns out that the Indian public policy space is also hobbled by a search for *Rambaan* equivalents. In this chapter, we zoom in on a few candidates.

Every year, July 31 is a day of trepidation for honest and dishonest income taxpayers alike. It's that day of the year when the dreaded income tax returns need to be filed.

In recent times, the income tax filing process has been digitized and does not require visiting government offices. However, such is the complexity of our tax laws that few taxpayers dare file income tax returns themselves. The myriad tax exemptions entice the tax filer to hunt for ways in which they can reduce their tax burden. On the other hand, the need to navigate and report the numerous income source categories means that even an honest taxpayer is never sure whether she has filed the returns correctly. The result is that most taxpayers end up seeking the help of a chartered accountant (CA) who can guide the taxpayer through the labyrinthine tax laws.

But have you stopped to wonder, why is tax filing so complicated? Why the need for so many exemptions; why can't the government just tax everyone at a lower rate instead? If you've pondered over these questions while haplessly staring at the income tax return filing spreadsheet, you've hit upon a key insight that pervades Indian public policy: the intention to achieve several objectives through one policy or institution.

Why Do Many Policies Fail?

This topic is a subject of deep research. Surely, there are many answers to this important question. But a part of the reason is how each of our policies is laden with several objectives—some of them in direct conflict with each other. Complicated goal setting mixed in equal parts with underwhelming implementation capacity is a perfect recipe for policy failure. In other words, policies and institutions fail when they are laden with several objectives, resulting in a system that fulfils none of them. We call this phenomenon hyper multi-objective optimization.

Multi-objective optimization is a step in any design process that tries to make a system suitable for several objectives at the same time. This concept is applied in several branches of science such as engineering, economics, and logistics.

In engineering, this process of multi-objective optimization translates into 'design constraints'. Some common design constraints are performance, cost, reliability, and usability. The whole design problem is about coming up with a solution that falls within the acceptable range on all these counts. For example, a hardware engineer designing a chip tries to optimize it for higher speed, smaller size, a wide temperature range of operation, and low costs.

Often, increasing design constraints (both in terms of their number and their strictness) makes the system design so complex that it becomes impossible to meet all the constraints. This is because objectives are often conflicting and trying to optimize for one leads to degradation with respect to the other. In such a case, system design can only proceed if one objective is traded-off to some extent. In other words, for a nontrivial multi-objective optimization problem, there does not exist a single solution that concurrently optimizes each objective.

Multi-objective optimization applies to government policies as well. Making any government policy or institution is a mighty difficult job already. There are five ex-ante design constraints to meet in a liberal democracy, even before you consider the specific problem at hand.

These are effectiveness, equity, efficiency and costs, political feasibility, and ease of implementation.

Now, the problem with government policies is this: governments try to optimize a policy or an agency for many additional objectives at the same time. And just like an engineering system design returns a null solution when strict conflicting objectives are applied at the same time, public policies trying to optimize for several objectives end up failing.

A more elegant way to formulate this intuition is the Tinbergen Rule, named after economist Jan Tinbergen. The rule states: 'To successfully achieve n independent policy targets at least the same number of independent policy instruments are required.'

A corollary of the Tinbergen rule is the *assignment principle*. Once a policy instrument has been mapped to a policy target, it becomes unavailable for pursuing other targets.

With these concepts in mind, observe a few cases where government policies flout the assignment principle.

Flogging Tax Policies Is Counter-Productive

Take the case of India's tax policy first. As we discussed, India's income tax policy is extremely complicated, with several layers of rebates and raises across sectors, income levels, and geographic areas. *The fundamental reason behind this complexity is that India's tax policy has been burdened with several objectives*. And hence, it is no surprise that such a system does not function as desired.

Dr M. Govinda Rao, an authority on public finance in India, describes this condition best:

> Although many countries' tax policy is used as an instrument to accelerate investment, encourage savings, increase exports and pursue some other objectives, India's obsession is perhaps unique. In addition to the above, India's tax policy is loaded with objectives such as industrialization of backward regions, encouraging infrastructure ventures, promotion of small-scale industries, generation of employment, encouragement to charitable activities and scientific research, and promotion of enclave-type development through Special Economic Zones (SEZs). These objectives are pursued through various exemptions, differentiation in rates and preferences which enormously complicate the tax structure and open up avenues for evasion and avoidance of tax and create rent-seeking opportunities.[1]

Another Ulta-Pulta Tax

You would have come across the news that the government is struggling to refund the Input Tax Credit (ITC) it owes to businesses, ever since the Goods & Services Tax (GST) was introduced. Essentially, the government didn't anticipate the volume of ITC being claimed. As a result, it is far behind its payments and has sucked out working capital

---

[1] M. Govinda Rao, 'M Govinda Rao: Tax Sops—Their Cost and Efficacy', *Business Standard India*, 4 May 2010, https://www.business-standard.com/article/opinion/m-govinda-rao-tax-sops-their-cost-and-efficacy-110050400031_1.html.

from businesses. But, have you wondered why the GST ITC refund claims are so high?

The main reason is something called the inverted duty structure. Since we expect a tax policy to perform miracles—solve India's inequality problem, create an *aatmanirbhar* Bharat, create employment, maybe even produce *vibhuti* (sacred ash) from thin air—we ended up with a GST that has way too many rates.

Inadvertently, this resulted in some raw materials being taxed at a much higher rate than the final product. For example, the tax on rubber used in *hawai chappals* is a mighty 18 per cent. Why it is so high, we have no idea. On the chappals itself, the tax rate is just 5 per cent presumably because we have to save this '*laghu udyog*'. This situation is what's called an inverted duty structure.

This results in refunds because input taxes claimed for credit exceed the output taxes payable. For example, assume the *hawai chappals* are sold at Rs 120 to customers. The output tax payable would be Rs 6/chappal (5 per cent of 120). However, since the GST is a value-added tax, the chappal maker can net out the taxes she has paid for the inputs. Assuming that she purchased rubber of Rs 50, she has already paid a tax amount worth Rs 9 to her supplier (18 per cent of 50). The net tax to be paid by her is Rs –3! This means the government needs to refund this amount to the chappal maker. Ordinarily, such a situation wouldn't arise if the value added by the chappal maker was really high or if the tax rate on rubber would have been the same or less than the one on the chappal.

Examples of such an inverted duty structure abound in the Indian GST. Textiles, housing, and many other sectors are afflicted with this problem. The government, of course, delays paying these refunds, resulting in even more emotional *atyaachaar* on businesses.

The lesson from this touching story is the same. Violating the assignment principle has real consequences. Hence, redistribution and equity should be the goals of the expenditure side of the budget alone. Raising revenues through taxes shouldn't be tasked with this goal at all. Broadening the base, lowering the tax rates for all individuals and companies, and getting rid of tax exemptions will avoid the follies of hyper multi-objective optimization.

Not to forget, the inverted duty structure is that it creates incentives for a new class of cheaters: professional refund creators. Read this extract from a news report:

> In a case from last year, authorities found that a group of people created a network of 500 firms, including fake manufacturers of 'hawai chappals', across states, other intermediary firms and fake retailers to claim and encash fake credit . . . the group managed to create fake credit amounting to Rs 600 crore before the tax authorities cracked down.[2]

Thus, it isn't surprising that tax evasion and tax avoidance have become a defining feature of India's tax reporting. And for this reason, we should be sceptical whenever the

---

[2] Remya Nair, 'Fake Firms, Fake Invoices and Credit Fraud—How It Went All Wrong for GST in Just 2 Years', ThePrint.in, 16 January 2020, https://theprint.in/economy/fake-firms-fake-invoices-and-credit-fraud-how-it-went-all-wrong-for-gst-in-just-2-years/349933/.

government uses tax exemptions as a means for another purpose, however well-intentioned the objective may be.

Compulsory Philanthropy

Philanthropy implies choice. It is an act of generosity, of empathy. But that's not how the Indian State sees it. Under the name of Corporate Social Responsibility (CSR), philanthropy was made mandatory starting in 2014. India is the only country to make CSR mandatory and statutory.

The underlying philosophy was hyper multi-objective optimization again. Not only should companies be responsible for maximizing shareholder value, but they should also be made responsible for social welfare. They should be made to plug the State's failures.

What have the results been? A paper 'Does Mandated Corporate Social Responsibility Crowd Out Voluntary Corporate Social Responsibility? Evidence from India' analysed the impact of government intervention on CSR funding since the mandatory CSR law came into effect and concluded:

1. Overall, there is a marginal increase in the average CSR spending since the law came into effect in 2013–14. But . . .
2. 'High CSR' firms—companies that used to spend 4 per cent to 5 per cent of their profits on CSR before the law came into effect—reduced their spending to the mandated 2 per cent level. 'Low CSR' firms— companies that used to spend less than 1 per cent of their profits on CSR before the law came into effect—

increased their spending to the mandated 2 per cent level.

3. CSR contributions became highly sensitive to negative shocks to profits. This meant that companies reduced their CSR spending during bad times but did not increase CSR spending by the same amount during good times.[3]

In sum, 'mandatory CSR crowded out voluntary spending.' It became a checkbox to be ticked, a tax to be complied with.

Azim Premji, India's most prolific philanthropist, has consistently highlighted the futility of mandatory CSR. Premji alone donated Rs 7904 crores in FY20[4] while the total contribution of nearly 22,531 companies under the CSR scheme was Rs 24,689 crores in the same year.[5] He has argued that:

I do not think we should have a legal mandate for companies to do CSR. Philanthropy or charity or

---

[3] Shivaram Rajgopal and Prasanna Tantri, 'Does Mandated Corporate Social Responsibility Crowd Out Voluntary Corporate Social Responsibility? Evidence from India', *SSRN*, 22 August 2021, https://ssrn.com/abstract=3909219 or http://dx.doi.org/10.2139/ssrn.3909219.

[4] 'Azim Premji Donated Rs 7,904 Cr in FY 2020, That's Almost Rs 22 Cr a Day!', *The Economic Times*, 11 November 2020, https://economictimes.indiatimes.com/news/company/corporate-trends/azim-premji-donated-rs-7904-cr-in-fy-2020-thats-almost-rs-22-cr-a-day/articleshow/79163112.cms.

[5] Ministry of Corporate Affairs, Government of India maintains a CSR dashboard at https://csr.gov.in/index20.php.

contribution to society must come from within, and it cannot be mandated from outside. But that's my personal view. As of now, this is the law and all companies must follow it.[6]

The violation of the assignment principle as mandatory CSR is problematic at a fundamental level as well. To think that companies can easily plug government failures is to delude ourselves. All of CSR expenditure in FY19, despite the mandate, was less than one-third of union government expenditure on the Mahatma Gandhi National Rural Employment Guarantee Scheme (MGNREGS) alone. Given how sensitive CSR spending is to profits earned, it means that this number would have gone down further because of COVID-19.

The assignment principle would have implied that it's only the State that has the resources and stamina to provide public goods. It must be held accountable for that. No amount of philanthropy can be allowed to provide an escape to the State. In sum, compulsory philanthropy is akin to the Indian State reprimanding markets and society by saying: I won't do what I'm supposed to but why the hell aren't you two doing what I'm supposed to do?

---

[6] PTI, 'CSR Should Not Be Legally Mandated, Philanthropy Must Come from within, Says Azim Premji', The Economic Times, accessed 28 January 2022, https://economictimes. indiatimes.com/news/company/corporate-trends/csr-should-not-be-legally-mandated-philanthropy-must-come-from-within-says-azim-premji/articleshow/81126383. cms?utm_source=contentofinterest&utm_medium=text&utm_campaign=cppst.

Some Other Examples

The National Rural Employment Guarantee Scheme's expanding job scope is also a consequence of flouting the assignment principle. It was originally meant to be a scheme to augment the income of households by providing wage employment opportunities in rural areas. However, several new objectives were subsequently added. For instance, creating sustainable rural livelihoods through the regeneration of the natural resource base and strengthening rural governance through decentralization. Thus, far from being optimized for increasing wages, this is also seen as a process of regeneration of natural resources and for strengthening rural grassroots democracy.

Similarly, you would have often seen traffic police trying their best to manage traffic flows even as motorists indiscriminately break the most basic rules of traffic. This situation can also be explained through the assignment principle. The traffic police system was created with the objective of upholding the rule of law on roads i.e., ensuring that the traffic rules are adhered to on roads. But this same police force is also tasked with the objective of reducing traffic congestion, i.e., ensuring a smooth flow of vehicles. Often, the two objectives of faster vehicular traffic movement and upholding traffic rules conflict with each other. The result is that neither objective is met.

How to Resolve This Multi-Objective Optimization?

Here's a three-fold heuristic approach to avoid this folly that characterizes many policies of the Indian State.

First, withdrawal, i.e., reduce the number of targets that the State is held accountable for. This is why, in Section 1, we argue for a State that does fewer things and does them well. This method requires a realization that a few objectives just cannot be optimized efficiently by government policies. They are better left to the market or by society.

For example, the traffic police can return to their original duty—ensuring that traffic rules are adhered to. The objective of managing vehicle flows can be left to automated traffic signals. Beyond that, it is for individuals to assess and build consensus for reducing travel times. Similarly, given that absolute poverty is its biggest concern, the government may choose to leave the moral question of relative poverty and the pursuit of zero inequality to a future date.

If a withdrawal is undesirable, it is best to increase the number of instruments or organizations, each responsible for a narrow set of targets. For instance, the Department of Telecom (DoT) was a service provider, regulator, and the chief policymaking organization for communications. These roles often came in conflict with each other, with the end result that none of these objectives was met. Later, the DoT's functions were divided into a service-providing corporate entity such as BSNL, an independent regulator called Telecom Regulatory Authority of India (TRAI), and finally a policymaking organization that decides the overall objectives.

Often, people would baulk at the mention of another government organization and more bureaucracy. But as we saw in Chapter 4, the Indian State is small where it matters. We need more capacity and more organizations with a razor-sharp focus.

Finally, if increasing the number of organizations is not possible, an option is to coordinate policy instruments within the same organization to achieve more than one target. This applies to tax policy reform. Until the 1980s, it was widely accepted that personal income tax shouldn't just be used to raise resources for important government functions but also for reducing inequality. As a result, income tax slabs used to be highly progressive (multiple tax slabs) even in countries such as the US and the UK. Not unlike in India, such tax regimes allowed for a number of exemptions at the lower end of the spectrum even as the marginal tax rates at the highest end used to be as high as 95 per cent. However, these highly progressive tax systems did little to reduce inequality.

An important empirical tax study in Chile in fact showed that the Gini coefficient—an indicator of inequality—slightly increased *after* a highly progressive tax system was put into place as the rich were able to evade the high-income taxes, while the poor bore the brunt of regressive consumption taxes.[7] The learning from this phase in taxation history was that it is futile to address multiple objectives through the tax system. Instead, it was better to deal with systemic problems such as inequality or women's low employment rates through the expenditure side of the budget and design tax rates for simplicity and effectiveness. This is a reform possible within India's Ministry of Finance.

---

[7] Eduardo Engel, Alexander Galetovic and Claudio Raddatz, 'Taxes and Income Distribution in Chile: Some Unpleasant Redistributive Arithmetic', *Journal of Development Economics* 59, 1999, 155–92.

The revenue department shouldn't be burdened with the objective of reducing inequality.

The default mode of operation in the Indian State is *jugaad*, i.e., try to execute option 3 haphazardly. Option 2 requires increasing state capacity. Internalizing option 1 requires a radical reimagination of the State's role, which seems distant given how the welfare State continues to increase in scope unabatedly.

III

Samaaj

21

A Short History of State and Society

Man is a social animal.

You would have come across this line in essays at school. But why or how did this happen? We see the proof of this all around us. Your family, the locality you live in, the apartment complex you are a part of—they are all inseparable parts of your life. We are so conditioned to live in a society with its own matrix of norms that it feels the most natural thing to do.

But is it normal?

The Need for a Sovereign

Our earliest ancestors lived as hunter-gatherers. A family unit would move around the forest looking for their next meal and finding a safe shelter. Over time, a few families began to band together to form a kind of proto-community that would hunt and gather in groups. This coming together as a tribe made sense. Hunting got easier, diverse skills within the tribe must have helped in making better tools, and the camaraderie would have provided a sense of security and well-being. Things would go on swimmingly until this tribe came in contact with another. It is difficult to imagine the two tribes finding a way to coexist peacefully, especially if the options to hunt and gather were getting scarce in that neck of the woods. As time went by and the population went up, these bands would come into conflict quite often. This couldn't have been nice. Life in such a natural state, as the seventeenth century English philosopher Thomas Hobbes famously wrote, would have been 'nasty, brutish and short'. It would have taken a few generations of bloodshed for these tribes to realize this cycle of violence wouldn't ever end. There must be a way to balance cooperation and competition between them. Wouldn't it be nice if someone powerful set the rules of peaceful coexistence among them and enforced those rules with a firm hand, they must have mused. But who would this powerful entity be? Who would restrain the entity itself from abusing their power? And if they did, what could they do?

It is likely some kind of an early philosopher must have proposed a solution to these questions. What if we agreed to *voluntarily* give away some of our freedoms to a powerful entity in exchange for order among our tribes? This powerful entity, let's call it a 'sovereign', would then do a few things drawing their power from the people's will—a set of rules to prevent violence among them, a police force to enforce those rules, a standing army to defend territory from outsiders, and some kind of forum to arbitrate disputes.

This isn't hard to imagine. Of course, these would need funding. So, the sovereign had to crowdsource it as taxes. It didn't matter who the sovereign was, the philosopher argued. It could be the strongest, fastest, most skilled, or the sharpest. So long as the people voluntarily gave the sovereign the power to control a few of their freedoms and the sovereign exercised this power fairly while managing order, the elusive equilibrium between cooperation and competition was reached. Now this was an idea of far-reaching consequences. It is likely *Homo sapiens* would not have 'settled' into an agrarian society without this voluntary act of finding order in their lives by handing over the right to a sovereign power to punish them if they fell out of line.

This is how society and a sovereign came about. It is not too difficult to see how society preceded the notion of sovereignty. In the post-industrial age, the idea of the State became *de rigueur*. The enforcer was no longer the royalty or the clergy of yore. Instead, a group of people chose their own enforcer who then took on the business of running the apparatus of the State. In very broad brushstrokes, this is the modern conception of the State.

Until the advent of nation-states, the State kept its area of influence limited in the lives of its citizens. Internal and external security, taxation, infrastructure, law and order—well-governed States rarely went beyond these. It isn't that the State didn't try. But the consequences were often terrible. Medieval world history is dotted with instances of kings using the powers of the State to promote a certain faith or to change the customs of their societies. The many civil wars in western European nations between the fifteenth and seventeenth centuries can be traced to the Protestant and Catholic divide in those societies with the king weighing in on one side. As nation-states and the idea of the republic became common in western Europe after the Industrial

Revolution, the State began consolidating more powers to itself. Monetary policy, trade, more laws for governing the society, what should be taught in schools and universities, social equity—the list is long.

Is society by itself capable of creating norms or reforming the older norms as it contends with new knowledge, advances in science and rational thought? Or should the State take it upon itself to nudge the society in the direction of change? That has been the crux of the debate between conservatives and liberals over the past two centuries.

The definition of who is conservative or liberal isn't constant over time. But loosely put, a conservative believes time-tested traditions and norms that have worked to keep a society stable and functioning are precious. They must be conserved. Any change to them should be gradual and with the consent of the society. It is better to create conditions for society to reform itself than to induce change from outside. Successful societies are complex and adaptive. They must not be tinkered with too often.

Liberals believe societies tend to continue with biases, prejudices, and entrenched hierarchies for far too long. Some changes cannot be left to the society to decide on how and when it will adapt to them. Slavery or the oppressive caste system won't go away merely because more people learn about values of individual life and liberty alone. These will need to be reformed with proactive force and passion. Lawmakers will have to be co-opted, new laws drafted, and reforms will have to be triggered. A liberal is unafraid of losing something precious of the past in search of a glorious future based on the progressive march of ideas.

The Indian *Samaaj* and Its Sovereigns

India is a unique case. For centuries it followed the classic model of a State (royalty) that restricted itself to a few areas in the lives of its citizens. Society lived by its traditions. The *Varna* system, the practices that were handed down over generations, and the ancient texts interpreted by the priestly class were the guides to the everyday lives of people. The restrictions on learning the ancient texts and the lack of access to Sanskrit (the language in which they were written) meant over time there was limited reinterpretation of these texts. Alternative philosophies like Buddhism and Jainism did emerge and had an impact on society. They spread widely across India but some clever appropriating of Buddha into the pantheon of Vishnu avatars and a resurgence of *Sanatana Dharma* by the tireless efforts of Shankaracharya stopped it in its tracks. These offshoots of Hinduism couldn't deepen their roots within India beyond the first millennium.

This absence of updating of the core beliefs of the society through a continuous process of enquiry and revision of the texts meant that the society harboured deep suspicion about any change from outside. The reformation movement in Christianity from the sixteenth century or the Islamic golden age from the eleventh century onwards are interesting cases to consider. These periods of social and religious ferment didn't strive to change the 'revealed' truth written in the holy books. Yet there was a reinterpretation of how that text should be read as human enterprise and knowledge expanded about the world around them. This is a process that continued in western Europe through the industrial age where the modern understanding of the natural world could co-exist with a deep belief in religion. Many are surprised to learn Newton was a professor of mathematics as well as of theology at Cambridge. Newton questioned the concept of the holy trinity while holding onto his deep Christian faith. His unravelling of the mysteries of the physical world wasn't seen in contradiction to his religious beliefs because the ground was being set for the two to co-exist by the clergy and the philosophers of the time. In contrast, for multiple reasons but chiefly the restriction on who could learn Sanskrit, Indian society didn't popularize the knowledge of scriptures. So, the question of continuous updating of the past beliefs in the light of new knowledge didn't arise.

That apart, there was also the continuous process of invasions and newer communities settling in India through the medieval age. The earlier intrusions of the Kushanas, Huns, and other tribes didn't carry with them the religious fervour that was a feature of the Islamic marauders. One way was to take them head on. But these were battle-hardened warrior tribes with the natural advantages of cavalry and arms. The other option was for the society to turn inwards to protect its identity. It is no surprise then that there was an almost simultaneous springing of the Bhakti movements with saints and singers across India between the twelfth and fifteenth centuries. This idea that we will devote ourselves to our gods while the world around us turns adversarial became alluring. The Bhakti movement also came with associated social reforms the likes of which were seen in the efforts of the great saints Basavanna in Karnataka and Namdev in Maharashtra. This was a rupture in the tradition of keeping knowledge of scriptures exclusive to the upper echelons of the Hindu society. But it wasn't deep enough and morphed into a paradigm for an individual searching for God instead of 'reformation' like it happened in Europe.

The Mughal era followed by the Maratha empire and the early consolidation of power by the East India Company was marked by advances in warfare, political manoeuvring, and statecraft. The coming of the Persian and Turkish communities and the mixing of the cultures did produce a mélange of new languages and evolution in arts, literature, and architectural styles. But there was no marked change in the societal norms. There was no equivalent of an Age of Enlightenment in the subcontinent. And no surprise then, we didn't have a scientific or industrial revolution that followed the Enlightenment.

The hundred-year period between the Battle of Plassey (1757) and the first War of Independence (1857) saw the Company take over the role of the State in large parts of the subcontinent. This period was the first time in ages that the State tried to intervene more directly into the social domain in India. The British-educated class who came over to the colonies were brought up on Enlightenment values at their schools and colleges. There was a zeal, often misplaced, to educate the 'natives' and reform their 'barbaric' practices. Many of them tried to replicate the process of European enlightenment by learning the languages of the older texts and translating them into English. Practices like Sati were banned. An education system modelled on the English system was set up to create a supply of 'natives' who could help the Company govern. It is likely this mix of State intervention in social practices, re-reading of our classical texts and their translations, and a generation of

Indians taught the modern scientific advances of the West could have spurred an Indian age of enlightenment. The mid-nineteenth century period suggested an emergence of something resembling a renaissance in the two key cultural centres of Bengal and Pune. And then the War of Independence happened in 1857.

1857 marked a change in the British attitude to governing India. Power was transferred to the Crown and Queen Victoria became the sovereign of India. The close shave of 1857 clarified British thinking about India. The primary objective now was to perpetuate their reign for as long as possible and to maximize the gains from India's abundant resources and wealth. The grand notion of reforming Indian society or enlightening the natives was given short shrift. What replaced it was the idea of using the existing fault lines in the society to keep it from coming together and encouraging new fault lines to emerge. The State was designed to be rapacious with short-term gains trumping any idea of long-term reforms. It appropriated enormous powers on itself to curb the liberties of its people. This was a State that was insecure and tyrannical with the sole objective of enriching itself. This is an important point to keep in mind. What we inherited in 1947 was a State apparatus that was designed to be predatory even more than what a State usually is. It had tremendous powers to say no and stop its citizens than to enable them to lead a life of liberty and self-development.

In 1947, we took over this apparatus. The winds of socialism blowing around the world influenced our founding fathers too. They saw the State as a force of positive change. Society was too riven with differences, and Indian capital was too weak and small to take the lead to change India. So, the State would have to do the heavy lifting. We didn't think too deeply about reforming the State itself. What's more, we decided that a society that had not reformed itself in any significant measure for ages needs to transform itself in a hurry. So, we designed a constitution that was not merely a rulebook for how we would govern ourselves. We also made it a tool for social revolution. We imposed a liberal constitution on a society that was illiberal, in a top-down fashion (a point that Amit Varma makes often in his popular podcast 'The Seen and the Unseen'). So, we handed over more powers in the social domain to a State that was designed originally to exploit and stymie its people.

So, in 1950 when we became a republic, we had a State that was already overbearing, given more powers, and a society that had not reformed itself for a long time. And that had resisted any top-down imposition of rules from the State in its history. This was bound to get fraught. What we have seen since Independence is this battle between the State and society. For a while it was felt that the State would be able to change society in line with the lofty goals of the constitution. Now, we cannot be sure.

In the chapters that follow in this section, we will present a view on how this tussle between the State and society has evolved in India over the years after Independence. In Chapter 22, we tackle the question of who should have been the primary agent of change in our society. This is an unresolved question from the time of our Independence and its repercussions are felt in today's India. We pick up the contentious issue of the State and its attempt to control or reform religion in Chapter 23.

Democratic ideals meant the old ways of organizing social life based on scriptures were to be subordinated to the constitution. This hasn't been easy in India. In Chapter 24, we trace how the individual incentives to act in consonance with the objectives of the State have changed over the decades in India.

In Chapter 25, we contest the commonplace narrative that India's huge population is the reason why its State is ineffective. Chapter 26 breaks down two State–society archetypes that have been projected as polar opposites in recent times, the so-called Gujarat and Kerala models of development.

How does a society with ancient roots that's visible in its everyday customs and traditions deal with a State that seeks to promote a scientific temper among its citizens? We discuss this tussle between tradition and modernity in Indian society in light of what can be construed as a trend of Hindu revivalism in Chapter 27. Finally, the idea of India has always been a subject of vigorous contestation. Chapter 28 surveys the directions this debate has taken since Independence.

Are we getting better or worse in the delicate balance between the powers of the State and society? There are no easy answers here but the incident or the thought that triggers each chapter is a good way to appreciate the task we have in our hands.

22

The Unresolved Question of *Naya Daur*

The Hindi movie *Naya Daur* (A New Era, directed by B. R. Chopra and released in 1957), made during the high noon of Nehruvian socialism, is often considered the defining cultural watermark of those times.

Far from it.

Naya Daur is, in fact, a stinging riposte to the Nehruvian State. It asks a fundamental question that split even the Constituent Assembly—who should be the primary agent of change to modernize India? The State, the society, or the market? In siding with the society, *Naya Daur* seeks a rethink on the role of the State intervening in the lives of its people.

That the newly independent India needed to change wasn't ever in doubt. Colonial rule had drained it economically. Its society was riven with ancient caste prejudices and practices. The enlightenment values of liberty, freedom, and equality that philosophically underpinned Western democracies were difficult to root in the Indian intellectual or social context. Democracy, with equal rights to all citizens, was, therefore, an audacious gamble.

All that remained was what means should we adopt to change India?

The market was quickly dumped as an option. The imperialist plunder that was seen as the handiwork of markets, the influence of Fabian socialism on Nehru, and the apparent miracle of central planning in the Soviet Union were enough to silence the pro-market voices. One would have assumed that the Gandhian vision centred on society would have seen the market—that emphasizes the merits of voluntary exchange between individuals—in more favourable terms. But that was not to be either. Gandhi had never taken a liking to market forces or economic modernity.

The society and the State, therefore, were the two poles around which the debates coalesced. This was a debate that had played out since the late eighteenth century following the revolutions in America and France. Burke was a traditionalist who defended monarchy, social hierarchies and orthodoxies; Paine argued for the State to advance change and the enlightenment values of liberty and reason. Burke believed in the power of community and emotions. Paine was all for individual agency and rationality. What transpired in India was the classic Burke versus Paine debate on new territory.

The proponents of the State during our founding moment included trenchant critics of Indian society like Nehru and Ambedkar. Deeply suspicious of Indian society, they wanted the State to remain consciously detached from it while working to change it from outside. Gandhi,

S. P. Mukherjee, and J. B. Kriplani viewed society as the most acceptable agent of change and wanted the change to emerge from within. Gandhi believed strong moral suasion and the efforts of the volunteers of the (disbanded) Congress who would fan out to the lakhs of villages would bring about true swaraj in India. The power of the State would devolve down to a village collective or a panchayat who would use that judiciously, not coercively, within its local context to bring swaraj for all.

The statists won. Our Constitution was to be more than a legal construct. It was to be a tool for a social revolution engineered by the State. And, so began a schism in the Indian polity. The State was run by liberal-minded modernists who viewed the customs and traditions of Indian society as impediments to progress. A popular song of the early 1960s from the movie *Hum Hindustani* captured this spirit. It went:

> *Chhodo kal ki baatein, kal ki baat purani,*
> *Naye daur mein likhenge, mil kar nayee kahaani,*
> *Hum Hindustani, Hum Hindustani*

> [Let's leave behind the past. The past is full of outdated notions. We, Indians, will write our own destiny in this new era.]

That was the optimism the State brewed in society. The common citizenry, on the other hand, viewed the rootless elite presiding over the State as a substitute of the colonial power who would 'rule' over them with, possibly, greater benevolence.

Rousseau in *The Social Contract,* a book that launched a thousand revolutions, describes an ideal society where 'the peasants are among the happiest people in the world regulating the affairs of state under an oak tree'. 'The simple and upright peasants' were happy because the 'general will' of the entire community was being expressed and was so 'manifestly evident that only common sense is needed to discern it'.

The village of *Naya Daur* is the Rousseau ideal. There are hardworking men and women who are deeply connected to their land with a benign feudal overlord who was part of the social fabric. There isn't a wisp of the casteist and superstitious cesspool that Ambedkar or Nehru so wanted to upend.

Naya Daur is a masterly crafted plot with multiple strands running through the movie—a love triangle, a friendship gone sour, man versus machines, and the village as the locus of change in society. It begins with a quote from Gandhi:

> Dead machinery must not be pitted against the millions of living machines represented by the villagers scattered in the seven hundred thousand villages of India. Machinery to be well-used has to help and ease human effort.

You know where the film's sympathies lie.

The lives of Dilip Kumar (the tonga driver, *tangawallah*) and Ajit (woodcutter) and their hardworking friends change when Jeevan, the son of the village zamindar, returns after his education in the city. Jeevan represents both the market and the instincts of the Nehruvian State that want to change the village from the outside. He automates the sawmill first that hits the livelihoods of the woodcutters. Things come to a head when Jeevan decides to introduce a bus service to the famous temple nearby. This route is what earns the *tangawallahs* their daily *daal-roti*. Dilip Kumar objects and a bet is placed. There will be a race between the tonga and the bus to the temple; whoever wins gets their way.

Meanwhile, Dilip Kumar and Ajit, vying for Vyjayanthimala's affections, fall out with some 'hand of God' support from Chand Usmani who plays Dilip Kumar's sister pining for Ajit. This rift has consequences. Ajit joins the dark side with Jeevan while Dilip Kumar and the villagers begin building a bridge that will cut short the distance to the temple for the tonga and give it a fighting chance against the bus. The usual last act drama ensues with man winning the race against the machine and Ajit redeeming himself. Dilip Kumar sums it up at the end when he claims that the villagers aren't against machines but want them in their lives on their terms.

Let society decide how it wants to change.

The cast, with an outstanding performance by Dilip Kumar, is first-rate. The film established O. P. Nayyar as a top-notch composer, and the script (by Akhtar Mirza, father of Saeed) and the direction move the film along briskly tying up the multiple sub-plots to perfection at the end.

The point that remains unresolved is why did Chopra name the film *Naya Daur*? Did man winning over machines herald a new era? Or was the title a touch satirical? That the new era won't arrive through a State-led intervention until you co-opt society into the modernization project. The role of the State still remains a principal axis of divergence in the Indian political discourse. These questions have greater salience today as society questions the shibboleths on which the Constitution and the modern India project was built.

Naya Daur was a huge commercial success. Not merely because the underdog won. Rather, it showed a mirror to the foundation of Indian society. The reflection we saw confirmed our biases. We weren't as bad as the State made us out to be. *Naya Daur* has a message for the liberals who wring their hands in despair about the path Indian society is going down today. Society isn't the problem. To mock it or to force a change on it is often counterproductive. Within it, possibly, lies the solution.

23

The *Purohit* Who Wore a Uniform

Raghu S. Jaitley

I grew up in a small industrial town in eastern India. The town beat to the rhythm of the factory that was at its heart. The factory was part of a State-run enterprise and it pervaded every aspect of our lives. The State ran everything—school, hospital, library, park, sports club, and even the temple.

The '*purohit*' (priest) uncle of the temple was otherwise an ordinary worker of the factory. He went to the temple every day wearing the factory uniform—light blue shirt and khaki trousers. He changed into his dhoti at the temple and put in his shift there performing *aartis*, *kirtans*, and pujas interspersed with playing the latest Bollywood songs during specific events like Ganesh or Durga Puja when a fair would come up nearby under a *shamiana*. '*Mere angane mein tumhara kya kaam hai*' (from *Lawaaris*, a 1981 film starring Amitabh Bachchan) was a particular favourite.[1] Then late every evening he would close the temple doors, change back into his factory clothes, and head back home on his cycle. No one questioned if the *purohit's* was a formal role in the factory. Maybe someone senior had just let him become the *purohit* of the temple while relieving him of his responsibility in the factory. It seemed to work for everyone. The town got a *purohit* who was always available and the man was happy doing something that he loved. Things were going well till a new general manager arrived who couldn't understand this arrangement. He threw the rule book at it. The *purohit* uncle went back to the factory, and we had a series of temporary *purohits* in the temple who were never as good.

Looking back, I find there is something emblematic in this incident about the relationship between the Indian State and religion over the years since Independence. Like we wrote earlier, the Constitution gave the State an extraordinary mandate to change society. In India, this would inevitably mean contending with social practices that were deeply rooted in religion. Two things complicated this.

One, Hinduism, the majority faith in India, is not rigidly codified. There's no single God and no single book to guide its adherents. There's a very loose set of uniformly defined practices but there are so many variations depending on region, caste, and community that it is impossible to agree on them. How do you reform something when that something is difficult to pin down?

---

[1] Literally translated, the lyrics run thus: What are you doing in my courtyard?

Two, there was very limited inquiry done of the extensive and fairly sophisticated philosophy of Hinduism present in the ancient texts over the last many centuries. This meant the society hadn't grappled with the issues of its ancient identity and heritage with the modernity that colonialism had brought about with it. There wasn't much intellectual groundwork already done that could then be built upon by the State. And the State didn't have much patience to create this intellectual scaffolding to support its revolutionary intent. This could only mean trouble as we will soon see.

The first real confrontation between the Indian State and religion was on what came to be called the Hindu Code Bill right after Independence. This was a battle over three decades in making.

By the early 1920s, as the British Indian courts spread across India, they were hearing cases on civil disputes from the Hindu community. The usual problems arose. There were claims made by disputing parties on the back of customs that were either backed by oral traditions or loosely interpreted in one of the many ancient texts that communities followed. The *Dharmashastra* was a common reference text in many regions but it was not the only one. Jurists and legal scholars gamely tried to blend the knowledge embedded in these texts and social practices to the common English laws that were prevalent in Britain then. But the sheer diversity of the Hindu religion confounded them.

Separately, many Indian leaders, including Nehru, were of the opinion that unity among Hindus could only be achieved if there's a common code of civil laws that created a sense of Hindu identity with a legal sanction. Clearly, something had to be done.

In 1941, the Hindu Law Committee was set up with B. N. Rau, an eminent civil servant and a judge in Calcutta High Court, as its chairman. The Rau Committee toured the country, sought inputs from scholars, jurists, religious leaders, and ordinary Indians and prepared a Draft Code.

By 1947, it had prepared a comprehensive report on the Hindu Code with a recommendation to draft a Bill that could be taken up by the Parliament for approval. The Draft Bill was taken up by a committee chaired by B. R. Ambedkar, the first union law minister. The committee gave the final shape to a bill that was far-reaching in its ambition to codify and reform Hindu society.

There were to be no caste-based differences in law among Hindus. A Hindu was a Hindu was a Hindu in the eyes of law. There were path-breaking proposals on women's right to property and succession, marriage and divorce, uniform definition of a joint family, and guardianship. This was revolutionary stuff.

The draft was presented to the Constituent Assembly in 1949 and met with immediate widespread protests and outrage. Congress stalwarts like Dr Rajendra Prasad and Purushottam Das Tandon, Hindu Mahasabha leaders like N. C. Chatterjee and S. P. Mukherjee (who later founded Jan Sangh), and religious leaders like Sant Karpatri Maharaj took public positions opposing it. The State had no business interfering in matters of religion that have guided the lives of people for centuries was their collective contention.

Nehru was surprised by the opposition and decided to take only the first fifty-five clauses to the Constituent

Assembly for debate. This didn't help matters. Only three out of fifty-five clauses were accepted after a week of debate. Mind you, this was the Constituent Assembly—a collection of the best and the brightest of Indians who knew their Locke, Paine, and Hume. Nehru, seeing the writing on the wall, had the committee make significant changes to the clauses. Even that didn't satisfy the Assembly.

Ambedkar, dissatisfied with the dilution of the Bill and not finding enough support from Nehru, quit the cabinet. Nehru put the Bill on hold and decided he would seek the mandate for the Bill in the upcoming first general elections of 1952. Congress won a majority, and Nehru took that as the approval of his people for the Bill. He split the Bill into four separate bills and passed them over the next four years in Parliament.

The Indian State had won the battle. But the Hindu Code Bill episode laid bare a few truths. The State that was controlled by progressive liberals could impose its agenda on the society in a top-down manner. But the society was conservative and it wouldn't take the liberal imposition of the State lying down. It might have been defeated for now but the war was far from over. Even the agents of the State weren't convinced about this imposition. They aligned to it though because of how the State set up their incentives. It wouldn't take a lot for them to turn. As the years since have shown, this turned out to be true. The State tried to change the social and cultural norms of the society for long till society struck back. It could be argued that the State now follows society on most of these issues.

The role of courts or the Indian legal system in framing social policies has been a matter of intense debate since the years of the Hindu Code Bill. Should courts be framing social policies? This is a question that animates discussions in the US too. In fact, the ability to nominate a judge of your political leaning to the US Supreme Court (SC) is possibly the most important reason for people to vote for a candidate in the presidential and senate elections.

At the heart of these debates is a deeper question about the larger role the SC has taken over the years in legislating social issues in the US. The two most famous examples, of course, are *Roe vs Wade* (1973) and *Brown vs Board of Education* (1954). The court turned into a lawmaker is how it appears. Seen from here in India, the US is a litigious country. As far back as 1835, Tocqueville had noted that 'sooner or later, every major dispute in the US ends up in the courtroom.' So, it is no surprise when women, minorities, and other under-represented sections started contesting the social norms handed down to them, the matters reached courts for resolution.

Over time, this has been true in India too. From caste-based reservations, rights of women (across religions), decriminalization of homosexuality, to adjudicating on the Ram *Janambhoomi* dispute, Indian courts have taken up social issues whenever the legislature has been coy about taking a stand. And the divide between conservatives and liberals on the role of the courts or the State in remodelling society has turned more fraught. We touched upon this in the previous chapter but it will be useful to go deeper into the issue of conservative anxiety and liberal activism in the context of courts here.

The conservative preference is for any social change to be gradual. Societal change is shaped through the many eddies of debates and protests that resist the flow of the mainstream. As they gain wider acceptance, they begin changing the course of the flow of social norms. This could be painstakingly slow, but it makes change acceptable and sustainable. For the conservatives, the role of the judges is to apply laws, not to create them. Going beyond this brief becomes judicial activism. So, the original conservative view was that all issues of public or social policy should be discussed and debated by the legislative and executive branches of the State that represents the society. Courts resolve disputes following the written down law while sending back any ambiguities to the legislative arm for approval. Courts shouldn't be making laws.

There is a lot of merit in this argument. It is difficult to imagine how a single complainant with a specific grievance in a combative judicial process would be the basis for drafting a norm or law for the society. Isn't there a risk of the courts overlooking the true costs and benefits to society while judging a single case? How representative is that case anyway? Would the second order impact of their decision on society be visible to them? How will we prevent the judges from bringing in their personal values into issues of constitutional merits? And let's not pretend judges are above this. Judicial activism is unavoidable if we let courts decide on such issues.

In fact, the heated debate between the two major parties in the US about nominations to the SC is an implicit acceptance that judges insert their personal code into judgments. When you consider the adversarial nature of many historic social judgments (both in the US and India) and the costs such a process extracts in polarizing the society further, it becomes clear that litigation is a blunt instrument to carve out social change. Courts shouldn't pre-empt social and political debates.

The liberal position, as it has evolved over time, is marked with suspicion about society reforming itself. The classical liberal approach to this problem was to accelerate the process of change within society. This was to be achieved through a combined political, social, and cultural assault on the bastions of conservatism in the society. This led to the portrait of a liberal as a perpetual activist in a constant state of mobilization to upend existing norms. The liberal belief that society must change from within was no different from the conservative stance. The difference was on the need to induce change through proactive measures and on the speed of change. This need for speed eventually led the liberals to the courts. To the liberals, this wasn't difficult to justify. The law isn't ever 'value neutral'.

Like Sahir Ludhianvi once wrote (*Chitralekha*, 1964):

Yeh paap hai kya, yeh punya hai kya, reeton pe dharm ki moharein hai,
Har yug mein badalte dharmon ko kaise aadarsh banaoge?

[What's right or wrong has always been a compilation of enforceable values by society.]

This is a forever changing or evolving construct. Since people use these values in their daily lives, the courts can define their boundaries of 'reasonableness'.

The old question of law and morality comes in. Should law intrude into the moral sphere of citizens? The liberals often make a distinction between public and private spheres. We use our intuition to guide our behaviour in public. This is different from our conduct in private space. The law should focus on maintaining this intuitive decorum that allows free individuals to conduct their business in public without the threat of private behaviour of others spilling onto the public. This is the freedom that law should guarantee.

The private space of individuals has been guided by the doctrine John Stuart Mill put forth in *On Liberty* (1859).[2] In Mill's view, the law shouldn't be used to prohibit the rights of people who are acting on the basis of mutual consent. This principle has been central to liberalizing social laws over the past century. Liberals believe judicial activism works in favour of protecting individual liberties based on this principle.

A few other reasons nudged the liberal position closer to supporting judicial activism.

---

[2] 'That the only purpose for which power can be rightfully exercised over any member of a civilized community, against his will, is to prevent harm to others. His own good, either physical or moral, is not a sufficient warrant. He cannot rightfully be compelled to do or forbear because it will be better for him to do so, because it will make him happier, because, in the opinions of others, to do so would be wise, or even right.

It is, perhaps, hardly necessary to say that this doctrine is meant to apply only to human beings in the maturity of their faculties.' Mill, *On Liberty*, p. 13, https://socialsciences.mcmaster.ca/econ/ugcm/3ll3/mill/liberty.pdf.

Firstly, it became clear that there can be no regime where every issue of public policy can be resolved through the executive or legislative arms of the State. How representative is the legislature anyway? Or, how compromised? This centralized policymaking unit that changes every few years in a democratic process cannot be expected to draft policies that will be considered the final word and stand the test of time. Also, there are common laws that precede the State and changing them requires the blunt force of law itself.

Secondly, as the legislative environment turned more partisan and dysfunctional, the drafting of laws became more imprecise or vague to accommodate political bargains. This has meant a constant need for interpreting or divining the legislative intent of laws. This act of precise interpretation and proofreading has turned judges into lawmakers by default. Lastly, the liberals who are often blamed for supporting activist judges argue this is a matter of perspective. Their argument is that only when the issue at hand goes against the conservative agenda, it is considered judicial activism. Not otherwise.

Based on the evidence in most democracies around the world, it can be argued that the conservatives have lost the argument. The courts are at the front and centre of social policymaking in many societies. The many historic judgments that cleave the US (abortion, racial intermixing, etc.) and Indian society (reservations, marriage, administration of temples et al.) are evidence of it. The legislative arms of the State representing the society aren't drafting these laws.

But here's the irony. The conservatives over time have co-opted the liberal model. With a few strokes of good fortune electorally, the conservatives have been able to control or influence the appointment or nomination of like-minded judges. The peril of pushing social change into the cabins of a powerful, centralized, and autonomous institution is clear to the liberals now when the shoe is on the other foot. A blunt instrument doesn't look blunt till it is in the hands of your adversary. It is possible that in both the US and India, society might turn liberal over the next generation while its legal system remains conservative. This will mean another round of State versus society battle fought in the courts in times to come.

Postscript: Back to the town I grew up in. The last I heard, the town folks, dissatisfied with the affairs of the temple run by the factory management, collected *chanda* (donations) and built a new temple. It was society telling the State—*Mere angane mein tumhara kya kaam hai?*

24

The Changing Fortunes of *Farz*

Dilip Kumar passed away on 7 July 2021. You might wonder why we should bring that up in this book. Well, there are reasons. For one, we have used the Dilip Kumar starrer *Naya Daur* to make broader points about the choices we have made as a nation. The other reason is that great artists shape our collective identity and contribute to national consciousness. It is no surprise that a lot of what was written about Dilip Kumar in his obituaries touched on this part of his legacy.

If you went past the usual hyperbole about his 'method acting' ways and how he had to seek medical support to get over his 'tragedy king' persona, you will find the more serious commentators usually hold forth on a couple of aspects of his life. First, how he was the embodiment of the Nehruvian ideal of India. Some went all the way to call him Nehru's hero.[1] Second, how in his death we have lost

---

[1] The economist Lord Meghnad Desai published a book on him in 2004 entitled *Nehru's Hero: Dilip Kumar in the Life of India*.

the last link with an era that was marked by idealism and innocence. In this chapter, we will use both these notions to further the discussion on how relations between the State and society have changed over the years.

What did it mean to be the Nehruvian ideal of India in the years after Independence?

Nehru, Ambedkar, and other members of the Constituent Assembly drafted the Indian Constitution as a project of radical forgetting of our past. This, to them, was necessary to build a new India. But a radical forgetting of the past for a land as old as ours isn't really an option. So, it was paired with the notion 'reawakening from slumber' that Nehru used in his famous 'tryst with destiny' speech. Nehru set the template for the reimagining of a new nation-state.

Benedict Anderson reached a similar conclusion in his book *Imagined Communities*. Anderson defined the nation as a social community that is imagined by people who believe they belong to it, while being different from other such communities. Every newly formed nation has to define this imagination. And at that stage, it faces a choice. Or, as Anderson puts it, a paradox:

> The objective modernity of nations to the historians' eyes
> vs. their subjective antiquity in the eyes of nationalists.[2]

This is a tough ask especially for nations that are formed after a period of struggle. There's a strong desire to start

[2] Benedict Anderson, *Imagined Communities: Reflections on the Origin and Spread of Nationalism* (Verso, 2006 [1983]), p. 5.

from a clean constitutional slate while paying homage to 'subjective antiquity' in areas outside the bounds of law and statecraft.

The reimagination project of a newly formed nation then usually follows a three-step template. First, newly independent nations like to make a new start that represents a break from the continuum of their history. Next, nations or communities that have a long history that can't be wished away easily use the trope of slumber and reawakening to represent the departure from the past. Finally, historians are pressed into service to reframe history that shows past events as serving the nation-building or myth-making objectives of the present.

Dilip Kumar was a Nehruvian ideal because he contributed significantly in mainstreaming this project of reimagination through cinema. His 'natural' style of acting, specifically his enunciation and dialogue delivery, was a marked departure from the theatrical or the singing style that was popular until then. Though Ashok Kumar and Motilal before him had started the trend, Dilip Kumar was a class apart. His style marked a break from how we watched and assessed a performance.

Secondly, as much as he represented a new beginning, he also fitted the trope of reawakening. He was well read, he spoke on a wide range of issues with acuity, and he could quote from Indian, Persian, or English literature with equal felicity.

Lastly, as an artist, he contributed to the reframing of history and served the myth-making objectives. His film persona of a sacrificing lover or son, his popularity among the masses who could see past his religion in the years right after Partition violence, and his social contributions (charities, supporting the troops, etc.)—all contributed to the strengthening of the syncretic culture or the *Ganga-Jamuni tehzeeb* that was part of the reimagination project of Nehru. He was indeed the Nehruvian ideal.

It will be hard to argue against the notion that with the passing away of Dilip Kumar, we have lost something precious that linked us back to the years of hope and idealism post-Independence. But we would suggest that era had begun its decline from the 1980s and was well and truly forgotten in the past decade. What remained was buried with him.

What was this era about and what ended with him? We will have to go back to another of his films to elaborate on this.

In his later years, Dilip Kumar often played an agent of the State (judge, police commissioner, etc.) who would place his *farz* (duty) above everything else. In these roles, where he effortlessly blurred the lines between method acting and sky-high racks of piled-up ham, Dilip Kumar would often shoot to kill or sentence his own kin to untold misery.

Shakti (1982), directed by Ramesh Sippy, is the prime example of this genre. Dilip Kumar chooses to not pay a ransom for his kidnapped school-going son at the beginning of the film and in a memorable final scene shoots his son down (Amitabh Bachchan) as he flees from justice. The audience saw this adherence to *farz* as a strong personality trait. Placing *farz* over your personal beliefs was the credo the Indian State hoped to inculcate among its agents. The popularity of such roles and films gave it comfort. In reality though, the *farz* of the agents of the State stems from their incentives. It used to be at odds with their personal values but they suppressed it for the material upside designed by the State.

The foundational premise of modern India is that the State is ontologically prior to society. The State should create legislation and structures that shape and change society. Its agents who emerge from that society itself have the incentives to adhere to the philosophy of the State regardless of whether it aligns to their personal convictions.

This created an unstable, yet desirable, equilibrium in newly independent India. The State was founded on values of equality, redistribution, secularism, fairness, and social welfare. The society from where agents were drawn hadn't fully accepted and internalized these values.

So, you had people leading double lives. A free-market economist would be drafting socialist policies of the State or a well-educated district magistrate would preach social equality at work but practise caste discrimination in his personal life. This was all good so long as the objectives of the State were met in their professional roles and the agents of the State could make peace with this dissonance in their personal sphere.

An episode of *Panchayat*, a well-crafted series available on Amazon Prime, subtly drives home this point. In one of the episodes, the protagonist, who is a young, city-bred, mid-level government officer, finds out that the science teacher of the village school has concocted a story about a ghost living in a tree on the outskirts of the village. Now, how should the somewhat timid government officer confront the teacher? Instead of directly telling the teacher off about his beliefs, the young officer asks the teacher how will the local district magistrate who values scientific temper as mandated by the State think of him if she were to know about his belief in ghosts? The teacher quickly confesses to having concocted the ghost story. He knew that continuing to believe in it would hurt his career. Personal values can easily be abandoned. Because incentives matter. The State drove the agenda for change in society through the right set of incentives. *Farz* was about creating the right incentives for people. This was classic public choice theory at work.

Things changed in the 1980s when the State started loosening its grip on the economy and was no longer the primary provider of employment for the middle class. This had an unintended consequence. The acceleration of economic reforms in the 1990s led to the creation of a large middle class that didn't depend on the State for its livelihood. This freed them from the incentives designed by the Indian State. Free-market incentives aren't the same as those of the State. It rewards efficiency and value creation.

For the middle class now, there was no need to live the dichotomous life their parents led—of having a professional code that was different from their personal code. Liberals today are often surprised how well-educated professionals working for multinational companies or having global exposure turn out to be bigots on so many social issues. The answer is simple. The State couldn't change society as it had expected during the time it had an iron-fisted grip on it. And once the incentives stopped mattering to citizens, the mask of *farz* they wore at work dropped.

There's no *farz* to adhere to because there's no incentive.

You can argue the democratic mandate now is for the idea that the society is ontologically prior to the State. This changes the incentives for the agents of the State too. No longer do they have to align their ethics to that of the State. The State itself is being made to align its incentives to that of society. So, you have a scenario where both, those who depend on the State and those outside it, have no conflict between their professional and personal codes.

If you believe that the Indian State, as it was founded, aspired for ideals that were universal and virtuous, then you would worry about this alignment. On the other hand, if you agitated against the imposition of ethics by the State and the false dichotomy that served us no good and impeded our growth, you'd see this as a greatly needed transformation of the State.

So, what has ended with Dilip Kumar?

For new India, a great actor of the past whose films were slow and sad is no more. That's about it. Life goes on. But what about for a generation and more who grew up believing the ideals of the Indian State as it was founded on? Those who invested in the idea of India that was shaped by Nehru?

For them, the death of Dilip Kumar is a painful reminder of how things were, how they could have been, and how far we are now from those ideals. Their loss is palpable.

Like lyricist Shakeel Badayuni wrote in the Dilip Kumar sci-fi starrer *Uran Khatola* (1955):

चले आज तुम जहाँ से, हुई ज़िन्दगी परायी
तुम्हे मिल गया ठिकाना, हमें मौत भी न आयी

[You have left this world today and we are bereft. You found your destination while we continue living in despair.]

25

Aabadi Isn't *Barbaadi*

There was a time not so long ago when a population clock (counter) would play for a few ominous seconds on Doordarshan (DD). During the 1980s, the State-run DD was the only channel in the country, and right in the middle of a film or an episode of B. R. Chopra's *Mahabharat* we would see the counter ticking away furiously, eighty-one crore Indians and counting. Thus, sobered about the grim reality of our population, we would go back to the fifth day of the great war wondering about Abhimanyu.

Over the years, governments of all hues have viewed our population as a problem. This is a view that most citizens also hold because this has been drummed into their heads. Population explosion or *janasankhya visphot* is a hook on which Indians hang a lot of their problems. People are seen as hungry stomachs to feed rather than enterprising brains that can contribute to prosperity. From an economic perspective, population is a neutral variable. It can be good or bad depending on the context. We will examine it in the Indian context in this chapter.

The supposed ills of a large population have an outsized influence in our policymaking. The near-death experience in the mid-1960s when we were in danger of being a global basket case casts its long shadow on our thinking. The idea that the human population would outpace farm productivity leading to hunger, pestilence, and deaths has been debunked over the years. The role of human capital, institutions, and ideas on productivity have been established by economists like Solow and Romer. Yet we persist with the Malthusian notion.

As Julian Simon argued in his 1981 book *The Ultimate Resource*, we are an intelligent race who innovate in the face of scarcity. Human ingenuity is the ultimate resource that can make other resources plentiful. More humans lead to more ideas, bigger markets, larger infrastructure spends, and, paradoxically, higher prices for scarce resources that leads to conservation or search for replacement products. There is empirical evidence to support this has been good for the world over the last century.

Pitted against Simon was Paul Ehrlich whose 1968 book *The Population Bomb* was a stronger and more logical update of the Malthusian argument for a different era. Ehrlich believed human exploitation of resources would make them scarcer and costlier until we ran out of them. Famously, in 1980, Ehrlich and Simon placed a bet on the future prices of five metals ten years later. Here's Ronald Bailey in his book *The End of Doom* about the bet:

> In October 1980, Ehrlich and Simon drew up a futures contract obligating Simon to sell Ehrlich the same quantities that could be purchased for $1,000 of five

metals (copper, chromium, nickel, tin, and tungsten) ten years later at inflation-adjusted 1980 prices. If the combined prices rose above $1,000, Simon would pay the difference. If they fell below $1,000, Ehrlich would pay Simon the difference. Ehrlich mailed Simon a check for $576.07 in October 1990. There was no note in the letter. The price of the basket of metals chosen by Ehrlich and his cohorts had fallen by more than 50 percent. The cornucopian Simon won.[1]

Population isn't a problem. The ability to tap human capital to produce 'catch-up' growth and 'cutting-edge' growth is the issue in India. We have failed to create institutions or policy frameworks that enable the ultimate resource. As Nitin Pai, director of the Takshashila Institution, a think tank, puts it eloquently: under-governance, and not overpopulation, is India's problem.

To say that our public institutions have the capacity to handle only so large a population is not an argument to reduce the population. It is an argument to enlarge the capacity of our public institutions. Like Procustes, we cannot chop off the legs of sleepers who were too tall to sleep on his bed. We need longer beds. Enlarging capacity is about better ideas, better technology, better people and more people engaged in governance. It is wholly wrong to attribute our failure to scale up

---

[1] Ronald Bailey, *The End of Doom: Environmental Renewal in the Twenty-First Century* (Thomas Dunne Books/St. Martin's Press, 2015).

governance to keep pace with population growth to 'overpopulation'.[2]

Nevertheless, we continue to blame our population. Several prime ministers in the past have failed to appreciate this, and PM Modi in his address to the nation on 15 August 2019 followed the same line. This sentiment is shared by large sections of our society too. It's not difficult to find Malthusians opposing migration on the grounds that there are just way too many people in their city.

We will get older before getting richer. That is the plain truth. At a mere $2000 per capita income, we are sliding below-replacement fertility rate in most of the States. This is a bigger problem than our imagined overpopulation. In 2040, we will be an old, low-income country lacking a social security net. At this time, the only moral imperative is income growth. Everything else pales in comparison. But we continue with false trade-offs between growth and other higher-order virtues—equity, environment, and national pride. This is not to argue that these aren't important. But we should consider our priorities as a $2000 per capita income economy. Not what we imagine ourselves to be.

The downside of viewing population as a problem is seen in the 'jobs for locals' reservation policies that have become common among many states. This is classic zero-sum thinking. Instead of focusing on growing the employment pie, state governments want to prevent migration of other Indians looking for jobs into their state. In 2021, the

[2] Nitin Pai, 'Acorn: Overpopulation Is Not the Problem—The Takshashila Institution', *The Acorn* (blog), accessed 28 January 2022, https://takshashila.org.in/acorn-overpopulation-is-not-the-problem/.

Haryana government passed an ordinance to provide 75 per cent reservation in the private sector for residents of Haryana. Nothing spreads like a bad idea. Andhra Pradesh did this the year before and Maharashtra has similar plans. There have been calls for such laws in Madhya Pradesh, Karnataka, and Telangana as well.

The law will require private companies to register every employee with a salary below Rs 50,000 per month on a state portal. Any employer with more than ten employees will be covered under the law. A domicile certificate would be mandatory for candidates to get the benefit under this scheme. If there's no eligible local candidate for a position, the company will have to inform the state government. They will then issue permits to employers to hire from other states. Yes, permits.

Then we have this—the survey results of Sample Registration System (SRS) 2018. SRS is a survey commissioned by the Census Commissioner that collates data about age demographics in India including births, deaths, fertility, and age-related milestones. A few things stand out.

One, the Total Fertility Rate (TFR) of India is down to 2.2. In simple terms, TFR is the average number of children that would be born to a woman over her lifetime. The replacement fertility rate for the developing world is pegged at 2.1. This is the rate at which each generation will exactly replace itself and the population will stop growing. Technically, the replacement rate is the average number of children a woman would need to have to bear a daughter who survives to child-bearing age.

Two, fourteen states of India are now at or below the replacement fertility rate. The population of these states will stabilize and after a decade start decreasing. Only eight states (Bihar, UP, MP, Rajasthan, Jharkhand, Chhattisgarh, Haryana, and Assam) have TFR above replacement rates.

Three, for the first time, more than half (53 per cent) of India's population is now twenty-five years or older. This is higher in urban India where the fertility rates are lower. We are getting older. The demographic dividend is starting to slip through our fingers. The death rate in India is down to 6.2 per cent from 7.3 per cent over a decade back. We are living longer, and our dependent population will get bigger over the next decade.

Seen through this prism, the policy of job reservation for 'sons of soil' will be an unmitigated disaster.

India is a union of states. The federal structure enables better governance through devolution of power and accountability closer to the citizens. At least, that's the design. The union enables free movement of citizens across the states, a common currency and monetary policy, and control over a large part of the fiscal policy. Despite many flaws, this is an arrangement that's worked. This job reservation policy left unchecked will hurt it.

There's nothing to redress that needs an affirmative action. There are instances when the moral argument in favour of reservation overrides everything else. A long history of subjugation of a race, ethnicity, or class of people is an example of it. Reservation becomes a tool to overcome prejudices and offer a level playing field to them. Philosopher John Rawls called it 'justice as fairness' that should take priority over the utilitarian lens to maximize social output. There's no evidence to suggest the youth of

Haryana or any other state that plans for local reservations have been discriminated against for generations.

In the long-run, employment in Haryana will be impacted. Does Haryana have skilled unemployed youth to fill up 75 per cent of all new jobs created in the state? If a blue-chip multinational company were to open a large technology development centre in Gurgaon with an intention of hiring 10,000 high-quality engineers, would Haryana be able to provide 7500 of them? The answer is no. Besides, why will any company constrain itself with this limited talent pool when it wants to tap the best engineering talent in India. Why would any company want to add capacity in Haryana? They will take their business to another state.

Next, what's the incentive for the Haryana youth to do well in studies? The reservation would mean with mere threshold qualifications, they will be a shoo-in for most jobs. Once they are in a job, what's their incentive to work hard? They can free ride because the 75 per cent 'local' metric will become the primary constraint for the company rather than competence. Haryana youth will not be competitive or motivated, and the employers will lose on productivity. It's lose-lose all around.

Besides, the whole arrangement is tailor-made for the State machinery to play its favourite sport. Rent-seeking. The 'business' of issuing domicile certificates will take off at the lower levels of the administration. Companies will have to receive permits to hire for skills they can't find in Haryana. How will they prove this scarcity? The bureaucrat will be the overlord deciding on this. This absurd, arbitrary clause will be abused. This is but a step away from a Kafkaesque bureaucratic nightmare.

Further, a possible scenario that will emerge is that of employers hiring temporary workers or pegging compensation for roles at Rs 50,001 p.m. to circumvent the law. The other option for smaller firms will be to keep their headcount below ten for as long as possible. If this can't be managed, entrepreneurs will start shell companies to hire new employees to stay below the threshold of ten. This is a textbook example of the State creating a bad law that forces its citizens to turn unlawful. This corrodes the moral fabric of society.

Haryana is doing what it thinks is good for its citizens. How will other states respond? This will trigger similar populist moves in states that have one or more regional parties. If that comes to pass, labour mobility will be restricted across states. This will distort the labour market and reduce the competitiveness of states. Any company planning to invest in India will have to contend with a labour market that is 'balkanized'. If this turns into a contagion with other states joining in, we will struggle to attract investments. The general equilibrium effect will be terrible. Also, the other states could choose a tit-for-tat response by discriminating against candidates from Haryana for jobs in their states. This is a slippery slope for a federal structure.

As is usual with the State, the draft law has threats, fines, and punishment for non-compliance. As the political ends of this law become difficult to achieve because of the lack of logic in the law itself, the State will overreach. The law will become more stringent with worse results for everyone.

Now, imagine 2035. If the trends as seen in SRS 2018 play out, we will have fourteen states running below-replacement fertility rate with a declining rate of population. These states already have better human development indices and higher capital investments. Expect them to have consolidated these gains further. Some states (let's call them category 1) will have a large productive workforce in the market for jobs while the other states (category 2) will be ageing but prosperous. This is a complex problem by itself with deep implications on centre–state relationships and devolution of grants to states. There's something deeply evil about a local job quota that applies below an income threshold. Migration still remains the most-powerful route for people at lower incomes to change their fortunes for the better. To block that route by balkanizing the labour market is reprehensible.

The better way to help 'local' labour is to clear the regulatory cholesterol so that more and bigger industries take shape in our states. The larger the pool of available jobs, the fewer the chances that this victimhood will resonate politically.

The preamble to the Indian Constitution begins with 'We, the People'. The social contract explicitly mentions that the Indian Republic has been constituted to secure justice, liberty, equality, and fraternity to all its citizens. 'We, the People' are the centre of this enterprise. It's the State's responsibility to strive and deliver the promised outcomes to every Indian. By blaming the population, governments are blaming the people for their underperformance. It's turning the social contract on its head. We shouldn't allow our governments to get off this easily.

26

Appam Is Appam, Dhokla Is Dhokla

Kerala and Gujarat are different. Their food, their society and, of course, their politics. It is a study in contrast. Perhaps, only a Verghese Kurien could straddle these differences with ease. But are they really different? If so, how did they turn out to be different? Is it because of who they vote for? Or is there something more to it?

It doesn't take a lot to happen in the political economy for analysts to start debating the Kerala versus Gujarat models of development. This is a shorthand for the left versus right debate in India. We find this debate symptomatic of how there's hardly any objective analysis of development models. Instead, any emerging data from these states are conveniently retrofitted to a narrative of how one 'model' is superior to the other. The pandemic period has proved this even further.

In the first six months of the pandemic (April to October 2020), Kerala did well in containing the pandemic despite the relatively higher risks of returning expatriates. By the end of May 2020, it had fewer than 1000 cases despite the higher risk factors in the state; its testing rates were among the highest in the country and its low TPR (test positivity rate) of below 2 per cent suggested it was able to get a good ground game going in tracing and containing the spread.

Gujarat, on the other hand, during this time didn't fare well. By the end of May, it had the third-highest number of cases, and its 'steady' increase in the number of cases raised questions on the extent of testing done in the state. It also had the highest mortality rate (7.8 per cent) in the country. This provided ammunition for the proponents of the Kerala model to declare victory and suggest to other states and to the centre to learn from it. This was in response to the supporters of the Gujarat model, who in the past, have missed no opportunity to highlight its economic superiority and advocated for the rest of the country to follow suit.

But this wasn't the end of the story. After a while, the numbers flipped and Kerala had a higher number of cases and struggled to keep the numbers down while Gujarat opened up for business by January 2021. Then the second wave struck in April 2021. The cycle turned back in favour of Kerala while Gujarat gasped for oxygen and hospital beds for patients. The Gujarat government was accused of persistent underreporting of deaths with local dailies tallying up the numbers from cremation and funeral sites with the official death toll. The Kerala model proponents found their voice again. By September 2021, Kerala accounted for more than half the total cases in the country while Gujarat was almost free from the virus. The Gujarat model partisans were back to mocking the Kerala model.

It is a stupid debate where political agenda has taken over any objectivity. Of course, the question of which model of development we should choose is an important one. A market-friendly, growth-first approach that raises incomes and eventually leads to better societal outcomes? Or, a State-led focus on human development parameters that creates a strong foundation for sustainable economic growth? There's a strong tendency on both sides to over-attribute any success of either model to the policies and actions of the recent governments in the states. There's always more than a whiff of evidence being cherry-picked to support ideological positions. The pandemic experience where both states yo-yoed from good to bad confirmed these suspicions.

We will try here to make sense of this debate without any intention of choosing a winner. Our simple conclusion is there is a significant path dependence on how these states have reached where they are today. Their histories matter. There is limited evidence to suggest there is truly a different Gujarat or Kerala model. So, the experience of the pandemic where both states seemed to be clueless at different times shouldn't be a surprise. We will go into the history to see how their present is shaped by their past.

Kerala and Gujarat have been the gateway into India for many centuries. Surat and Kochi were great, cosmopolitan port cities that attracted traders from all over the world. The open and liberal nature of people and the royalty in both the states provided a safe harbour for various communities looking to set up a new base or fleeing persecution (Parsis, Jews, Dawoodi Bohras and others). Their paths diverged in the early nineteenth century.

The Model Native State of Travancore

The princely states of Travancore and Kochi and the British controlled Malabar comprised the region that is present-day Kerala in the early nineteenth century. The Hindu society here had the *jenmi*, the landed upper caste aristocracy, that lorded over the remaining castes who worked in the fields. There was no significant Hindu mercantile caste. The Muslims, Christians, and Jews filled in and controlled commerce in these regions. The arrival of Christian missionaries in the early nineteenth century led to more conversions from non-*varna* Hindus. More importantly, the missionaries set up schools that were open to all, which further increased the allure of conversion for backward Hindus.

A somewhat alarmed but progressive Hindu royal family of Travancore issued a proclamation in 1817 and became the first state to provide free education to all its subjects. Similarly, the three regions were among the first to focus on public health and vaccination in India. The Queen of Travancore inoculated herself and her entire family in 1813 to demonstrate her commitment to the programme.[1]

By 1846, the Travancore medical department was established, and in 1879 vaccination was made compulsory for all government servants, children, and those dependent on the state. Kochi and Malabar followed suit with a lag. Travancore was keen to be seen as a model 'native state'. It privatized landholding and introduced commercial crops in

[1] Parthasarathy K. S., 'History of Vaccination and Anti-Vaccination Programmes in India', *BMJ*, 25 February 2022, https://www.bmj.com/rapid-response/2011/10/29/history-vaccination-and-anti-vaccination-programmes-india.

the state. Private property rights meant a greater incentive to improve farm productivity. The results were immediate. The state ran a budget surplus for a better part of the nineteenth century and used it to invest in education and public health.

In a way, the state implemented the so-called 'Gujarat model' and followed it up with social spending about 150 years ago.

Between 1871–72 and 1946–47, the state expenditure on education and healthcare increased seventy-one and twenty-six times, respectively. By 1900–01, Travancore had over 1000 schools of which more than half were run by private management. It also had thirty-five hospital beds per 100,000 persons at that time. To put this in perspective, in 2019, India has fifty-five hospital beds per 100,000 persons while Gujarat has thirty-three. Travancore and Kochi were ahead of the rest of India by about half a century on human development indicators by the beginning of the twentieth century.

Social Reforms and Lal Salaam

Two other factors strengthened this in the early twentieth century. Since the British didn't rule directly over Travancore and Kochi and the royal families were welfare-oriented, the freedom movement didn't take off here. Instead, there were strong social reform movements that aimed to secure basic civil rights of the lower castes. Sri Narayan Guru and Ayyankali established organizations like Sree Narayana Dharma Paripalana Yogam (SNDP) and Sadhujana Paripalana Sangham

(SJPS) that encouraged education for all (specifically girls), political representation, liberation from caste tyranny, and freedom to enter temples. This Kerala renaissance was different from the Bengal or Pune renaissance in that it was led by non-*varna* Hindu leaders, and it truly involved a large section of the society.

This spirit of social reform and consciousness continued after Independence, and it had a direct bearing in the rise of communism in the state. The communists came to power in the first elections to the Kerala legislative assembly in 1957 and in keeping with history, focused on education, health, and land reforms in their short tenure of about two years. That set the agenda and successive governments in future toed the line.

The suspicion of the State towards markets and industries and militant trade unionism meant the state saw limited industrialization. It ranked outside of the top ten on most economic indicators till the mid-1990s. An educated workforce without employment prospects within the state led to the 'Gulf' migration boom of the 1970s and 1980s. Despite high Human Development Index (HDI) parameters, the revealed preference of the citizens was to leave the state. The remittances from this boom now account for more than 14 per cent of the state GDP. These have single-handedly kept the state economically viable.

The 73rd and 74th amendments to the Constitution that gave recognition and devolved powers to *nagar palikas* and panchayats were enthusiastically adopted by Kerala. It is among the states with higher allocation of state expenditure delegated to the local bodies, who then have greater control on health and education investments in their areas.[2] Kerala was the first state to be impacted by the H1N1 virus in 2009, and it set up a state nodal centre for emergency response to outbreaks at that time. This nodal centre along with the district nodes were responsible for containing the H1N1 and Nipah outbreaks. When COVID-19 struck, Kerala with its robust grassroots healthcare capabilities was more ready than any other state in India initially. But that initial advantage was just that. As the pandemic continued, state capacity and focus wavered. Things started slipping and soon the numbers went up.

Mercantilism in Blood

Gujarat, in contrast, followed a very different path. It also had multiple princely states but barring Baroda, they weren't stable or progressive like the states of Travancore or Mysore. Gujarat also had a strong Hindu and Jain mercantile community that was well-entrenched. Further, the trading communities from outside that settled down in Gujarat (Parsis, Bohras) weren't evangelical in their faith. The limited Christian settlements in the state also meant a significantly smaller missionary footprint. Unsurprisingly, there wasn't a boom in education or healthcare investment in Gujarat in the nineteenth and early twentieth century, unlike in Kerala.

---

[2] For an analysis of how Kerala is an outlier on the financing of public health, check this paper: Pavan Srinath et al., 2018, 'A Qualitative and Quantitative Analysis of Public Health Expenditure in India: 2005–06 to 2014–15', *The Takshashila Institution*, July 2018.

There was a continued focus on enterprise, trading, and industrialization with the hub of activities shifting to Mumbai as the Surat port turned shallow for large ships. For almost a century between 1850 and 1947, native capital and industries were concentrated in the hands of Parsi and Gujarati communities who emerged from the various trading hubs of Gujarat. It hasn't changed a lot since. The first half of the twentieth century saw Gujarat becoming one of the fountainheads of freedom struggle in India. Three of the four most important figures of the Indian subcontinent in the twentieth century (Gandhi, Patel, and Jinnah) emerged from Gujarat. While this meant a strong sense of political awareness developed in the state, it didn't lead to any significant social reforms. The Gandhian attempt at Sarvodaya to reform society withered away after his death.

Things didn't change significantly post-Independence. The middle-class route to prosperity remained through enterprise or commerce instead of education. Gujaratis took to newer markets outside of India in East Africa and later to the UK and the US. But unlike Kerala migrants, they set up their own businesses and developed roots in those countries. This reflects in remittances that account for less than 1 per cent of the state's GDP.

That both the Navnirman Andolan—which eventually led to the proclamation of the Emergency—and the electoral rise of Hindutva started from Gujarat shows it stays ahead of the political awareness curve. While Gujarat continues to lead on economic development parameters (among the top three on almost all indicators across various reports) as it has for the better part of the last two centuries, its public health infrastructure and education outcomes are poorer than most states (outside of top ten on most parameters). This follows a long legacy of spending meagrely on social infrastructure. These are long-term investments whose benefits show up much later, often indirectly. This isn't apparent in a state where the focus is on short-term returns on investment. This was evident in its response to COVID-19 in the initial period.

Convenient Falsehoods

In trying to carve out the developmental paths of these two states into a neat binary, many facts are overlooked.

For instance, India's first new-age world-class airport was Kochi Airport. Cochin International Airport Limited, the owning company, is not a public sector unit. Instead, the Government of Kerala owns about 34 per cent of the company while the rest is owned by individuals, banks, and companies.

While it is true that Kerala has the largest number of State PSUs in the country (about 130), Gujarat ranks third on this list, with eighty-six companies, out of which fourteen are in a non-working limbo state. So, Gujarat is not exactly an apostle of free markets either.

Nurses from Kerala are a common sight across hospitals in India. However, what's less understood is that of the 17,600 nursing college seats in Kerala (2016 figure), more than 90 per cent were in private colleges.[3]

---

[3] Krishna Rao et al., 'From Brain Drain to Brain Gain: Migration of Nursing and Midwifery Workforce in the State of Kerala' (World Health Organisation), accessed 25 February 2022, https://www. who.int/workforcealliance/brain-drain-brain-gain/Migration-of-nursing-midwifery-in-KeralaWHO.pdf?ua=1.

Finally, it's incorrect to label Kerala as a communist state. It is a part of the Indian Republic, which means it cannot be a communist state. Instead, it would be accurate to say that a few favourite policies that rank high on the agenda of communist regimes have had their way in Kerala.

Nobody's Credit

The Gujarat and Kerala models, as we like to see them, have been in existence for over two centuries. The current outcomes of these models owe more to the history and evolution of multiple social and political trends in these societies than specific policy decisions over the last few decades. The COVID-19 crisis was a challenge to both models. Gujarat had to make up for its poor public health capabilities by seeking outside help and diverting state capacity from other areas to manage this. It had an uphill battle. Kerala will have to eventually weigh the impact of a significant drop in remittances as people returned home because the economies of 'Gulf' struggled. It might be in for a significant contraction of its GDP. All models are inaccurate; some are useful, and the utility of understanding them is in drawing lessons from one another.

A good state 'model' should consolidate the legacy policy gains it is endowed with while breaking away to address policy areas that have been its Achilles heel. Any state that successfully makes this marked departure should be considered a good 'model'. The rest is mere narrative building.

27

Poorab Aur Paschim

Never Shall the Twain Meet

An objective study of the civilization that flourished around the Indus valley and its culture, texts, and artefacts suggest that it was a triumph of imagination of some of the earliest human settlers. But nothing suggests it was significantly more advanced than other such settlements that came up in the Nile or the Mesopotamian valleys. Further, it is unlikely our forefathers had solved the great mysteries of the universe or knew what modern science hasn't known till date. They may have mused over such topics, but musing doesn't mean knowing. Quite like good science fiction isn't the same as real scientific progress.

Yet, there has always been a strong undercurrent in our society that our forefathers had most of the science figured out, and it is only a matter of recovering the wisdom from the many ancient texts we have supposedly abandoned. Over the years, politicians, mystics, philosophers, and charlatans have weighed in on this. Of late, judges, academic scholars, and scientists have joined in on the chorus. WhatsApp messages on our scientific legacy abound—the panacea that's ayurveda, the secrets of quantum physics embedded in the *Upanishads,* the advances of surgery in the works of Sushruta, the air travel of Pushpaka, the in-vitro miracle that was Drona—these part myths, part fantasies with a minimal kernel of truth are now staging a comeback in popular consciousness.

What explains this? There are similar instances in the myths of other ancient civilizations—Norse, Egyptian, Greek, and Roman. So what explains the persistence of our belief that our forefathers knew what we call modern science today all those centuries ago? Why do we get longer and longer WhatsApp messages showing how quarks were known to those who wrote the *Vedas*?

Thus far, this section discussed how the Indian State and society differ in their attitudes to social change. We will now tackle modern scientific knowledge and the attitude of the State and society towards it.

The Indian Constitution cites the development of scientific temper among its citizens as a Directive Principle of State Policy. It is not difficult to see why this would have mattered to the members of the Constituent Assembly during Independence. To them, Indian society with its superstitions, traditional practices, and a reluctance to embrace new ideas was still stuck in the medieval age. This was largely true.

But it would be useful to also point out here that some of this image of Indian society was created by the British intellectuals and thinkers who contrasted the native knowledge of natural sciences with what they learnt in their universities in the post-enlightenment age. Anyway, we chose an education policy that laid emphasis on the scientific method derived from Bacon and favoured the western philosophical thought as a way of making sense of the world. This approach also reflected the backgrounds of the founders of modern India, led by Nehru, who were educated in the western thought and felt it was a necessary pre-condition for modernizing India. The knowledge and philosophy of the ancient Indian texts were to be respected, but they weren't going to be used to propel India forward. You could pursue them in your own time, but the State was only marginally interested in them.

This was not easy to pursue in practice. Most elite or middle-class Indians grew up with the knowledge of these ancient texts passed on to them at home. The philosophy of Bhagwad Gita, the holistic system of wellbeing that is yoga, the traditional calendar system, the power of ayurveda—our past affected our everyday lives in many different ways. These were not memories of a dead past. They were alive in our traditions. As the State pushed the western methods, these practices became the 'alternative' ways, not the mainstream. Traditional society always suspected an agenda in the push of the State towards westernization. It complied to a large extent but continued to preserve its past in the hope of a resurgence sometime in the future.

It wouldn't be wrong to say that the time of resurgence is here. And what we have now is a more direct confrontation between the western philosophical and scientific thought with what is now often referred to as the Indic alternative. In this chapter, we will look at this confrontation using two perspectives—the difference between science and pseudoscience and the challenges of using ancient Indic knowledge in current times. A clearer understanding and articulation of these will be instrumental in bringing the useful elements of our ancient texts into our modern education system than summarily calling all of it mumbo-jumbo or giving them an exalted status of being superior than all Western thought.

Science and Pseudoscience

Sometime in the first week of July 2020, at the peak of the first wave of COVID-19 pandemic in India, Patanjali Ayurved claimed their ayurvedic drug Coronil could cure COVID-19 based on trials on mild to moderately ill patients. Yoga guru Ramdev, who founded Patanjali, was soon seen in the presence of the union health minister launching Coronil, the so-called 'wonder drug'.

Ramdev is followed by millions who tune into his morning yoga shows beamed on multiple TV channels. Over the past few years, he has built a remarkable food and beverages empire that has taken on multinational companies like Unilever and Nestle while positioning his products as pure and free of chemicals with the goodness of ayurveda blended into them. It has been a runaway success though there have been questions raised on the many claims the company makes about its products. The public announcement of Coronil as a cure for COVID-19 and the dubious scientific endorsements, including a fake WHO certification, were met with outrage. Patanjali backtracked and later called it a product for COVID-19 management.

A fairly significant section of the Indian population has always looked at Western medicine with suspicion. There is a fear of 'side effects' from the chemical cocktail that modern medicines contain. For a lot of minor ailments that affect daily lives, Indians use a combination of home remedies and ayurvedic concoctions. These are considered safe and have proven to work for them. Even during the COVID-19 pandemic, there was a widespread use of remedies such as *kadhas/kashaayaas,* herb-based steam infusions, and other traditional remedies that were believed to improve the health of the lungs. It is in this context Coronil was launched, and after some initial hiccups it seemed to have done quite well.

But this begs the question—is ayurveda scientific?

The modern medicine system (allopathy) follows a rigorous multi-step trial process to prove a simple hypothesis—a drug must be both effective and safe for its use by humans. Drug acts and clinical trial guidelines set out as laws in India are meant to ensure that any drug has to go through a process where these two parameters are tested. The molecular structure of the drug, its dosage, and its method of ingestion are all tested; first on animals and then over three stages on humans. The clinical trials must be 'controlled' and blind or double-blind. It means there must be a group that's given the actual drug and another that is administered a placebo without either of them knowing it. However, the same laws aren't applied on the traditional medicinal systems like ayurveda, *unani,* or *siddha.* The medicines in these systems are tested on two other criteria—how faithful the drug is to the recipe as written down in traditional texts and the hygiene of the location where they are manufactured. This received wisdom is the basis for introducing a drug. If there is a new disease, the usual approach in traditional medicines is to look for the proximate underlying cause and then develop a drug based on prescribed literature that cures that cause.

With that context, there are three points to consider as we think of ayurveda as science. First, ayurveda or any traditional healing method works based on empiricism. Over many generations, traditional healers observe that certain natural products help in healing common ailments. A meticulous record of these ingredients and their healing properties is formalized. These cures are then used over the centuries to treat people. A study of these ingredients and the chemicals contained within them using modern knowledge of biochemistry often reveal these are effective cures. But ayurveda doesn't isolate these molecules and arrive at the optimal dosage for these cures.

Two, these traditional techniques are tried over time on a population with a common ethnicity or a similar gene pool and factoring in the local climate, food, and lifestyles. These healing techniques, therefore, are endogenous to a specific ecosystem. These might not be universal.

Three, if you consider the two points above, it is clear that ayurveda or any traditional healing technique follows loosely what modern medical science refers to as 'trials' over generations before formalizing it. Therefore, any cure for a new ailment or a new virus should follow a similar process and timeline before it can be considered a legitimate ayurvedic formulation. So, maybe ayurveda can cure coronavirus, but we are possibly 200–300 years of 'trials' away from it if we were to respect the science behind it.

Modern medicine and biochemistry emerged because we couldn't wait for this long with a low probability of success at the end of it. Also, the 'germ theory' was a clean break from the three-'dosha' belief system of ayurveda. But the idea that ingredients within herbs, flowers, or other natural substances could heal wasn't discarded. Instead, this knowledge, along with the development of disease science and the synthesis of new chemicals was used to develop medicines. Patanjali wasn't just ignoring the ayurveda code for new products but circumventing the accelerated mechanism of trials for modern medicines using tradition as a fig leaf. This is unfortunate in a country where people trust ayurveda and traditional methods based on their empirical experience.

Is ayurveda pseudoscience then? Interestingly, in May 2021, Ramdev came under fire when he made disparaging remarks about Western medicines and doctors who were at the forefront of battle against the second wave of COVID-19 then. He backtracked but made this statement that summed up the views of those who believe in ayurveda:

> Everyone should progress through self-evaluation. Some allopathic doctors too consider Indian medical science, Ayurveda, yoga as pseudo-science, which hurts crores of people.[1]

The point about pseudoscience made by Ramdev is of interest here. Who defines it? If crores of people follow something, does that mean it shouldn't be called pseudoscience? Palmistry, astrology, homoeopathy, ayurveda—where do

---

[1] '"When Allopathy Doctors Call Ayurveda Pseudoscience": Ramdev Replies to Minister, Withdraws Controversial Statement', *Hindustan Times*, 23 May 2021, https://www.hindustantimes.com/india-news/ramdev-withdraws-statement-on-allopathy-but-says-self-evaluation-is-necessary-101621789708240.html.

they stand on the spectrum of science and pseudoscience? Since some kind of revivalism is seen in Indian society these days, it will be useful to explore this further.

Refer to the newsclip from the *New York Times* cited in the footnote of this page.[2]

Why was the eclipse on 29 May 1919 that was mentioned in this clip such an event?

A hundred years ago, Albert Einstein wasn't a household name. He was a professor in Berlin, known to scientists, intellectuals, his divorced wife and the first cousin who would soon become his second wife—but not to the world.

His rise to superstardom began on 29 May 1919, when the moon and sun lined up just right for a solar eclipse. Photos of the astronomical event showed something strange. A few of the stars visible during the blackout were in the 'wrong' place according to the conventional wisdom of astrophysics.

Einstein had foreseen this a few years ago. Using his theory of general relativity, he made the seemingly crazy bet that the stars' positions in the sky would shift during an eclipse, and even calculated by how much. As the data came in and the results were confirmed, the general theory

---

[2] Special Cable to *The New York Times*.

'LIGHTS ALL ASKEW IN THE HEAVENS; Men of Science More or Less Agog Over Results of Eclipse Observations.

EINSTEIN THEORY TRIUMPHS; Stars Not Where They Seemed or Were Calculated to Be, but Nobody Need Worry.

A BOOK FOR 12 WISE MEN; No More in All the World Could Comprehend It, Said Einstein When His Daring Publishers Accepted It', *The New York Times*, 10 November 1919, sec. archives, https://www.nytimes.com/1919/11/10/archives/lights-all-askew-in-the-heavens-men-of-science-more-or-less-agog.html.

of relativity was proven. Newtonian physics that was considered science for over two centuries was no longer the complete truth.

'Revolution in Science', the front page of *The Times of London* proclaimed. 'New Theory of the Universe: Newtonian Ideas Overthrown' *The New York Times* followed suit with 'Men of Science More or Less Agog'.

Following this with interest was a precocious seventeen-year-old student in the University of Vienna.

His name: Karl Popper.

This event would leave a deep impact on him as he thought about the nature of truth and the philosophy of science in his later life. The idea that Einstein could precisely postulate in advance what would happen during a solar eclipse and then have the courage for it to be proven or be 'falsified' publicly was in sharp contrast to other 'sciences' that were in fashion during those years in Europe, namely, Marxism and psychoanalysis.

For over two centuries, scientists had empirically tested Newtonian laws and it worked in all known cases. New inventions came up based on these laws including the steam engine and the power loom that revolutionized societies. Kepler showed how the laws worked for planets and other celestial objects. Haley predicted a comet would reappear again in seventy-six years based on it. The scientific method that Bacon had proposed involving observation, hypothesis, test, and conclusion was proven over and over again for Newtonian physics. That's how the universe worked. Yet, when Einstein argued that they didn't work for the special case of really large objects and it was proven during the eclipse of 1919, the entire community of physicists updated their priors. They followed where science took them.

For Popper, this was the 'demarcation' between what he called science and non-science (later termed pseudoscience by others). To him all observation is selective and can be used to prove anything. Psychoanalysis was a prime example. Therefore, he dismissed inductive reasoning as the method of drawing scientific inference. Because every single observation so far has followed Newtonian law, doesn't mean it is the truth. Because the sun rises every morning doesn't necessarily prove it will rise tomorrow. More has to be done.

Popper instead offered 'falsifiability' as the test to 'demarcate' science and non-science. As he put it, you can always cherry-pick evidence to prove any theory. Like the psychoanalysts and Marxists of his time were doing or what Ramdev is doing with his claims. That's not enough. For him what really counted as science was if you could stake your theory on a future prediction that could turn out to be false like Einstein and the physicists did with the solar eclipse. A million instances of something working aren't enough to prove something is science but a single counter-instance is enough to falsify the claim that it is science. That's how the claim should be tested. On falsifiability. So, science is always about a provisional truth till someone falsifies it. The moment it is falsified, it is no longer science. Science, to Popper, therefore, was a grand pursuit to solve big problems and not about making a series of tiny empirical observations and figuring out the cause behind them. The observations were only to be made to serve the grand pursuit of truth.

Now, there were others who debated with Popper on the philosophy of science, most notably, Kuhn who coined the term 'paradigm shift' to explain how science evolves. Those debates are best left for another day. For now, let's consider 'falsifiability' as explained by Popper and view modern medicine as it is practised today. The entire drug discovery and development process involving identification of likely compounds useful in curing a disease, synthesis, characterization, validation, optimization, and assays that will make it ready for clinical trials follows the principle of finding a single counter instance that would falsify the results. The clinical trials, multiple reviews by the regulators, and then the monitoring of the drug performance after it has been launched in the market are all meant to ensure that any instance of failure is captured and studied to eliminate the root cause. This is a rigorous process to stand the test of 'falsifiability' and keep modern medicine as close to true science as possible.

If you consider the criteria above, none of the 'sciences' mentioned here come off well.

To be clear, this isn't to overstate the primacy of science in our lives. You might find comfort and peace of mind through astrology. Yoga and ayurveda might help you to stay fit and build your immunity. You might have personal experience of homoeopathy working for you. A scientist who retired from ISRO (or IISc) or a former Nobel prize winner might believe in past life regression or Vedic chants to cure something. There could be observable truths for those instances. It still won't make them science. Because they can easily be falsified.

The other argument about modern medicine deriving its compounds from nature like ayurveda also needs to be understood better. It is true that many modern drugs have compounds that are extracted from plants and herbs that we often use in ayurveda. But the modern medicine process is quite exact about the compound, the amount, and how it should be delivered into our system. Eating the same plant or herb as a paste or in food isn't the same thing though it might occasionally yield the same results. There is a difference.

The same as that between Sanjeevani and the Dronagiri mountain. Between specifics and generalization. And no, searching for Sanjeevani isn't exactly a scientific pursuit.

Is the Indian State Eurocentric?

The difference between science and pseudoscience is possibly easier to establish. But what about the philosophical perspectives from our ancient texts like the *Vedas, Upanishads* and *Dharmashastra*? The Indian State has often been accused of being too Eurocentric in its approach. There is the lament that we don't teach Indic philosophical perspectives in our schools and colleges.

This is largely true. The question is how should we approach the absence of Indic perspectives in our thinking? Should you dismiss it or should you engage with it at the cost of learning something else?

This is where the philosopher Richard Rorty who taught at Stanford for many years had a few things to say. Rorty followed in the footsteps of Isaiah Berlin in recognizing the inevitability of the plurality of ideas in a society. For Rorty, society was diverse and plural with conflicting ideas, beliefs, and biases. It was futile to expect that universal truth of any kind (even the most liberal kind) can be imposed on it by ivory-tower intellectuals top-down.

Rorty questioned the dogma of liberalism that prevailed in Europe in the centuries after enlightenment. To him, enlightenment was a movement against dogma. The prevailing dogma in seventeenth-century Europe was religion. In the twentieth century, liberalism had turned into a dogma, according to him. To impose it anywhere without a context is wrong for any society. For Rorty, the social policy that we seek for a nation must be compatible with its history, culture, and language. It has to emerge from within. Once it does so, a strong sense of community and solidarity will shape the society. There is no universal truth except what the society agrees on within the traditions of its culture, history, and language. In fact, Rorty contested the idea of truth itself.

There are three philosophical constructs Rorty advanced that are useful to consider while thinking about political or ideological arguments.

First, Rorty questioned the correspondence theory of truth that stated that 'the truth or falsity of a statement is determined only by how it relates to the world and whether it accurately describes (i.e., corresponds with) that world.'[3]

---

[3] Marian David, 'The Correspondence Theory of Truth', in *The Stanford Encyclopedia of Philosophy*, ed. Edward N. Zalta, Winter 2020 (Metaphysics Research Lab, Stanford University, 2020), https://plato.stanford.edu/archives/win2020/entriesruth-correspondence/.

Rorty debunked this. When we say it is warm in the month of April, we are using language to express multiple ideas—the feeling of the weather being warm, the notion of April as a month, and our ability to connect the two. And we believe it is true because the sentence in its construction corresponds to the reality we perceive. But in reality, there's no truth about the world being warm in April. Only our description of it, based on the language of what we feel.

Rorty summed it up in his book *Contingency, Irony and Solidarity* as: 'Truth cannot be out there—cannot exist independently of the human mind—because sentences cannot so exist, or be out there. The world is out there, but descriptions of the world are not. Only descriptions of the world can be true or false. The world on its own, unaided by the describing activities of humans cannot.'[4]

This was an important premise for him. If there's only a descriptive notion of truth, why should we give primacy to any universal notion of truth or rationality? After all, it is only our language (or in his words, vocabulary) that gives structure to the truth. It is, therefore, futile to debate if reality has an intrinsic nature. Say, you may believe living in harmony and justice for all are universal truths. But are they? Go back three of four centuries and prejudices were rampant and people were hung, drawn, and quartered for the pettiest of crimes. Truth is malleable. It depends on what we seek to achieve. Focus

---

[4] Richard Rorty, *Contingency, Irony and Solidarity* (Cambridge University Press, 1989).

on justifications for your argument rather than seeking universal truths.

Second, everything we read, listen to, watch, or discuss helps build what Rorty called our 'final vocabulary'. He defined it as:

> All human beings carry about a set of words which they employ to justify their actions, their beliefs, and their lives. These are the words in which we formulate praise of our friends and contempt for our enemies, our long-term projects, our deepest self-doubts and our highest hopes. I shall call these words a person's 'final vocabulary'. Those words are as far as he can go with language; beyond them is only helpless passivity or a resort to force.
>
> It is 'final' in the sense that if doubt is cast on the worth of these words, their user has no non-circular argumentative recourse. Those words are as far as he can go with the language.[5]

The 'final vocabulary' is a beautiful construct to make sense of a lot of arguments on social media. When someone says 'India first, always' or 'don't you trust your own traditions?', it means they have reached their final vocabulary. You will hit a circular argument if you further debate him on these points. It is 'India first' because it is India first. There's nothing beyond it.

Lastly, Rorty suggests a way to find a common ground among people who have different final vocabularies. This

---

[5] Ibid.

is important. This is the way we can find common ground among people. He suggests an 'ironist' perspective for an individual to participate in political debates while fashioning the self through continuous improvement. He cited three conditions that form the ironist perspective that will allow us to keep an open mind on all belief systems. An individual is an ironist if:

- She has radical and continuing doubts about the final vocabulary she currently uses, because she has been impressed by other vocabularies, vocabularies taken as final by people or books she has encountered;
- She realizes that the argument phrased in her present vocabulary can neither underwrite nor dissolve these doubts;
- Insofar as she philosophizes about her situation, she does not think that her vocabulary is closer to reality than others, that it is in touch with a power not herself.

This is the best way to engage and debate with others in the current world. Show humility, have radical doubts about your own final vocabulary, and engage with others in good faith believing their vocabulary might be as close to the reality as yours. If more of us did so, we might improve our final vocabulary while nudging others to see beyond theirs. We might then arrive at what Durkheim called collective effervescence, which is what most political projects seek to achieve for nation-building.

I'm sure there is something of value in our great Indic texts. Rorty would encourage us to read them to improve our final vocabulary. He would caution us on jettisoning the western philosophical thought with the wisdom of those texts. That would be a self-goal like no other.

Since we are on this topic, it will be pertinent to debate the point on the usefulness of our ancient texts in current times further. There's a view that deracinated Indian historians and intellectuals along with Western Indologists have conspired to devalue the civilizational merits of ancient India. These rootless and unmoored elites have done a terrible disservice to Hindu civilization by devaluing its lofty achievements in areas of science, arts, metaphysics, and philosophy. This has meant a nation of people who feel ashamed of their past, mimic Western ways of thinking, and lack authenticity. For real progress to be made, we must reclaim our heritage, regain self-confidence, and meet the world on the foundation of our traditional knowledge. Or so goes the line of thinking among the advocates of Indic thought. So, what to make of it?

Firstly, we agree with them about India being a civilizational State and Hinduism or Sanatana Dharma being a common cultural thread that runs through the length and breadth of this land. This is a lived experience for all of us, and there are many examples of common rituals and practices that have been around for centuries to back this assertion. Denying this is an exercise in futility and serves no useful purpose except alienating a large section of Indians.

Secondly, we are happy to concede that ancient Hindu civilization was the pinnacle of human achievement during its time. There's no proof for it but let's assume it was. My question is what do we do with such an ancient but highly complex intellectual construct now?

Almost every text that is believed to be foundational to our civilization was written hundreds of years before CE. Many of these are metatexts unmoored from their context or what formed the basis for such scholarship. One could read the hymns of *Rig Veda* on the conception of the universe today but what does that do to our understanding of science? To merely say it is similar to what quantum physics postulates today has limited meaning. It is the equivalent of saying Da Vinci designed all sorts of futuristic machines, so let's study him for scientific insights today.

Even *Arthashastra* can be read to appreciate the philosophy of statecraft and economics of ancient India but beyond a concept or two that might be relevant today, what purpose will it serve? The problem here is there has been no reinterpretation or updates on these texts over two thousand years. One of us comes from a town that houses one of the four *mathas* (seats) of Shankaracharya. Ever wondered what stopped the scholars of the *matha* to do more to make their knowledge accessible? Resources? Scholarship? Interest? It is difficult not to conclude that they do not know what to do with this knowledge in the modern world.

To draw a parallel, the reason a few texts of Greek philosophers are still taught selectively in Western universities is because many philosophers of the renaissance and enlightenment used them to build further on their thoughts on ethics, politics, and the State. Nobody reads their views on science, for instance, anymore. That's because later philosophers falsified it. Similarly, there's an unbroken chain of thinking from Adam Smith to a Piketty or a Sowell (choose your poison) today. So, it makes sense to selectively read Smith to get a basic understanding of how economic thought has evolved and then apply it further today. This is missing with the great ancient texts that hold Indic advocates in raptures. How will reading texts of Aryabhatta and Bhaskara help mathematics students today? Knowing about them could be useful to impress others about our great mathematical tradition but what beyond that? Some kind of pride and a sense of identity could be possible benefits, but we fail to appreciate their material manifestations.

Thirdly, most advocates of our civilizational achievements talk about caste and patriarchy almost in passing. Even while mentioning them, the usual tropes are laid out first. That the original Hindu texts were suffused with liberal doctrine, how Shankaracharya came across a Chandala in Kashi and placed him at par with the Brahmin, or the usual list of women of ancient India—Gargi, Maitreyi, or even the possibly fictional Draupadi—to suggest how open Hinduism in its original version was.

Was the oppressive nature of the caste system and the pervasive patriarchy mere failings in an otherwise lofty, liberal philosophical belief system? Or, is it, as it has been often argued, the inevitable outcome of our civilizational construct? Who can tell? If after all these centuries, the one pervasive cultural reality that has prevailed in our society is caste, how should we think about it? The same argument holds for patriarchy and the place of women in our society. The reclaiming of the wisdom of the texts that is advocated— can it be done without facing up to the 'material' reality of caste and patriarchy that will accompany it? In the abstract, they may be right. But the act of reclaiming won't restrict itself to the realm of the abstract.

Fourthly, is the current ferment to question the version of our history that has been fed to us by the colonialist academia a first in our recent past? Have other intellectuals also lamented the state of the culturally unmoored Indian elite and educated class who need to be brought home to the glory of our ancient civilization?

If yes, what happened to previous such attempts?

This is an area that has held my interest for a few years. And I'd like to highlight two twentieth-century intellectuals who spent their lifetime studying ancient Indian texts, translating them, and looking to find their relevance in the modern context—Shri Aurobindo and Hazari Prasad Dwivedi. These are no ordinary names. They were first-rate intellectuals with rare felicity in both Western and Eastern philosophies.

So, what did they conclude?

We are going to stick my neck out and make some broad generalizations here. Aurobindo started this pursuit with an aim to find the modern relevance of our ancient texts and to spread it far and wide. What did he end up with? A very personal journey into the self that was mystical and detached from the material. Anything else couldn't be transferred. That's what he concluded.

Dwivedi was an intellectual powerhouse who was deeply rooted in the Indic tradition and philosophy. A great Sanskrit linguist who spent a lifetime studying the Sastras and writing beautiful expositions on them, Dwivedi should be more widely read today. His essays, their themes, and his arguments betray no trace of Western enlightenment influence. He had a clear-eyed view of the richness of our heritage and its relevance in the modern age. But, in the end, he had to contend with the reality of the present. If we were such a great civilization, why is our present the way it is? And he wasn't content blaming colonial rule or our lack of appreciation of our past. There was something else that was missing.

In his anthology, *Vichar Aur Vitark* (Thoughts and Debates), there's an essay titled '*Jabki Dimaag Khaali Hai*' (While the Mind Is Empty) published by Sachitra Bharti in 1939, which is often quoted by scholar and columnist Pratap Bhanu Mehta to make a specific point about our current obsession with our glorious past and the identity crisis among Hindus. As Mehta writes:

> This identity is constituted by a paradoxical mixture of sentiments: a sense of lack, Hinduism is not sure what makes it the identity that it is; a sense of injury, the idea that Hindus have been victims of history; a sense of superiority, Hinduism as the highest achievement of spirituality and uniquely tolerant; a sense of weakness, Hindus are unable to respond to those who attack them; a sense of uncertainty, how will this tradition make its transition to modernity without denigrating its own past; and finally, a yearning for belonging, a quest for a community that can do justice to them as Hindus. This psychic baggage can express itself in many ways, sometimes benign and creative, sometimes, malign and close minded. But these burdens cast their unmistakable shadow upon modern Hindu self-reflection, often leading to a discourse on identity that Dwivedi memorably described as one,

where the heart is full and the mind empty (*dil bhara hai aur dimag khali hai*).[6]

Dwivedi's original essay reads (translation ours) as follows:

But when the mind is empty while the heart is brimming over, there cannot be any possibility of an engaging exposition of the Sastras.

Otherwise, there isn't any reason to be anxious about a race whose writ once ran from the shores of River Vaksh in Central Asia to the end of South Asia, the imprint of whose culture transcended the Himalayas and the great oceans and whose mighty fleet once controlled the waters of the eastern seas. It is true that this mighty race is a pale shadow of itself today. The sons of Panini (the great Sanskrit grammarian from Gandhara) sell dry fruits and heeng on the streets today while the descendants of Kumarjiva are involved in the basest of trades. Yet, there's a hope that there must be a semblance of that glory still running in the veins of this race. And it will show its true colour some day. But then I wonder. After all, a tree is known for the fruits it bears. The state of disrepair that the Hindu society is in today must trace its cause to that once glorious civilization of the past. How can that tree be so glorious when its fruits we see all around today are so terrible?

---

[6] Pratap Bhanu Mehta, 'The Heart Is Full, the Mind Empty', *The Indian Express*, 21 December 2003, https://indianexpress.com/article/news-archive/the-heart-is-full-the-mind-empty/.

There was indeed an age of prosperity for this race. That is true. Those verdant streets of Ujjain, the gurgling sounds of River Shipra and the celestial music of the *kinnaras* still echo in the Himalayan valleys—these memories remain fresh in our minds. And amidst these riches, our eyes can clearly see the attack of the Huns and the defiant stand of the Aryans, the numerous rise and fall of empires, the thunderous roar of Vikramaditya. The glories of Magadh and Avanti were unparalleled. Its elite could wield the sword and the brush with equal felicity. They could fight fire with fire and let their hair down when they wanted. But things changed. The elite suppressed the masses; they paralysed the polity. The chasm within the society began to open up. The elites immersed themselves in the pleasures of the material world while the masses were tied down to scriptures and their orthodoxy. One took refuge in merriment while the other was often lampooned for their outdated beliefs. And the fissure in the Hindu society widened further. Over the centuries every invader used this to their advantage—Huns, Sakas, Tartars, Muslims, and the British. They divided us further and they ruled. Today that Pathan dry fruit seller asked me if that beautiful house belonged to a Muslim or a Christian and could scarcely believe it could be that of a Hindu. And I wondered if the chasm continues widening every day. But then the Sastras don't bother about such identity issues of the Hindus and I lack the courage to intellectually confront this issue any further. When the mind is empty and the heart full of passion, isn't it enough to have even mentally contended with the existential conundrum of our race.

Now, you could persuade us to believe it was the 'foreign' invaders for over a thousand years that's responsible for our present. Maybe it is true. But that rupture is a reality, and that discontinuity is so large that any attempt to bridge it through a modern reinterpretation of ancient texts can only be an academic 'feel good' exercise. Not a way forward to the future.

Fifthly, any 'nationalist' exercise of reclaiming the past after the advent of modern nation-states runs the risk of 'instrumentalizing' this past for political gains in the present. This holds true everywhere—in pre-Second World War Germany or Japan, in current-day Turkey, and in communist China. For instance, there's nothing that the Communist Party in China learns from Confucius or some ancient Han dynasty view of the Middle Kingdom that it sincerely wants to apply today. It is a mere 'instrument' to homogenize its people, perpetuate the party supremacy, or use it for diplomatic parleys with other nations. There is always a danger of 'lumpenization' of this phenomenon of reclaiming the apparent greatness of our past.

It is difficult to 'thread the needle' by taking the great and the good from the past while avoiding the instrumental use of it that manifests in the form of bigotry and minority persecution. But it is a difficult task.

So, here's the thing. How should we think of Nehru, Ambedkar, and other 'liberals'? Those who decided to use the Constitution to rid India of the 'deadwood of the past'. One way to think of them is as intellectuals who appreciated the glory of our ancient past but realized any kind of reclaiming of that past in the modern conception of the State will bring along with it all the baggage and the 'deadwood'. They feared the good of that past will be buried soon under the 'unforgivable failings' that accompany it. So, they let it be. And decided to begin afresh.

We are in a different reality today. The 'instrumental' use of religion for narrow purposes by those who don't understand it at all. The likes of Nehru feared this would happen and tried to avoid it. We already find those fears materializing around us and yet we want to go down that path. The State will have to reclaim some of its moral legitimacy to find the right balance between letting society nurture its traditions while helping it embrace modernity.

28

The 'Idea of India' Narratives

Alice laughed. 'There's no use trying,' she said. 'One can't believe impossible things.'

I daresay you haven't had much practice,' said the Queen. 'When I was your age, I always did it for half-an-hour a day. Why, sometimes I've believed as many as six impossible things before breakfast. There goes the shawl again!

—Lewis Carroll, *Alice in Wonderland*

Some days it feels like we are living in the world that the Queen was talking about. There are more than six impossible things we are made to believe before breakfast. The WhatsApp university works overnight to feed you with good morning messages and convoluted takes on events around us that align with a particular narrative. The university never sleeps.

Narratives Are Important

Narratives have the power to make the unreal real. One such powerful narrative is the story that defines the largest body of 'us'—the nation. It follows that since a nation is a mental construct, it can be and is reimagined. This is an illustration we use to understand the concept of a nation:

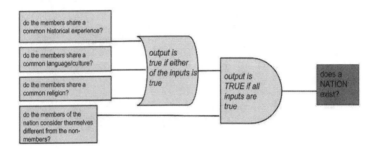

Nation—An Engineer's Imagination

Source: Authors

At the time of the Independence struggle, the modern Indian nation was imagined in the backdrop of a shared historical experience—the British colonial rule. That reimagination conceptualized all Indians traumatized by colonial rule as one people, one nation. That narrative seems to be changing over the last few years. Whether it's due to a generational shift, changing State versus society dynamics, or global influences, we don't know for sure.

Narratives are central to how governments communicate their policies because we think in terms of stories. No matter how good a policy proposal might be, constructing a powerful story around it is equally important.

Specifically, three reasons make narratives important. One, building narratives helps to decide whether the 'time has come for an idea'. Two, a good narrative makes the policy recommendation easy. And three, politics itself is a contestation for narrative superiority and dominance as opposed to ideological dominance. Stories, narrative arcs, images, symbols, numbers, and causes are some building blocks for creating powerful narratives. The kinds of things we write about in this book—unintended consequences, cost–benefit analysis, economic reasoning—are necessary but not sufficient in countering terrible policies. Good policies need not just good evidence but also good stories.

That's an important lesson to keep in mind. Narratives and the nature of public discourse are important. Instead of focusing on a single instance of a narrative, we will zoom out a bit in this chapter to take a broader view on the narrative arcs used in India that has brought us to the present day and the challenge of building a counter-narrative in the current time where public discourse is controlled by social media trolls and high-decibel news channels.

Narratives about India

Let's start with the beginning of India's narrative arc at its founding moment in 1947 and see the choices we made using this lens. India had to present Independence as a break from its long history. This was necessary to build a new 'imagination' of India in the minds of its people. Why was this necessary?

India was the very definition of diversity—over 600 princely states, fourteen provinces, dozens of major languages, scores of castes, and six large religious groups. It was impossible for such diverse people to have an imagination of its past that was common and uncontested. It made sense to start afresh with a new narrative.

There was also the question of what phase of our history should be considered an aberration that this founding moment needed to correct. Should it be restricted only to the period of British rule or should we go back to the founding of the Sultanate in Delhi in the eleventh century? We made a choice that British rule would be considered 'colonial' or 'foreign' and nothing beyond it in history. That we felt would have the broadest consensus and foster long-term harmony in society. We must remember that the horror of Partition was still unfolding at that moment, and any contentious definition of the imagination of our past would have made things worse.

Two other coincidences helped. One, in Ambedkar and Nehru, we had two towering personalities involved in the drafting of our Constitution who viewed our society with suspicion while privileging the State as an agent of change. Two, the assassination of Mahatma Gandhi at the hands of a right-wing Hindu zealot obliterated any opportunity for an alternative imagination to emerge from the society in the immediate term. This suppression, as we have written earlier, had long-term ramifications.

Once this break from the past was agreed upon, it was a question of making it palatable to a traditional society. Nehru, who had a deep understanding of Indian history, took it upon himself to position this not as a departure from the past but as a waking up from slumber. His 'Tryst with Destiny' speech is a delicate balancing act between setting aside our history for a fresh start while playing up the continuity of the current moment with the past:

> At the stroke of the midnight hour, when the world sleeps, India will awake to life and freedom. A moment comes, which comes but rarely in history, when we step out from the old to the new, when an age ends, and when the soul of a nation, long suppressed, finds utterance.
>
> At the dawn of history India started on her unending quest, and trackless centuries which are filled with her striving and the grandeur of her success and her failures. Through good and ill fortune alike she has never lost sight of that quest or forgotten the ideals which gave her strength. We end today a period of ill fortune and India discovers herself again.

This project of a new imagining and waking up from the slumber was then passed on to historians. The historians went about 'speaking for the dead' since 'the silence of the dead was no obstacle to the exhumation of their deepest desires'. In newly independent India, this meant different things: a disproportionate attribution of our woes to British rule, labelling provincial wars against British armies as a struggle for independence, airbrushing contentious parts of our history, like Islamic invaders who plundered and left, that would muddy this imagination, and amplifying elements that furthered the chosen narrative.

The specific positioning of events that are familiar to us today followed from here—the Anglo-Mysore wars led by Tipu Sultan, the papering over of the destruction of our cultural heritage by the invaders in the name of Islam, the playing down of the importance of Hindu kingdoms of Vijayanagara or Suheldev, and the deification of Sufism and Ganga-Jamuni Tehzeeb. This was narrative building in action based on the objectives the government had set for itself.

We pass no judgement on this project by those who were at the helm then. As Benedict Anderson argued, once you have chosen, in good faith, your narrative that is a break from the past, you will need to rework history. This was neither a unique attempt nor in any way insidious. This is what every nation-state did. In India's case, it was logical, constructive and forward-looking.

The critical question though is this—how deep did this imagination seep into the consciousness of the society? Seventy-five years later, the evidence suggests, not a lot. The alternative imagination of India as a nation that was suppressed by foreign invaders for over a millennium didn't transmute itself into the official narrative. Neither did it die out. It remained subdued, biding its time.

This strength of the mainstream narrative weakened in the decades of the 1970s and 1980s. The undermining of institutions by Indira Gandhi, the political rehabilitation of the Jan Sangh and the RSS during the Emergency, the stifling nature of a socialist economy that hemmed in the enterprise of people, and the naked pandering to minority vote banks led to disillusionment with it. The Ram Janmabhoomi movement strengthened the alternative and the second decade of this millennium made it mainstream.

Now, there is an alternative imagination that has the political mandate to unseat the original. It believes the lack of real reckoning with our past before the British era, the choice by Nehru and his ilk of an imagination that wasn't true to the belief of our society, and the constant peddling of this fake narrative have not allowed us to move ahead with conviction and confidence. Once free of this burden, we will flower to our real potential. This is a deeply held belief among the proponents of the alternative. The question now is of the political will to make a change and the extent of opposition to such a move by the adherents of the old imagination.

A concerted effort to formalize the change in the imagination will see a repeat of the series of steps that played out during our Independence. There might be constitutional amendments that will signal a departure from the original imagination. The last seventy-five years will be seen as a period of slumber from which we must awake. And there will be a reworking of history to fit past events into this imagination. This is already in progress. That it will gather pace shouldn't surprise anyone.

Since we are discussing this, we might as well try to make sense of the public discourse in India. Why now, you may ask? Are we giving in to the familiar tendency of over-reading the current moment and drawing broad conclusions from it? We'd say no. There's something afoot that suggests we are in the midst of a more fundamental shift.

The Present

We have a dominant political party with a PM who enjoys high approval ratings. An overwhelming majority believe we have a hardworking leader with a single-minded objective of building a stronger and more prosperous India.

The results of these efforts have been mixed. On most objective economic measures, even prior to the pandemic, we were faring below expectations. Things have gotten worse since. This dissonance between efforts and outcome is one factor in the current discourse. The partisans are in search of answers to reduce this dissonance.

Also, there has been a continuous shrinking of the liberal space over the past few years. Arguably, this is a worldwide phenomenon. There are many reasons for this including the inability of these liberal voices to persuade a public that sees it as fake, is suspicious of the elitism and hypocrisy that is often associated with it, and the opportunists among its ranks who lack credibility based on their track record when they were in office. What's made it worse is the splintering that has accompanied this shrinking. Indian liberals have been quick to imitate the worst instincts of ideological purity that pervades the US liberal discourse. This has meant attacks on anyone who is otherwise a fellow traveller in your cause but might hold one divergent view from you. This narrowing of the definition is a self-goal in a scenario where few are willing to stand up for the liberal cause.

There's a strong groundswell of sentiment that we haven't done as well as we should because there are saboteurs dragging us down with diversions. There has been a relentless bid to position the strawman of the 'establishment' as the reason for the dissonance between efforts and performance. An example of this is the '9 PM debate' spectacle that plays out every evening across TV channels. There is hardly any political opposition left in the country, and there are few voices that are willing to be on the panels to be on the other side of the debates. Yet an 'establishment' is defined, built up, and fought against every day. Often it is the opposition that is castigated for not supporting the government or the nation. Other days, it is history and Nehru that let us down. In some debates, it is the bureaucracy that is stymieing progress. Then there is the permanent 'establishment' of the elites, liberals, and minorities who are forever to be damned. There are many names given to them—Lutyens cabal, Khan Market gang, *tukde tukde* gang, etc.

Viewed in the cold light of the day, this 'establishment' has no real power left except for writing a few op-eds or running niche online news sites. Even that space is shrinking. The real establishment has corralled all the power, yet it projects itself as a victim of history and the elites. Then this imagined victimhood is internalized and outraged over on social media platforms. This has become the default battle line and any contemporary event—from Chinese incursions at the Line of Actual Control (LAC) to the death by suicide of a young actor—is easily framed within it. A faux establishment is propped up, a few known voices speak against it, and a craftily structured message is then broadcast far and wide on media platforms. It is quite a feat in setting a narrative.

We are developing our indigenous models of the chilling effect and cancel culture. The extreme left has its stringent code of who qualifies as a 'legit' voice. Nobody knows anymore what is acceptable while talking about a liberal cause. A well-known writer and lyricist writing against caste privilege is accused of appropriating the cause while old tweets are dug up to prove some stringent ideological purity test. Someone isn't liberal enough because she once praised former PM Vajpayee. Another isn't good because he let a far-right voice use his platform to write on his area of expertise. Advocating or writing for a free and liberal society seems like a long race with hidden hurdles. You can trip up anytime. Is it any surprise that there are fewer people willing to stick their necks out?

To compound the problem, the far-right has become bolder and creative by the day in labelling people as Jaichands, imagining offences, and dispensing punishment. It is no longer fringe. It is mainstream now. What was considered controversial is now acceptable because of this amplification. Further, nothing is too small to outrage about or to draw a false equivalence. The example of a stand-up comedian receiving death threats over a joke on a statue is an example of this.[1] The spate of apologies that follows establishes the chilling effect. People will think twice and not speak the next time. Our experience during Emergency has shown there's nothing that pleases the powerful more than self-censorship. Between these two extremes, free speech is in for rough days ahead.

A strong and prosperous India is our core policy objective. Like we have argued through this book, good policies require a rational, data-oriented, and reason-driven approach. Often this approach yields formulations that go against the grain of conventional thinking. They are tough decisions to sell to people because they appear counterintuitive to them. That is where the true use of

---

[1] 'Mumbai: Comedian Agrima Joshua Apologises for Joke about Shivaji Statue', *Scroll.in,* accessed 28 January 2022, https://scroll.in/latest/967237/comedian-agrima-joshua-apologises-for-joke-on-chhatrapati-shivaji-after-row-erupts.

narratives come in. We have taken only a handful of such steps in the history of independent India. Instead, we have largely relied on emotions, used slogans, and hoped for the best. There is merit in rallying people through emotive appeals. But they must be supplemented by a realistic plan to find a way out of these crises. There is enough in our history to suggest that we have used emotions as a substitute for policy and let things drift.

We wrote earlier in this chapter, there appears to be a fundamental shift in discourse in India. The coming together of the three trends—an all-powerful and ideological new establishment that questions the choices we made at our founding moment, the shrinking of the 'middle' space in public discourse, and relying on sentiments to defend questionable policies—portends a different social compact than what was established post-Independence. It might lack a moral force, but it has democratic legitimacy.

Its counter can only emerge from We, the People.

Epilogue

The primary reason for writing this book was to make public policy and the issues relating to governance accessible to more people. Since we are no experts, our approach was to use stories and news from the everyday din of public life in India to explain the role played by the State, the market, and the society in them. We liberally used existing frameworks from economics and sociology, picked extracts from papers and books written by intellectuals we admire, and applied a few of our original mental models to explain the many persistent issues that plague India.

Through the book, we have gone back to the texts from the European age of enlightenment to appreciate the root of a democratic ideal found in our Constitution. The concept of equality, individual liberty, and primacy of reason are best understood by reading the original thinkers of that time who questioned orthodoxy and freed knowledge from the realm of blind faith. Wherever possible and to the extent of our knowledge, we turned to the classics of Indian philosophy and thought to support an argument. Often, we have gone back to the founding moment of the modern Indian State to make sense of the high-quality discourse that led to our Constitution and to discover the origins of the faultlines that persist till date in our polity.

We have used these tough yardsticks, these high benchmarks to assess the policies, and the practices of our State. A State that emerged from the crucible of colonial plunder, Partition, a fragmented polity, and a deeply fissured society. A State that is only seventy-five years old. To put it in context, America was going through a bloody civil war that was threatening to tear apart the union when it had turned seventy-five.[1]

So, yes, you may accuse us of holding our State and society to an impossible standard given our starting position. It is easy to lapse into cynicism while talking about India. There are policy failures galore, economic reasoning is scarce, our politics can be depressing, and the public discourse is terrible. These are all true. We take no pleasure in bringing these up. We have been disapproving of almost everyone; equal-opportunity offenders you might say. But we have discussed them with passion here because we believe in India, in what we have built so far, and what we could become in future. Indifference shouldn't be an option for anyone who believes in India. It isn't for us.

We wrote this book with a critical gaze. Of course, there are many good things happening in India. Apart from the glaring policy failures, there have also been many shining

---

[1] The American Civil War took place between April 1861 and April 1865. While the Declaration of Independence was adopted in 1776, the first president assumed power in 1789. Seventy-five years after the presidency began, the US was three years into a bloody civil war.

examples of policy successes over the last seventy-five years. We haven't covered them because we believe there is more that can happen. And can happen easily. For that we need *we, the people* to think better, question more, and improve the nature of public discourse around them. We believe changing the demand side of the political equation will automatically bring the right kind of change on the supply side. The road to a sustained improvement in our politics begins from here. We remain optimistic about India because we believe our people have the ability and the resilience to do the heavy lifting that is needed to change our destiny by the time we celebrate the centenary of our Independence. Our people are our strength. If we didn't believe in this, we wouldn't have bothered writing this book.

So, don't let a few trolls or a handful of screaming anchors colour your view. We Indians are nice people. Many wrote us off at the time of Independence. Ours was an experiment doomed to fail. There are naysayers even now about our prospects. We survived then. We will survive in the future too. Because we are a unique people.

We are a compassionate, friendly, and a stoic lot. We confound those who measure us using conventional metrics of success. Like Shailendra wrote:

जो जिससे मिला सीखा हमने, ग़ैरों को भी अपनाया हमने
मतलब के लिए अँधे होकर, रोटी को नहीं पूजा हमने[2]

[We are open to strangers; to new knowledge,
We don't worship at the altar of greed and self-interest]

---

[2] From the Hindi Film *Jis Desh Mei Ganga Behti Hai* (1961).

We take life in our stride. This isn't fatalism. This stems from a deeper understanding of our place in the universe. As Sahir Ludhianvi summed up:

जो मिल गया उसी को मुकद्दर समझ लिया
जो खो गया मैं उसको भुलाता चला गया[3]

[We accept that which comes our way as destiny,
And we don't bemoan that which could have been]

We draw our inspiration from the deeper wellspring of an ancient philosophy. We have seen the many cycles of fate and despair. Yet, we survived. Don't bet against us.

The guiding light of the modern Indian State, our Constitution too has its flaws. Some consider it too liberal; others think it makes the State overbearing. Some find it too long; others feel it comes up short. This may all be true. However, there is no doubt our Constitution has strengthened our democracy, protected the weak, and continues to act as a tool for social change.

Tagore wrote:

Where the clear stream of reason has not lost its way
Into the dreary desert sand of dead habit
Where the mind is led forward by thee
Into ever-widening thought and action
Into that heaven of freedom, my Father, let my country awake.[4]

---

[3] From the Hindi Film *Hum Dono* (1961).

[4] Poetry Foundation, 'Gitanjali 35 by Rabindranath Tagore', https://www.poetryfoundation.org/poems/45668/gitanjali-35.

Our Constitution is still our best bet to reach that 'heaven of freedom'. Its structure has stood firm in the face of attacks while being flexible to adapt to the needs of a modern society. Seventy-five years is not too long in the history of a nation-state. Yet, given how it has fared so far, our Constitution will most likely stand the test of time.

Despite the cacophony and noise in our public discourse, there is a strong consensus on what is good for India and how to achieve it. Surveys, polls, and elections over the years have shown our preference for an open and progressive society, our belief in the fairness of the system, and our confidence about our future. Our preoccupation with the fault lines in our polity blinds us to the obvious reality that is around us. We continue to move past historic prejudices, suspicions, and biases that fractured us. Ties that bind us get stronger every passing year.

There have been occasional blips in this journey, and there are times we appeared lost, yet history will judge us favourably for what India has done in these seventy-five years. Of course, the work is incomplete and the pledge that Nehru spoke of at the stroke of midnight hour still remains unfulfilled:

> To bring freedom and opportunity to the common man, to the peasants and workers of India; to fight and end poverty and ignorance and disease; to build up a prosperous, democratic and progressive nation, and to create social, economic and political institutions which will ensure justice and fullness of life to every man and woman.

> We have hard work ahead. There is no resting for any one of us till we redeem our pledge in full, till we make all the people of India what destiny intended them to be.

We are all in it. Together.

What we have achieved so far is precious. It is worth reminding ourselves every day about this. Notwithstanding the many pages in this book lamenting our state of affairs.

We have done so because we know it's worth it.

Acknowledgements

This book is a result of several happy coincidences. It's tough to come up with a linear origin story. Nevertheless, we must tell one, if only to acknowledge the help and kindness of several people and organizations who played a part in making this project happen.

First up, thanks to the Takshashila Institution and the Graduate Certificate in Public Policy (GCPP) course for opening our minds to the fascinating world of public policy. Moreover, without this unique course, the two of us would have never met.

Our common interest in public policy led to a weekly newsletter on public policy called 'Anticipating the Unintended'. Thinking about a wide range of public policy issues every week for two years gave us the confidence to attempt a book. So, a note of thanks to all our newsletter readers for their encouragement.

Special thanks to Nitin Pai and Lt Gen Prakash Menon (retd.), who first put the idea of this book in our heads. Endorsements by Amit Varma, Rohini Nilekani, and Vijay

Kelkar greatly motivated us. For two first-time authors, having a kind, seasoned, and skilful editor is like a *vardaan*. So, thanks to Karthik Venkatesh, who saw value in this book, and backed us for this project.

Many a weekend has gone into the process leading to this book. It is only due to the understanding, encouragement, and help of our spouses (Asha and Smitha) that we could accomplish this task.

And finally, thanks to you all for picking this book. We do hope you will reflect on India's governance issues through a new lens.

Aati Rahengi Baharen,

Pranay Kotasthane

Raghu S. Jaitley